BORDEAUX

Published under the Superintendence of the Society for the
Diffusion of Useful Knowledge.

SCALES

REFERENCES

1. Foundling Hospital
12. School of Medicine
14. Hotel de Ville (Town Hall)
21. Courts of Justice
23. Royal College
26. Criminal Tribunal
27. Prison
28. Royal Chateau
29. Cathedral
34. Post Office
36. Custom House
38. Police Office
39. Great Theatre
40. Museum
45. Mint
46. School for the Deaf & Dumb
49. Admiralty

NOTE.

C. Calle. Passage
Mag. Magazine
Pl. Place. Square
Pds. Poids. Weights
Pte. Petite. Little
Q. Quai. Quay
R. Rue. Street
St. S. Saint

PLACE DE LOUIS XVI

Jardin Public

RIVIERE

D1612510

In
Vino
Veritas

*Inspired by Cyril Ray's **The Compleat Imbiber** –*
'the quintessential late-evening or bedtime book for
those who like wine'.

IN VINO VERITAS

A COLLECTION OF FINE WINE WRITING
PAST AND PRESENT

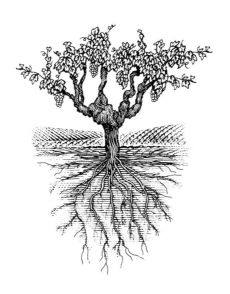

Edited by Susan Keevil

ACADEMIE DU VIN LIBRARY

Published 2019 by Académie du Vin Library Ltd.
academieduvinlibrary.com

Publisher: Simon McMurtrie
Editor: Susan Keevil
Designer: Anna Carson
ISBN: 978-1-913141-03-5
Printed and bound in Italy by LEGO, Vicenza

Contents

Introduction – Hugh Johnson OBE 7

CHAPTER 1 **GOOD VINTAGE, BAD VINTAGE**

Le Pin: the First Day of the Harvest – Fiona Morrison MW (2019) 10

My Best Claret – H Warner Allen (1951) 14

In Search of Bordeaux – Charles Walter Berry (1935) 18

My Wife and Hard Wines – Michael Broadbent (1981) 25

CHAPTER 2 **BORDEAUX, BURGUNDY… OR NAPA CABERNET?**

Burgundy is Better – Maurice Healy (1940) 34

Burgundy, the 'Cannibal' Wine – Ian Maxwell Campbell (1945) 36

The 'Judgement of Paris' Revisited – Steven Spurrier (2018) 40

CHAPTER 3 **POWER TO THE UNDERDOGS…**

Notes on a Barbaric Auslese – George Saintsbury (1920) 50

The Debut of Dom Pérignon – Henry Vizetelly (1879) 55

'Ah, the Sérinity…' – Randall Grahm (2019) 61

The English Wine Bubble – Justin Howard-Sneyd MW (2019) 71

Cyril Ray and the Rise of *The Compleat Imbiber* – Kathleen Burk (2013) 77

CHAPTER 4 **WINE TRAVELS…**

The Wilder Shores of Wine – Hugh Johnson (2019) 84

A Viking in the Vineyard – Peter Vinding-Diers (2019) 88

Giuseppe Poggio: Home Winemaking in Piedmont – Simon Loftus (1986) 102

Out of California's Shadow – Jason Tesauro (2019) 108

CHAPTER 5 **THE MISCHIEF OF TEA**

A Nice Cup of Tea – George Orwell (1946) 116

Tea Works its Mischief Slowly – Cecil Torr (1918) 119

Tea vs Bollinger – PG Wodehouse (1965) 120

CHAPTER 6   SHOULD PORT BE FORTIFIED?

A Call to Ban Port's Fortification – Cyrus Redding (1833) 124

The Best of Both Worlds? – Dirk Niepoort (2019) 128

The Scandal of Elderberries – H Warner Allen (1951) 131

The Port Trials – Ben Howkins (2019) 134

CHAPTER 7   TO THE TABLE AT LAST...

To Decant or Not to Decant? – Jane MacQuitty (2019) 138

Beyond the Banyan Tree – Hugh Johnson (1980) 140

Wine on Wine – Gerald Asher (1996) 143

Memorable Menus – Steven Spurrier (2018) 150

CHAPTER 8   AND FOR SOMETHING A LITTLE DIFFERENT...

Sting like a Bea – Dan Keeling (2019) 158

Mint Julep, a Cocktail to Crave – Jonathan Miles (2008) 162

CHAPTER 9   WINE AND ART

Art, Wine and Me – Andrew Caillard MW (2019) 166

Is Wine Art? – Elin McCoy (2019) 177

Best Dressed and Bottled at Home – Joan Littlewood/Philippe de Rothschild (1984) 185

For a Piece of the Glamour – Tony Aspler (2017) 194

CHAPTER 10   WINE WORDS FROM THE POETS

Wine and the Outcast Poet – Giles MacDonogh (2009) 202

Colette and Wine – Alice Wooledge Salmon (1983) 210

In Vino Veritas – Harry Eyres (2014) 217

INTRODUCTION

HUGH JOHNSON OBE

People like us have been enjoying wine since... let's settle for the Pharoahs. They chose amphoras, labelled with vineyard and winemaker names, to go with them to Paradise. You can see them in the British Museum. Did they not have sommeliers, scribblers and people sipping away somewhere in the palace, choosing, discussing, maybe scoring? May we not someday find the hieroglyphs for colour, bouquet and, er, minerality?

Language has never quite been adequate to pin down the flavours of wine or the pleasures they give us. We've never quite cracked it, but we keep trying. Wine, in fact, has provoked one long conversation over several thousand years. The Greeks had their symposia, lolling around on couches, their wine-bowls topped up as they analysed their Samian or Chian. Then they tossed their dregs at the *kottabos* in the corner. The best shot, who rang the bell, got a cuddle from a serving girl, or paid for the next round. The details varied.

The Romans were serious enough about it to ship wines in remarkable variety and huge quantity around the empire. Falernian from northern Campania, the district of Pompeii, was once all the rage; then the lighter, drier Rhaeticum from the Veneto came into fashion. The best vintages – famously the Opimian, a Falernian of 121BC – drank well a hundred years later. Read Columella on viticulture and Pliny for his tasting notes.

Omar Khayyam wrote beautifully about it. Samuel Pepys defined Classed Growth claret in one phrase: 'A good and most particular taste…'. Particularity; the essence of fine wine. Later writers, often physicians, became more learned – a quick way of losing readership.

There was a crisis at the turn of the 19th century, in the aftermath of the French Revolution, when many of the great vineyards came into the hands of merchant and peasant families. Napoleon's minister Chaptal – he advocated adding sugar from beet to inadequate wines – produced his *Traité Théorique et Pratique sur la Culture de la Vigne*, drawing on the work of such experts as the Abbaye Rozier and Parmentier (of the potato). He begins with a diatribe against vignerons for their idleness and lack of effort. His two-volume work of statistics and practical instruction remained on the mantelpiece of every vigneron in France for a century. Even now you can occasionally see the battered old tomes there.

The man who really founded modern wine writing, in his bid to explore and classify the wines of the whole world, was a sommelier from Paris, André Jullien. His *Topographie de Tous les Vignobles Connus* (1816) predated my *World Atlas of Wine* by 155 years. If geography, history, abstruse detail and sheer curiosity turn you on, Jullien is still a gripping browse. His summary of the differences between the four First Growths of Bordeaux can be said to stand for all time. Whether he is equally reliable on the wines of Astrakhan or Aderbijan is harder to judge. But he has a go; in fact three goes; his 1866 edition is the best.

English writers joined in. The journalist Cyrus Redding wrote his *History and Description of Modern Wines* in 1833. Redding was obsessed with falsification; above all the addition of spirits that was all too common in Britain. Another journalist, Henry Vizetelly of the *Illustrated London News*, having covered the San Francisco Gold Rush and translated Emile Zola so literally that he went to jail for obscenity, in 1879 produced an excellent and accurate account of Champagne which did much to promote its growing fame and success.

There were many Britons, some wine merchants and more amateurs, moved to share their experiences. The architect P Morton Shand described his delightful *Book of Other Wines than French* as 'frankly, a book of prejudices'. Many amateur books can be described in that way and are none the worse for it. H Warner Allen and Maurice Healy are good prejudicial entertainers. With Professor George Saintsbury, on the other hand, much the best-known of the school, his *Notes on a Cellar Book* never out of print in a hundred years, the prejudice is more in evidence than the entertainment.

We come to modern times with my own patron, André Simon, the Frenchman who, sent to London as agent for Pommery champagne, started the first wine education in England in 1911 – indeed, founding a tradition which led to the Masters of Wine and the Wine & Spirit Education Trust, which now has 100,000 students in 75 countries. Simon wrote 104 books. At the age of 86 he set off for Australia and New Zealand to write about their wines. At 88 he did the same for South Africa. I edited his last book, *In the Twilight* (1969).

Michael Broadbent, with his *Wine Tasting* of 1968, opens another era; that of science and precision in appreciating wine. Many brilliant practitioners are at it now, rather fewer can really be considered writers. It would make a long list, which I shan't start.

The conversation not only goes on: now, with the invention of blogs, it is a sustained bellow of information. It is hard to discern any pattern. Or distinguish sense from nonsense. But through it all runs the passion and frustration that wine engenders in its lovers. It is a drink piled high with opinions, judgements, jungles of science and thousands of years' worth of cultural baggage. It is its baggage that defines it   and makes it fill a huge and fascinating library. Which brings me to *In Vino Veritas*: the good bits, the juicy bits, the useful bits and the unsettled arguments that bring your favourite drink to life. You'll find them here.

Hugh Johnson, London, October 2019

CHAPTER 1

GOOD VINTAGE,
BAD VINTAGE

Le Pin: the First Day of the Harvest – Fiona Morrison MW (2019)

My Best Claret – H Warner Allen (1951)

In Search of Bordeaux – Charles Walter Berry (1935)

My Wife and Hard Wines – Michael Broadbent (1981)

Le Pin: the First Day of the Harvest

FIONA MORRISON MW (2019)

Master of Wine and author Fiona Morrison is married to Jacques Thienpont, maker of one of Pomerol's – and Bordeaux' – most prestigious wines, Le Pin. Here, she shares the drama of the first day of the 2019 harvest at this acclaimed property.

We always sleep with the windows open. Our northern souls relish the cold, fresh air and the bed is layered with duvets, quilts and an old horse blanket. We witness the moon, the stars, the clouds; we relish the rustling of the leaves on the huge beech tree outside our window; we wait for the metallic smell on the road outside and the pittering of raindrops on the tarmac. And it comes, the rain, at about 4.30 in the morning, and we lie in bed listening to it.

There was a time when we would have dreaded rain on the night before harvest. That was before climate change turned our preconceived notions of grape growing and wine-making on their heads. Then, we dreaded the cold, damp and threat of rot. Today, we are more confident that the rain will wash off the drought dust and perk up the acidity levels.

This is the witching hour when it is too early to get dressed and too late to hope for deep sleep. So we talk, we repeat the steps of preparing the *chai*, we visualize the different vineyard parcels, we worry about our cellar-hand who has just gone into hospital with appendicitis. It is all so familiar and yet our nerves are up, butterflies tug at our insides and we are as apprehensive as if we were doing this for the first time. I gently remind my husband Jacques that this is his 40th harvest.

The team arrives at 8.30am – a stream of old Renaults and Citroëns lines up along the road. Spirits are rather dampened as we see leaden clouds slouch along, hugging the hillsides, and tufts of mist hop over the vines. Jacques gives his opening talk; many have heard it before. Locals mostly: cousins, sons, daughters, sisters – we have given up trying to trace the family lines that link them. Meanwhile I punch into my phone, checking the five or so different weather apps that I will consult several times throughout the day. There is a glimmer on the horizon: for two this afternoon, all sites display a bright, happy sun.

Jacques and I have already walked the vine rows; the rain has not made much impact and is already packing its bags and moving on. No puddles, no swelling of the berries, but the grapes are cold and the ground greasy and slippery. Now the team is here it would be madness to send everyone home. Finding a good picking team is getting increasingly hard; keeping them for the duration of the harvest can only be only managed by cajoling with bonuses if they turn up each day. We decide to occupy the workers with some leaf stripping, to expose the bunches on the western side of the vines so that the grapes can dry off (those on the side of the rising sun are already free of moisture).

When we start to pick, the team moves quickly and we laugh as we see how swiftly scarves, raincoats, jumpers and gloves are peeled off as the pickers reach the end of the rows. The clip, clip, clip can be heard first; then the shouting begins: *'Porteur'*, *'Pas des Feuilles!'*, *'Allez, allez, allez'*. If the sun was shining, they would have broken into song by now.

I rather regret the mechanical drone that interferes with this timeless, bucolic scene. The noise of the generator that drives our selection table perched on a trailer at the end of the rows. But this is an ingenious invention that allows the picking and sorting teams to work closely together. The constant arrival of grapes keeps the sorters engaged, attentive – under pressure to sort rather than just stroke the berries. A bad load that includes leaves and sticks is frowned upon, and the porter who has just emptied his bin in a balletic twirl which pivots the large plastic pannier on his back over the first set of vibrating slats, is sent back to his two rows of pickers with a sharp reprimand. The tractor driver has the masculine gravitas to instill order in the troops better than I. I am up there with the sorters, relishing the viewpoint from the selection table looking out over the sea of vines.

A fleeting moment of mourning strikes me as I look at the freshly picked rows, empty, naked, stripped. Will it really be almost a whole year before I admire the heavy clusters of midnight blue grapes again?

We use bicycles, Jacques and I. They're perfect for getting ahead of the tractor as it leaves the vineyard for the winery with its new load, and for to-ing and fro-ing between Le Pin

These boots were made for working: Fiona and Jacques' footwear at the ready during harvest at Le Pin.

and Vieux Chateau Certan, our sister château barely 500 metres away where our cousins Alexandre Thienpont and his son Guillaume are such an important part of our family. We park our bikes and are ready for the grapes as they arrive at the winery.

You won't read this elsewhere, but there is always, always a certain amount of mechanical fiddling that goes on during the first day of harvest. It takes a moment to remember which direction a lever or a valve needs to be turned, or to repair a fuse or plug.

We have a moment of reckoning as the trucks appear. Jacques has chosen a vat, estimating that it will be large enough for the yield from the parcel that we are picking. But this choice isn't by any means guided by perfect science. There is a fair amount of starting again when we need a bigger or smaller vat. After all, the vessels will be the scene of that amazing alchemy of turning grape juice into wine. It is important to get it right.

Parcel selection is one of the key advances in winemaking lately. Being able to keep the different grapes from each plot separate, so that the individual character of that part of the vineyard is allowed to shine through, has led to more precise decisions tailored to the wine in each small vat. So what if the winery resembles a nursery of cots in a new borns' maternity ward?

And then that smell arrives – that gorgeous fruity, yeasty, gassy, heady smell of new grapes as their skins split and crack open, spitting out their peanut-flavoured pips and spilling their glamourous crimson purple juice into the bottom of the tank. The vat fills rapidly and it is time to note the density of the wine. We will check this every time we do a pumping over to homogenize the fermenting must and help the yeasts do their work with a good, deep breath of oxygen. After about 10 days, the grapes' sugars have all been converted into alcohol and the yeast's work is done.

Jacques moves calmly around the cellar; not for him rock music and crashes and clattering. When he built the new cellar in 2011, he employed an architect friend who had designed the great concert hall in Bruges to get things just right. Acoustics are important to him: the cellar's bridges and walkways are lined with oak undersides to reduce the jangle of cellar work. Le Pin is a peaceful place.

The tractors and sorting equipment, pumps, presses, tubs, hoses have all been washed down. It takes ages and we are all tired, but it is an essential part of the day. It's true what they say about needing an enormous amount of water to make a great wine. But hygiene is just so, so important and having once entered the cellar on an early autumn morning to the dreaded smell of nail-varnish remover – the combination of ethanol and acetic acid that can arise when rogue bacteria turn wine into vinegar – the memory spurs us on to ensure that all the equipment is clean and neatly stacked, even if in a few hours' time we will be using it again.

Across the vineyards, the house beckons; rich odours of hearty stew waft over the vines (we never have time for more than a bowl of soup and a hunk of baguette at lunchtime) and makes our stomachs rumble. The sun is an orange globe gently slipping behind the hill of Fronsac. *Ça y est*. It's done; the first day is over. 🍂

*Fiona Morrison MW is author of **10 Great Wine Families: a Tour Through Europe**, published by the Académie du Vin Library (London) 2019.*

MY BEST CLARET

H WARNER ALLEN (1951)

H Warner Allen admits that his 1951 book, A Contemplation of Wine, *indulges in 'hair-brained chatter of irresponsible frivolity' concerning everything from the first vineyards of Noah to the 'austerity of today and yesterday'. Here he alights on the more serious matters of Château Lafite's 1864 vintage and the demerits of Professor Saintsbury's handwriting.*

never had the honour of meeting Professor Saintsbury* in the flesh, but half a century has passed since he first became to me a very real and living personality. When I was at Oxford in the first years of this century, my best friend, Francis Tower Gray, had been one of Saintsbury's favourite pupils at Edinburgh University. Gray and I saw a great deal of one another, so much so that a wag coined the portmanteau name of 'Grallen' to cover us both on the ground that we were unthinkable apart, and Saintsbury's pupils were never tired of talking about him. So I heard a great deal of Saintsbury lore, and in particular I remember an evening made memorable by the Professor and a great claret.

My friend was the nephew of the Edinburgh physician Dr Bell, who was famous for applying to his patients the deductive method applied by Sherlock Holmes to criminals, and who was the actual model for Conan Doyle's classic detective. That evening he had just been to Scotland where he had enjoyed the Professor's hospitality. I rather think he had been one of the guests at the dinner numbered IX among the menus appended to *Notes on a Cellar Book*, in which Château Latour 1895 was the crown of the feast. I know

---

* Professor George Saintbury (1845–1933) was a wine critic and connoisseur. His much-admired *Notes on a Cellar Book* (1920) made him the 'Hugh Johnson' of his day. *See* pages 50–54.

Master of wine: Professor George Saintsbury, photographed by James Lafayette, c1910.

that we had been drinking an 1893 claret with our meal as preparation for a wine of which I was inordinately proud.

In my last year as an undergraduate, when I was dead broke, as all fourth-year men were in those unregenerate days, I led myself into temptation one afternoon and dropped in at Jones's, the wine-merchants in the High. A wily salesman with a reverend white beard made a casual remark that there was just one dozen of 1864 Lafite left in the cellar. I was tempted and fell. One hundred and twenty shillings a dozen seemed, in those days, a fantastic price to pay even for the best claret the world has ever seen. This wine was reposing under my window seat in the recess which was the nearest approach to a cellar in my digs, when certain sons of Belial, flown with insolence and wine, paid me a visit as they were wont to do, and, finding me out, hunted round for something to devour. Some of them helped themselves to whisky as was right and proper, but more enterprising members of the gang explored the cavity below my window seat. To this day I shudder to think of what followed. They laid sacrilegious hands on my best claret, and when I came in I found them drinking Château Lafite 1864 out of tumblers with no better excuse than that it seemed to them quite decent red ink.

I had decanted one of the surviving bottles of that precious claret for Gray and myself that evening when he discoursed on Saintsbury's hospitality. We were enjoying that incomparable wine after the table-cloth had been removed from the polished table, true to the Professor's dictum that the time to appreciate the finest wine comes when the more prosaic and vulgar business of eating is over and done with.

There is nothing to be added to Saintsbury's own account of his own hospitality in *Notes on a Cellar Book*, and so there would be little point in repeating my friend's account of that dinner, even if I remembered it. What I do remember is how he tried to show me Saintsbury as the man and critic he was by quoting one of his comments on the famous poem by Herrick that opens with the lines:

> *Bid me to live and I will live*
> *Thy Protestant to be.*

'I have no idea,' Saintsbury used to say, 'what Protestant means in this connection, but I am quite sure that it is the right word in the right place.' These words presented him to me as a hater of humbug and a critic eminently gifted with the soundest common sense, and as such his image has always remained in my mind.

After the World War I, I was brought into personal contact with Professor Saintsbury by correspondence, and, when he wrote some articles for the *Morning Post*, learned that he was to be numbered among the world's major cacographists. At the *Morning Post* the palm for bad writing had been awarded to Andrew Lang*, and all his articles were set up by a special compositor who was regarded as the expert in difficult hands. When Lang was out of town, if this compositor was away on holiday, the usual weekly article had to be held over till the printer came back, as no one else could make head or tail of what it was all about. When Saintsbury's manuscript came in, after one glance I sent it up to that same compositor, who boasted that anyone who could decipher Andrew Lang could read any script. Some hours later he came down to see me, a broken man, confessing that in an article about 1,500 words long there were at least 20 words that had absolutely baffled him. When Saintsbury received a proof with 20-odd blanks in it, he wrote back a letter, which, so far as we could read it, was lavish with compliments to our printers for having sent him the cleanest proof he had ever known. His handwriting was execrable, but his typing was even worse; for he seemed to strike the keys of his typewriter at utter haphazard, and there was no clue at all to what his arbitrary groups of unassorted letters might stand for.

I have pleaded guilty to the crime of omnibibulosity, and perhaps in his universality I may find an excuse for my error. It may be that his appreciation and sympathies both in wine and literature were a trifle too all-embracing. No doubt in this age of mass production fastidiousness should be our watchword; yet there is a great deal to be said for the ancient Jewish maxim, that on the Judgement Day every man will be called to account for every good thing that he has failed to enjoy, when he could legitimately do so. A Cambridge historian of English literature says of Saintsbury: 'His foible of omniscience is so transparently ingenuous as to be attractive rather than offensive,' and worthily lauds the immense vitality of his enjoyment, that magnificent zest of life, which endeared him to all who knew him. As in letters, so in wine, and it is to be remembered that he boasted never to have given a second-hand opinion either on wine or book. ❧

*First published as chapter II, A Wine Lover of Yesterday, in **A Contemplation of Wine** by H Warner Allen, Michael Joseph (London) 1951.*

---

* Andrew Lang, 1844–1912, Scottish poet, novelist, literary critic and anthropological commentator who said: 'An unsophisticated forecaster uses statistics as a drunken man uses lampposts – for support rather than for illumination.'

In Search of Bordeaux

CHARLES WALTER BERRY (1935)

Charles Walter Berry of Berry Bros & Rudd was one of the first British wine merchants to venture abroad and taste wines on their own terroir. In 1934 he spent eight weeks on a road trip of France, making diligent – frequently humorous – notes on the local food, wine and surroundings. Here are the jottings from his time in Bordeaux, where his celebrated skills for judging very young wine were put to good use.

We arrived at the Hotel d'Orsay in time for *déjeuner*, and sat down to a modest repast, accompanied by a bottle of 1923 Cos d'Estournel, second growth, Saint-Estèphe; a pleasant enough wine, but much too old for its age. Some of the 1923 wines, especially of the Graves and Saint-Emilion, are particularly pleasant, but they will not make 'old bones'.

As usual, when drawing the cork, it broke . . . Oh, those corkscrews!

On the table was standing a bottle of Château Latour, 1930 (*see* tasting note page 20) 12 francs, marked 'for propaganda'. What mentality! To me, it is almost unbelievable that one should introduce to the would-be drinker of red Bordeaux wine a Château Latour, first growth, Pauillac – one of the few names to conjure with – with the 1930 vintage! If ever there was a bad vintage, here you have it. Run through your mind the two together: Latour, 1930, and then imagine what the public will think, especially when the vintage 1930 is being used for this purpose.

Château Latour, which everyone regards as the acme: 'This must be good, we will try it!'

And then comes the fall – the great disappointment. 'If this is a specimen of the finest red

Bordeaux' (they probably know nothing about the vintage), 'then may I be spared from drinking it again!'

It might be argued that, for 12 francs per bottle of Château Latour, what can they expect? That is not the point. An inferior wine, even if it is given away, can never create a good impression, much less so when even 12 francs is asked for it. This is not of the way I am to popularize the excellent wines of the Médoc, of that I am certain.[1]

. . .the next morning, Monsieur Danglade took us off to his part of the world. The first property we visited was Château Nenin: a good estate, and good wine. We tasted the 1933, but I thought I detected a dry finish (which would mean too much tannin), and yet it still seemed to be suffering from a slight fermentation . . . it may come round all right.

We then visited Château Cheval Blanc, one of the most famous growths of Saint-Emilion: a fine property is this, and well kept. We tasted the 1933 wine, of which we were able to procure but very little – it was good, but perhaps somewhat light. It may easily turn into a fine wine, something between a 1900 and a 1923. (*See* tasting note page 20.)

We then tasted the 1934, which of course was not in a proper state to taste . . . it is very difficult to say what it will be like. The sample was fermenting, in spite of which I could detect softness by virtue of sugar, and a certain bitterness by virtue of tannin. I think it will develop well, it seems so well balanced. We shall certainly have a say in the purchase of the *totalité* of this famous wine![2]

We tasted the wine with a feeling of pride, while speaking of its fine future, yet realizing how very difficult it is to foretell how it will turn out. Young wines, so full of life, and 'noisy' with their fermentation, always lead me to compare them with humans: consider babies, they all look much alike, and although we know their 'parentage' we remember that 'good wombs have borne bad sons'. . . so Mother Earth is dependent on the elements, and on proper treatment during her 'travail'; the offspring likewise requires the most patient and studious attention in order that we may enjoy later what we fervently hope for.[3]

We then passed on to Pomerol again, and called at Château L'Evangile, which one of my clerks persists in calling 'Evanguile!' Unfortunately there was no responsible person on the premises and we had to retire without tasting.

---

[1] CWB was a shy man but a brilliant salesman, with a 'horrid commercial instinct'.
[2] Berry's purchasing confidence had been bolstered by the repeal of Prohibition in the US in 1933; his budgets had also been helped by Bordeaux's very successful 1928 vintage.
[3] It developed into a 'Vin Manifique'.

TASTING NOTES FROM THE MASTER

Michael Broadbent is known for his eloquent tasting notes. Over 6,000 of them have been published, each describing the wines he experienced in intricate (if occasionally florid) detail. Here are a selection of his views on the wines from this chapter (noted in 2002):

1930

Poor weather, execrable wine, no market and generally hard times for everyone.
Château Latour: *The only 1930 I have tasted but on two occasions. In 1983, at first glance, it had quite a good ruby colour; a light spicy bouquet trying to lift off but the palate was thin and acidic. More recently, a similar note, but seemed chunkier and more chewy, ending on a sour note. Last tasted dining at the Château in November 1990.*

1933
***

Another small crop but this time because of high winds during the flowering period.
Fairly light, attractive wines. However, apart from La Mission, no 1933s tasted during the last decade. For me the lightness and charm of the vintage was epitomized by Château Margaux which I drank in the 1950s and 1960s and Château Cheval Blanc in the 1970s.

1934
****

The decade's best vintage. The grapes were saved from a two-month drought by September rain. An abundant harvest, very good wines. Now risky, but the best kept still drinking well [in 2002].
Château Cheval Blanc: *Arguably the finest, certainly – in my experience – one of the most reliable of the 1934s. First noted 'rich, delicate, ethereal, exquisite' in 1978, and several admiring notes since, including a glowingly coloured magnum in 1986, its beautiful bouquet ripe, subsiding gently but not decayed. Well constructed. All the component parts in balance. Most recently another magnum with upper-mid-shoulder level, a bit hazy; nose disappointingly neutral though much better on the palate; sweet, complete, fading gracefully but still drinking well. Last tasted Dec 2000. At best *****
Château Beychevelle: *Lovely bottling . . . Translucent; delicate; fragrant. A delicious drink. Last tasted September 1989****.*

Ratings at a glance
***** *Outstanding*
**** *Very good*
*** *Good*

We then called at La Conseillante, where fine wines are made, but the proprietors always, in my opinion, ask too much to begin with. The 1933 was a very attractive proposition… fruity, perhaps a little more body than the Cheval Blanc, but too expensive. I could not entertain it. It was developing beautifully; I would like to have had that wine!

We tasted the 1934. Of course, as with the other 1934s, it was impossible to give any opinion, but I was a little surprised that it did not show more than 12% alcohol. I might add that there had been beautiful weather . . . sun, without excessive heat, also a little rain from time to time. Melons, peaches, figs, and table grapes were in fine condition, which is a good 'portent' for the grape harvest. (*See* tasting note, opposite page.)

The weather had now commenced to clear; in fact, the sun was beginning to shine. We went over to Saint-Emilion, and at Yon-Figeac we tasted the 1933. I did not find it very interesting…but others[4] did, and no doubt they know better than I. I made a point of asking what the 'ac' at the end of the name of so many towns signified (such as Figeac) and I was given to understand that it was an equivalent to 'village'.

While we were at Saint-Emilion I was anxious for Reg to have a look at this ancient and attractive town. The ruins of the old castle are very interesting . . . there are besides the six gates and ramparts which deserve every attention, but we were only able to have a glance.

The Arch de la Cadène was a picture, dating back to the 13th century, a fine sight meets the eye at Porte Brunet (I only mention these particulars as worthy of notice, in case any of my readers visit Saint-Emilion. They must make a point of seeing La Collégiale, which is well worth a visit, and the 12th century ancient church which is to be found beneath another . . . it is indeed remarkable!). The cloisters of Les Cordeliers are interesting too . . . and there is a sparkling Saint-Emilion associated with this.[5]

Before one leaves, time should be found to visit the first manufacturer of the delicious '*Macaroons du pays*' . . . do not forget this, they are indeed delightful.

From Château Pavie, we enjoyed a very fine view: Fronsac was pretty country. Here we tasted a Côte de Fronsac, Château Jeandeman, a 1933 wine, good, and almost elegant. It showed only 11%, which after all is not far short of an average.

---

[4] CWB's companions were his son Reggie, Ian Maxwell Campbell's son Lorne and Samuel Thresher, all with 'oenological propensities' and a willingness to share a joke about their observations – a few at the expense of fellow diners. They travelled in a car they christened 'Little Auk', to agree with its number plate.
[5] Vines climb the 14th century walls of the cloisters and underground lies a labyrinth of tunnels in which sparkling wine has been made since 1892 – a proud, if unusual tradition, that continues today.

This was the morning's work, and we were glad to accept Madame Danglade's very kind invitation to lunch.

With a 1928 of the Graves...a trifle sweet and sulphury...we enjoyed some of the Champignons de la Maison. Monsieur Danglade has some wonderful natural caves in which he cultivates fine mushrooms.

With a pheasant and a *pâté aux truffes*, we were allowed to indulge in a Saint-Emilion wine, Château Bel-Air 1923, which was light, very old, but very pleasant, and also a bottle of 1914 Château Haut Brion. This wine still possessed character, but I do think its best days are over.

With a pâté – a special *pâté de foie gras aux truffes* – we had a magnum of 1895 Château Cheval Blanc. Monsieur Danglade had asked if I would like it then or wait a little... Having heard what the wine was, I remarked: '*Le plus tôt possible...! Tout de suite...* the "tooter the sweeter".'

It was grand! I am glad we did not wait for the cheese... in this wise I had a double share!

Madame Auschitzky was seated next to me. Madame is Monsieur Danglade's daughter... very charming! Under the influence of the 1895 Château Cheval Blanc (bless the wine), I confided to this young lady that her name was too difficult to pronounce... would she teach me her Christian name... it was Madeleine. And now, Madeleine, I thank you for your charming company, and the happy conversation we carried on during this sumptuous repast. I only wish I could speak your language as happily as you do mine – *au revoir*, good friends. Thank you so much![6]

We had to be off, as we had work to do in the Médoc. The first visit we paid was to the Château Palmer Margaux... I always like these wines, and I tasted the 1933 feeling sure I would not be disappointed – but I was – it was light and elegant, but there was something I did not quite approve of... maybe the influence of the 1895 Château Cheval Blanc was still upon me. The others thought it excellent, so I was well in the minority. There is a fine landmark here, the Church of Lamarque. A guiding star in a wilderness of vines.

We were at Saint-Julien, and felt that we must call at Château Beychevelle, for had we not purchased the whole output of 1933? A grand tasting immediately took place. First of all we had to see the 1933, all the casks of which already bore our name. The sample from the

---

[6] Not always so shy: CWB welcomed a joke or two with the women on his travels.

first hogshead was agreed to be very good and elegant, so, in case this happened to be a particularly favoured cask we tasted another . . . it was better! I turned to Reg and said 'We're in clover!'

Although there are such excellent wines of 1933, I cannot help but think that they must be bought with considerable discrimination. The summer was hot, and in the vineyards where the roots of the vines did not penetrate sufficiently deep to retain the moisture, it is feared that the grapes suffered, and that the wine made from them will also suffer.

However, do not worry, trust to your Wine Merchant. These are the details of which he should be cognizant.

We then sampled the 1934: as I have already mentioned once or twice regarding 1934, it is too difficult to express an opinion, but it promises well. 1930, 1931 and 1932 we tasted; the only expression we allowed to escape us was: 'NG.'

The *chais* are important and imposing, and I was glad to be able to compliment the *maitre de chais*, Monsieur Branon, on the excellent way in which he kept them.

After leaving Beychevelle, we made our way to Château Latour, passing Château Ducru Beaucaillou on the way, where we saw the Tri-color and the Union Jack flying side by side.

We noticed a somewhat remarkable thing when we alighted, which was a number of small pegs in the ground, indicating that certain rows (*sillons*) in a given vineyard belonged to other vineyard proprietors; for example, here and there we found inscribed on these pegs: 'Château Latour', 'Château Beychevelle', etc.

I omitted to tell you the origin of the word 'Beychevelle'. Some 300–400 years ago, a Duc d'Epernon, Admiral of the Port of Pauillac, lived here, and when the ships passed his dwelling it was customary to '*baisse la voile*' – lower the sail – by way of salute; hence 'Beychevelle' (in the Gascon tongue '*beyche*' = *baisse* and '*velle*' = *voile*).[7]

We proceeded to Château Latour, and here tasted the 1933: undoubtedly a fine wine. It had been racked once, and showed up beautifully. There is no doubt that some of the 1933 wines are excellent. Most of the *régisseurs* are very competent men, but one would have to go far to find a more knowledgeable and enthusiastic man than Monsieur Brugiére, who

---

[7] The words of Jancis Robinson MW's introduction to this book in 1987 ring true when she says it is 'a cocktail composed of 101 often disparate ingredients, which CWB has done little to shake together. Read 50 years on, it is none the worse, and arguably even more entertaining, for that.'

controls the destiny of Château Latour, Grand Cru Pauillac. Out of 1,386 growths there are 60 'classed' growths of the Médoc, including Château Haut Brion which lies in Pessac, Graves.

During a conversation with this gentleman I learned the following rather interesting details: that four-fifths of the vines were of the Cabernet, the other fifth, Merlot. Some of the vines were upwards of 100 years old and these he regarded as being the small portion that gave the wonderful character to Château Latour. There are upwards of 350,000 vines in the vineyards, and the soil is mostly sandy. The vines are planted at least one metre apart, as was also the distance between the 'sillons'. Monsieur Brugière was very emphatic about the way in which his wines were 'equalisé'. He assured me that on no condition was the wine allowed to touch any metal of any description, and it was not even passed through the cask to the vat by means of a pump, which is usual, but was taken in wooden buckets by hand.

We were not sorry to return to the hotel. We had had a long and somewhat tiring day, and therefore decided to have a bath, a quiet dinner, and early to bed.

I cannot remember the menu, but we had a bottle of champagne nature, which we enjoyed. With the coffee we inquired for a really good 'Fine'; the waiter brought us a bottle: it looked its part, that of 1875 Champagne, and I thought it the best I had ever tasted in a French hotel.

I asked if they had any stock, being willing to pay, say, 30 shillings a bottle for a few bottles to last me on the journey.

The answer came back that there were only two bottles, and the proprietor desired to keep one for himself. If, however, I would like to have the other, it would be 60 francs . . . did I not!! 🍂

*Excerpt from Chapter VII of **In Search of Wine, A Tour of the Vineyards of France** by Charles Walter Berry, Sidgwick & Jackson (London) 1935.*

Tasting Notes reprinted by kind permission of Michael Broadbent.

MY WIFE AND
HARD WINES

MICHAEL BROADBENT (1981)

Michael Broadbent and his late wife Daphne often spent their holidays carefully unpacking the contents of stately old wine cellars ready for sale at Christie's, where he was auctioneer and head of the prestigious wine department – it was cold, damp and frequently dirty work, but the rewards could be sublime…

Glamis, Sir George Meyrick's, Fasque, Lord Rosebery's: what were these cellars actually like? I suppose I should have taken a camera but just as the description of a wine and its background in one of Christie's catalogues is often more evocative than the sight of the bottle itself, so the 'feel', smell, chill and content of an old cellar are infinitely more appealing written down than seen in a somewhat foggy photograph of dank walls and bins. Certainly a bigger contrast to the neat, informative and map-bedecked modern American air-conditioned cellars cannot be imagined – those cellars furnished with tables and chairs, I simply cannot understand. How can a room comfortable enough to sit in for several hours can possibly be the right temperature for storing fine vintage wines?

The first really great cellar I became involved with was Lord Rosebery's, thanks initially to the Marquess of Linlithgow, for it was the latter who, after I had spent a profitable morning in the vaults beneath the hall of Hopetoun House, suggested I should approach his neighbour at Dalmeny who had a large collection of old Lafite. The Hopetoun cellars housed older wines, including a quantity of 18th century Madeira, but the immaculately cared-for cellars at Dalmeny, Lord Rosebery's estate on the outskirts of Edinburgh, contained the greater treasures. Though not very extensive, the cellar itself was in two sections, with dark granite walls and a neatly raked gravel floor. Against the end wall, nestling on the gravel bed, were three double magnums of 1865 Lafite, unlabelled, glistening black, like World War I howitzer shells. Every bin had a label accurately detailing its contents which I checked against the cellar book clearly kept by a generation or two of immaculate butlers. My first job was to list the wines and put on Christie's slip labels – for once an unlabelled bottle has left its bin, identification can be difficult and its value lost. It was in this cellar that I learned another lesson: seconds after I put a gummed label on the bench it started to curl. I have since used this as a simple measure of humidity, essential to prevent corks drying out.

This visit took place in the autumn of 1966, shortly after the first sale by Christie's reorganized wine department. I next took stock of Lord Rosebery's cellars at Mentmore Towers (Buckinghamshire). During lunch, he told me that at his age he no longer gave big dinner parties: certainly not big enough to warrant opening a triple magnum of pre-phylloxera Lafite. In any case, he mused, how many guests would really appreciate it?

It struck me then, as it strikes me now, that it is fair and reasonable for those who have had their fill of beautiful, old and rare wines to allow others an opportunity to buy, cellar and drink them; and that the problem common to all owners of fine wines is wondering with whom to share them.

I remember as if it were yesterday: my visit in the spring of 1967 to Mentmore, a monumental pile, rambling cellars, a big dining room with a vast sideboard bearing a jar of every sauce and pickle one had ever heard of, its centrepiece a gun carriage with a huge bottle of Old Grandad Whiskey – and on a butler's tray, in a decanter, His Lordship's everyday port, Taylor's 1920. Mentmore and its earls have passed on a wealth of vinous treasures. The cellars held easily the greatest collection of pre-phylloxera Lafite in private hands (his Lordship's mother was a Rothschild), and the contents were sold at Christie's in May 1967. Occasional bottles still re-cross our threshold – at ever-increasing prices – though most must be consumed by now.

At least Lord Rosebery was aware of his cellar. The descendant of another British Prime Minister, Sir William Gladstone, who inherited both the baronetcy and the Scottish property, came across his great cache of wines by accident. The cellar door at Fasque near Montrose had not been opened since 1927, when the third baronet, a bachelor, died.

When Quellyn Roberts, the wine merchants in Chester, telephoned and started naming the wines on the list, I gasped and took the next plane to Aberdeen to meet the new owner. Fasque is a handsomely severe red stone mansion, but its gardens were ill-tended and it was cold as a morgue inside. The cellar was dark, damp and the coldest (a steady penetrating

9˚C) I have ever come across. It was the dark, the lack of disturbance and cold that had preserved the wines, and, incidentally, a dead rat, which turned up later during unbinning. I returned with my wife a few weeks later and spent Whit weekend packing up the wines I had listed but left in bin. It was freezing: we had an open fire and an electric fire in our bedroom, a fire in the breakfast room and a roaring log fire in the study where we drank malt whisky after dinner to keep out the chill. The house reminded me of a scene from *Great Expectations* – everything had come to a stop in 1927. There was a Post Office directory and Social Register of 1927 on the desk where I wrote up my notes. The drawers contained boxes of pen nibs of the sort one now sees on stalls in the Portobello Road. As for the cellar, we kept the chill off by lighting the place with oil lamps and dressing like Icelandic fishermen.

Readers might ask why my wife and I chose to spend a holiday weekend packing cases of old wine. Well the plain fact of the matter is that this sort of thing cannot be entrusted to a local carrier; and it is quicker and easier for me to identify wines than explain the layout etc to unqualified staff. Looking back, virtually every really great cellar of rare wines sold at Christie's over the past 15 years – from the far north of Scotland, through Wales and down to the south of Bordeaux – has been packed by the Broadbent family. It has been cold, dirty and thankless work, yet fascinating to look back on. Incidentally, this might just sound like cheap labour. And so it is: for it is really quite uneconomical to send a professional team to sort out and pack private cellars. For me it is more a labour of love. And of course it has its amusing and grand moments – like the Easter weekend spent southeast of Poitiers, the guests of the Marquis de Vasselot. By day, in gumboots and overalls, my wife, daughter, son and I sorted out mountains of old wine in cellars beneath a cow shed. It was snowing. We turned the billiards table in the château into a tasting bench and later consumed the various sample bottles of Lafite 1895 and Margaux 1890 followed by Filhot 1896 and Yquem 1890 at dinner with the Marquis, sleeping off the day's work and evening repast in the most beautiful old beds I ever encountered.

During two other Easter holidays in France, in 1974 and 1975, I remember we packed up marvellous collections of Latour for the de Beaumont family, former owners of that château. The countess had a cellar full of wine in Brittany, also inhabited by a white snake: clearly neither bottles nor snakes had seen the light of day for many generations. The head of the family, the Marquis de Beaumont, had another collection in rather macabre cellars, next to 13th-century dungeons complete with *oubliettes*, beneath the keep at Beaumont-la Ronce, near Tours.

One of the most wide-ranging and valuable of all French cellars was that of the Restaurant Darroze at Villeneuve de Marsan in the Armagnac area. Monsieur Jean Darroze, a most charming old man, had really lost interest in the business. Though the

Michael Broadbent, relaxing with a glass of wine during his days as Director of Christie's Wine Department.

place still had tremendous style, the restaurant was no longer patronized to the same extent and had latterly lost its two Michelin rosettes. After a long, arduous day in the cellar we dined in great elegance, more or less the only people eating and sleeping there.

Another most interesting cellar in that corner of France was that of Madame Teysonneau-Zamboni, beneath her most beautiful 18th century mansion in a small square off the central park in Bordeaux. I had known of this cellar for some time. Through a mutual friend in the Bordeaux trade, she cautiously sold a couple of bottles of 1877 Haut-Brion, which fetched a good enough price finally to allow me access to the treasure trove. It was an eye opener: quite the widest range of pre-phylloxera claret I have ever come across.

After spending the whole of one Sunday taking stock in a rather small dank cellar, Madame Teysonneau asked me if I would like to see the 'young wine' cellar. Frankly, I had had enough; but somewhat wearily said 'why not?' It was unlocked to reveal a huge cache of wines – the youngest of which was from 1933, the vast majority being Bordeaux and burgundy (all Calvet wines; she was of the Calvet family) of the 1919, 1920 and 1921 vintages. At lunch the next day we sampled two wines, both new to me, of which she had substantial quantities: 1892 Château Canon (Saint-Emilion) which was excellent, and the *deuxième vin* of Château Margaux 1900. She told me she had produced the 1900 *grand vin* at her daughter's wedding reception not all that long ago. Family and guests consumed over 100 bottles. I swallowed hard and just hoped that they had appreciated one of the greatest ever vintages of Margaux.

The knowledge that so much fine wine has been, and doubtless still is, wasted haunts me: cellars-full tipped down the drain either because the wine was considered passé or because a generation had lost interest or turned teetotal. Yet quite a few cellers have survived because the original wine lover was succeeded by a son who had no interest, then, in turn, by his son who then finds his grandfather's wines too old. This was exactly the case with one of the finest of the more recent English collections we disposed of. Sir John Thomson's cellar came to light, as do so many others, quite fortuitously. He was selling up his very beautiful house in Oxfordshire. A friend of mine, a young Master of Wine, sat next to Sir John at dinner and, talking about wine, learned of the collection, which he was shortly after offered, lock, stock and barrel, for £300. After inspecting the cellar, he promptly recommended that Christie's should be called in, and I made the journey to see it myself. It was a three-part cellar, the two rear sections containing old wine and the nearest a lot of fairly ordinary stuff for everyday drinking. Lady Thomson told me that they occasionally dipped into the old wines but it usually turned out to be a hit and miss affair (clearly an ullaged bottle occasionally found its way to the table) and their friends not only didn't like the old wines but thought their hosts were just being mean! It was another treasure house: 1867 Coutet in beautiful condition (there were only seven bottles so no question of opening one to taste: happily I was given a bottle by a grateful and generous American client some time later), 1870 Lafite in magnums, and one bin containing over 13 dozen 1874 Lafite, binned in sawdust. The original cellar book entry ran: 'Bin XXXII, Claret – Lafite 1874 – 1 Hogshead – 22 dozen. 11 purchased from Wicks *le tout première* quality, bottled at the château, full brand on corks. Laid (binned) in July 1877.' 'Moved owing to dampness to bin XXXIII Aug 7th 1882.' Sawdust packed between the lathes was quite an original way of drying off the bottles. After nearly a century it was a messy job to unbin. My wife and I, in boots and overalls, sorted them into 'firsts' (high to top of shoulder), 'seconds' (hovering either side of mid-shoulder) and low shoulder, discarding the dozen or so below that as unsaleable. We came out exhilarated but looking like a couple of coal miners.

At midday we gave ourselves a break and drove to the nearest village for a pub lunch. By chance we stumbled across a delightful old hotel where we had large Bloody Marys followed by toasted sandwiches, immaculately served. It turned out to be Studley Priory. But that's another story. Incidentally, the '£300' cellar sold for £13,000. If the honest MW failed to profit to this extent, at least his introductory commission exceeded the original offer price, which was some consolation – apart from an easy conscience.

Sir John Thomson, his grandfather's wine merchant, Geo Claridge of Rood Lane, London, and the cellarman who binned the wine so ably in the 1880s, are all immortalized in the Christie's catalogue of June 25th 1970.

I had been aware of the existence of Sir George Meyrick's collection of old claret at Hinton Admiral in Hampshire for some time but the opportunity to see it did not occur until early in 1970. The old wine was all binned at the far end of an L-shaped cellar which curled round the family silver vault. As usual I started methodically in the top left bin, pulled out a bottle and held it to the light to inspect cork, level and colour. My heart dropped. It was amber: too old, lost all its colour and life. To confirm my worst fears I drew the cork – and it turned out to be old pale sherry! There were two bins full. Of the 1953, half a dozen were packed on July 25th 1885, little had ever been drunk. The next two bins, against the end wall were clearly bin-labelled 'Claridge – Claret No 288 Château Montrose 1869, 25 dozen @ 120/-. Packed 30th May 1888. Mr Taylor.' And a very good job Mr Taylor had done: the binning was immaculate, the wooden lathes in excellent condition. The cellar yielded a small range but large quantities.

A little later Sir George told me *en passant* that he also had some old sherry, at Bodorgan, his country seat in Anglesey. Daphne and I promptly invited ourselves to spend Easter with friends whose holiday house, by the most extraordinary coincidence, had been built on Meyrick family property. The Bodorgan cellar was one of the most unusual in

Treasure trove? The irresistibly alluring contents of a dusty cellar.

structure and content I have ever come across. The walls and ceiling were of brick, and vaulted. It was extremely damp. Apparently in wet weather water streamed through the middle of the cellar. There was indeed some sherry, but more important than that, a long horizontal shelf upon which were lying 11 dozen and two bottles of 1865 Lafite: original corks and capsules and only three bottles with levels lower than the top of the shoulder! Also, in a little galvanized iron bin, with plain capsules, no labels and no bin labels or records, were some very anonymous claret bottles. I rarely open bottles in situ, but I really had to establish whether this was worth the expense of packing and removal to London. The cork turned out to be branded Château Kirwan vintage 1865 – the wine was perfection. Sir George had half the bottle for his lunch and I decanted the remainder to share with my holiday hosts. We enjoyed the quality if not the quantity.

Glamis. What this name evokes! Scenes from *Macbeth*; the birthplace of Elizabeth the Queen Mother; and the resting place of the most famous collection of magnums ever to find its way to (and occasionally revisit) the saleroom: 1870 Lafite with the thin but clearly embossed red wax seal 'Claret, Coningham & Co' and the bin label '1870 magnums Lafitte (sic) Coningham'.

The cellar itself was, most unusually, at ground floor level, right in the centre of the castle. It had certainly the easiest access of any cellar I have worked in. It was also dry and in immaculate condition. The famous magnums had apparently not been moved since they had been originally binned, for quantity and bin number tallied with the contemporary and later cellar books.

Clearly Claude Bowes Lyon, the 13th Earl of Strathmore, was a keen wine buff. But the 1870 Lafite must have proved an immense disappointment. It was an enormous wine, black as Egypt's night, severe, tannic – undoubtedly like red ink when young. The 13th Earl died before the wine had matured enough to drink; indeed it took half a century (as did the 1928 Latour) to come round. We opened one magnum before the sale – absolutely essential, for had it not been up to scratch the whole collection would have been suspect and its value negligible. To make the most of the occasion I invited some of the best English 'literary palates' to diner in the Christie's boardroom, including Hugh Johnson, Cyril Ray, Edmund Penning-Rowsell and Harry Waugh. Naturally, we had some interesting wines, the pièce de resistance being immediately preceded by one of the most exquisite of clarets: the 1900 Léoville-Las-Cases. With bated breath I drew the cork of the magnum of 1870 Lafite: the original cork was perfect, the level of the wine amazingly high. As for the colour, it was so deep and so red that it could almost have been mistaken for a 1959. The nose was equally miraculous: not a hint of old age, of oxidation or over acidity – just gentle rich fruit. It was a lovely drink: full yet soft and velvety, with great subtlety and length of flavour; still tannic, with years of life left. The greatest of great clarets. It just seemed to get better at every sip. After the initial relief, the rapture, and we toasted not only the 13th Earl but the long-dead cellar master at Lafite who, with nature's ripening sun, old fashioned skill and without the benefit of a consultant oenologist, had quietly and efficiently made so magnificent a wine. 🦋

First published in **Christie's Wine Companion,** *Christie's (London) 1981.*

CHAPTER 2

BORDEAUX, BURGUNDY
...OR NAPA CABERNET?

Burgundy is Better – Maurice Healy (1940)

Burgundy the Cannibal Wine – Ian Maxwell Campbell (1945)

The 'Judgement of Paris' Revisited – Steven Spurrier (2018)

BURGUNDY IS BETTER

MAURICE HEALY (1940)

First published in the 'dismal wartime winter of 1940', Maurice Healy's
Stay Me With Flagons met with a success that surprised and delighted the
author. Healy was an Irish lawyer, author, and co-founder of the wine trade's
elite Saintsbury Club. His wise words here, 'Burgundy at its best overtops
Bordeaux at its best', raised more than a few eyebrows…

Every journey I make by Underground is the source of a certain amount of irritation. I find myself faced with elaborate quotations from George Meredith[1] in praise of burgundy; and these appear on the advertisements of a wine that has just as much right to call itself Irish Whiskey as to take the name of burgundy. Closer examination reveals that the article advertised comes from Australia, or from some other part of the Empire; and I am prepared to believe that it has been made honestly, in the burgundy manner, from Pinot grapes. It is a perfectly genuine wine, straightforward in everything but its name and its attempt to attribute to itself what Meredith said about burgundy. [2] For it is not burgundy; and in fact it only faintly resembles burgundy. Mind you, for those who like that kind of wine, it is just the kind of wine they would like. It is strongly tonic, for it is very ferruginous; but only once, and then by a rare accident, did I succeed in finding an Empire wine of burgundy type that had been allowed to age; and at 10 years old it did taste rather like burgundy, although not a very good burgundy.

---

[1] George Meredith, 1828–1909, seven-times Nobel prize-nominated English novelist and poet, who famously contrasted port, Rhône and Mosel wines with burgundy…
[2] He said: 'Observe, I do not compare the wines; I distinguish the qualities. Let them live together for our enrichment . . . Were they rivals, a fourth would challenge them. Burgundy has great genius . . . An aged burgundy runs with a beardless port. I cherish the fancy that port speaks the sentences of wisdom, burgundy sings the inspired ode. Or put it that port is the Homeric hexameter, burgundy the Pindaric dithyramb.'

When Meredith went into dithyrambs about burgundy he was speaking of one of the noblest and greatest of red wines that has gladdened the hearts of generations of mankind. That wine is made in France, and nowhere else; it comes from a very strictly delimited area in the neighbourhood of Dijon. When Burgundy was a Duchy, this area was at the heart of the Duke's dominions. His rule varied from generation to generation; there were times when he also ruled over Flanders and the Low Countries. The inhabitants of these parts were his richest subjects; and they were able to pay for the very best of the wine made each year. They created a tradition that has lasted to our own time; and the seeker after the best burgundy today will be well advised to travel to Belgium or Holland.

In England there are certain wine-merchants that have the burgundy tradition, and one can count upon them to produce something good; but for one really good bottle of burgundy sold in this country there are 50 mediocre and 100 bad. I can only remember two lots of burgundy in my own cellar that were outstanding. One was a magnificent Clos de Vougeot 1904 that I got from Christopher's in about 1925, the other was a Les Bonnes Mares 1921 that came from Avery's of Bristol. The latter was a less expensive wine, because it was younger and the vintage year was not classic; but it really proclaimed the true merit of burgundy as loyally and satisfactorily as its elder superior in rank, which, however, was a superb wine; probably the best I ever had in my cellar. For let there be no doubt about it: burgundy at its best overtops claret at its best.

You will only drink four or five bottles of truly first-class burgundy in your whole life (and you will be lucky if you find so many; only three have rung that bell with me; good as the 1904 and the 1921 were, none of them was the really outstanding thing I have in mind). But you can drink claret of the highest class several times in the year: claret that should be drunk kneeling with every sip consecrated as libation to heaven.

I wonder if I can get an image from the orchestra. Everyone knows how tender and beautiful the flute can be in a solo part; but whosoever has had the luck to hear the solo played by the recorder recognizes a fullness, a roundness and a pathos of tone to which the flute cannot attain. Now claret flutes for us all the time, while burgundy is usually content to grate on its scrannel pipe of wretched straw. Occasionally it, too, will flute with grace and tenderness; but, once in a blue moon, it will produce the recorder, and then, indeed, our hearts are melted. Such a moment occurred to me the other day, when at the hospitable table of my good friend, Sir Francis Colchester-Wemyss, I partook of a bottle of Richebourg 1923 that fulfilled all the conditions that govern the best of burgundy. I had honestly forgotten how good burgundy could be, and this was like a new revelation. 🥂

*Excerpt from **Stay Me With Flagons** by Maurice Healy, Michael Joseph (London) 1940.*

BURGUNDY, THE CANNIBAL WINE

IAN MAXWELL CAMPBELL (1945)

The much-loved commentator, Ian Maxwell Campbell, was a source of wisdom on the wines made during both World Wars. He believed wine was a gift 'ordained to promote health of mind and body', and he occasionally felt that burgundy was better than Bordeaux, being particularly impressed with its 'cannibalistic' ability to absorb its own sediment.

I t may seem strange, but it is true, that I have never been able to acquire such an intimacy with burgundy as with claret. They are so often classed together and served at table in succession that a knowledge of one would seem to imply or perhaps necessitate a knowledge of the other. There are many far better judges than I am who consider burgundy to be the superior wine. I agree that, taken all over, it displays a more pungent and powerful bouquet than claret, more body and more evident sugar, and a robuster flavour in its masterpieces, but not an all-round equal refinement or gentility of quality: its sweetness is not so natural, nor do its humbler denizens show comparable breeding.

It is impossible ever to draw a real parallel between the produce of different wine-growing districts. Common burgundy is very common and harsh to the taste, but common clarets – particularly the common clarets of years like 1893, 1899 and 1928 – were pleasant to drink, soft and supple and satisfying. How diversely dictatorial, too, human or physical idiosyncrasy is in each one of us! I find red Bordeaux (claret) much easier to digest than red burgundy, and on the other hand I find white burgundy much easier and more agreeable to drink than white Bordeaux. Some of my friends find the exact opposite. So each gets its mead of approbation.

Burgundy's historic Clos de Vougeot: the essence of Burgundy or the tragedy?

The consequence, as far as I am concerned, is that I am much more intimate and on speaking terms with claret than burgundy. In the Côte d'Or the ill effects of burgundy, curiously enough, do not make themselves felt, and I can enjoy a whole *déjeuner* and dinner, accompanied by a formidable array of burgundy wines, without any forebodings of discomfort to follow. Most wines taste well in their native environments. Of modern burgundy vintages, and by that I mean vintages of this century, I bracket 1904 and 1906 as very fine all through the Côte d'Or, and what was then known as Romanée La Tâche was superb in both years and neither heavy, nor stodgy, nor heating, as so many of the older burgundies were. Then, although there were some attractive wines in 1908 and 1911 (perhaps the latter were unsally dry for burgundy), we had to wait for 1915 for another outstanding vintage, good but disconcertingly variable. This was only to be expected as it was a war baby and many agencies were at work ill-suited to satisfactory development of the wines when young: their later transport across France to the port of embarcation was also hazardous, and many casks arrived over here with the foetid smell and flavour of canal water and the truth was not in them. We forget, amid the travail and difficulties of the present post-war days (I am now in September 1945), the troubles that had to be encountered and overcome at the close of the World War I. Some Chablis my Dijon firm shipped to us came over in red burgundy casks and had acquired a pinkish tinge of colour. It gave us a lot of trouble, because people in the country began sending it back to us as 'not

Chablis'. One well-known London restaurant proprietor, however, put it on his list as 'Chablis-Rosé' and scored a big success. An intelligent use of their inventive faculties would frequently help people through troubles as often as not imaginary. But the 1915 burgundies were on the whole pleasing wines for many years though they hardly fulfilled their early promise. This autumn (1945) I tasted 1915 Nuits, of a good growth, and Clos de Vougeot, and much preferred the former; the latter was acetic. I look upon Clos de Vougeot, as long as it is shared by 40 different owners, as the tragedy of the Côte d'Or.

There were many good 1919 wines, especially those bottled and binned in the country of origin. The Bourguignon is a clever and resourceful fellow and, some years ago, he invented a sort of syphon which, in the guise of a thin strand of wire, he could insert between the cork and the glass neck, into a bottle of wine, and, with its aid, extract the heavy sediment which in burgundy is often both plentiful and shifty, like sand.

All wines, and certainly all red wines, ought to throw a sediment in bottle, and burgundy does not fail in this duty. There are different ways of dealing with the deposit or sediment, but careful decanting is the best because it is an operation performed by yourself, and you know quite well that, rather than see a speck of sediment go into your decanter, you will sacrifice a glassful of wine and sometimes a bit over. It is more economical, indeed, to lose a whole glass of wine than ruin, by parsimonious greed, a whole decanterful. Some wine-waiters need reminding, however, that the mere act of pouring wine out of a bottle into a decanter does not of itself clarify the wine! Quite the contrary, the operation requires care, watchfulness and steady handling.

I have seen burgundy eat up its own sediment and by doing so increase its sweetness as well as its softness in old age. The attractive, but eccentric, 1895 burgundies were an instance of this and gave a lot of trouble as the majority of them threw a very heavy deposit which, if you turned the bottle upside down and looked through it, you could see floating down like a cloud of soot. Most merchants, I think, emptied their bottles into casks again and rebottled them, and private people probably emptied theirs down the sink and forswore burgundy in the future.

I happened to have taken a fancy to an Aloxe-Corton and had put a little of it down in my cellar and, being of a frugal Scottish mentality, instead of throwing it away when it developed this excess of deposit, I left it alone where it was, and, to my gratified surprise some years later, I found that the sediment had almost entirely gone, leaving a mere film round the inside of the bottle. Where had it gone to? There was only one answer – cannibalism! The wine had eaten it up; my remaining bottles were child's play to decant and a pleasure to drink. I always had a warm corner for the 1895s which, without perhaps being great wines, were sweet and amiable all through the gamut.

This is not a textbook or a training manual and, even if I were properly able to do so, I am not going to try to explain the chemical reactions responsible for the above strange phenomenon: it is evidently not so strange as all that in the birthplace of burgundy, and the logical ingenuity of our friends there has, as already mentioned, sought, seemingly with success, to dispel the heavy clouds and help their wine once more to exhibit its bright and sunny nature. On my last visit to the Côte d'Or I dined with Georges Faiveley at his pretty and daintily furnished house in Nuits St-Georges. We were a gay party and started off the evening with an apéritif in the shape of port; it was served clear. I draw attention to this fact because, as a rule, the port aperitif in France, however good a wine in itself, comes to you as thick as pea soup. The series of wines at dinner was well selected and, though I drank my fill of choice growths of 1923, 1915 and back to 1904, I experienced no ill-effects.

I kept a copy of the menu, as, in its way, it was rather unique with its greetings to me as Chevalier of their pseudo-mediæval Confrérie of the 'Order of Tastevin' – of which Georges Faiveley is the grandest of Grand-Masters – that breathes the self-conscious pride, one might almost call it the boastfulness, the *panache*, of your true Bourguignon. Each of my fellow guests, when he signed his name, added an epigram, a jest or a complimentary word of welcome. I am afraid this much-treasured memento, as well as my gaily illuminated certificate of Tastevinous chivalry, was amongst my many valuable belongings that perished in the historic Blitz of 10th May 1941, when Burns Pye and I, and our faithful staff, meeting amid the smoke and stench of the 40-hours' blazing furnace that had been Mark Lane, fared forth into the unknown future, as all other Britons did, determined to carry on somewhere and somehow. 🍂

Extract from *The Wayward Tendrils of the Vine* by Ian Maxwell Campbell, Chapman & Hall (London) 1948.

Steven Spurrier outside his shop, La Caves de la Madeleine, in Paris, 1981.

The judges' table at the Judgement of Paris, which took place in Paris on 24th May 1976. Obscured by Steven Spurrier (6th from left) is Odette Kahn, doyenne of French wine writers and editor of La Revue du Vin de France.

THE 'JUDGEMENT OF PARIS' REVISITED

STEVEN SPURRIER (2018)

Steven Spurrier, creator of the controversial 1976 wine tasting that placed California wines ahead of the First Growths of Bordeaux, looks back at the rematches two, 10, 30 and 40 years on.

The results of 'The Paris Tasting' have been the subject of more discussion and debate than any other wine event since the Bordeaux classification of 1855. According to George Taber's book *Judgement of Paris: California vs France and the 1976 Wine Tasting That Changed the World*, they have even been the topic of high-level scientific interest. Two Professors of Economics at Princeton University, Orley Ashenfelter and Richard E Quandt (both wine connoisseurs), recalculated the tasting of the red wines using a more rigorous academic methodology than my simply adding up all the scores out of 20 and dividing by the number of tasters. This study was published in the summer 1999 issue of the statistical magazine *Chance* and they concluded that: 'It was no mistake for Steven Spurrier to declare the California Cabernet the winner.'

The scores from the Judgement of Paris were as follows:

White wines
1 Chateau Montelena 1973 – 14.67
2 Meursault Charmes Roulot 1973 – 14.05
3 Chalone Vineyard 1974 – 13.44
4 Spring Mountain Vineyard 1973 – 11.55
5 Beaune Clos des Mouches Joseph Drouhin 1973 – 11.22

6   Freemark Abbey Winery 1972 – 11.11
7   Bâtard-Montrachet Ramonet-Prudhon 1973 – 10.44
8   Puligny-Montrachet Les Pucelles Domaine Leflaive 1972 – 9.89
9   Veedercrest Vineyards 1972 – 9.78
10 David Bruce Winery 1973 – 4.67

Red wines
1   Stag's Leap Wine Cellars 1973 – 14.17
2   Château Mouton Rothschild 1970 – 14.00
3   Château Montrose 1970 – 13.94
4   Château Haut-Brion 1970 – 13.55
5   Ridge Vineyards Monte Bello 1971 – 11.50
6   Château Léoville Las Cases 1971 – 10.78
7   Mayacamas Vineyards 1971 – 9.94
8   Clos du Val Winery 1972 – 9.72
9   Heitz Wine Cellars Martha's Vineyard 1970 – 9.39
10 Freemark Abbey Winery 1969 – 8.67

The outcome surprised me as much as anybody that day, May 24th 1976, and the results were to be validated time and time again. The first rematch took place on January 11th and 12th 1978 at the Vintners Club in San Francisco. I flew in for this and was stunned to see that the Club, which normally had 30 or so tasters at their weekly tastings, had capped the attendance at exactly 100. In the Chardonnay flight the 1974 Chalone (my favourite in Paris) was placed first, followed by the 1973 Chateau Montelena, 1973 Spring Mountain and 1972 Puligny-Montachet Les Pucelles. Of the Cabernet Sauvignons, Stag's Leap 1973 again took the lead from Heitz Martha's Vineyard 1970 with Ridge Monte Bello 1971 third and Mouton Rothschild 1970 fourth.

By 1986, the Bordelais had seemingly forgiven me, but their concern that a decade earlier their wines had been too young to show their true quality against the 'up front' Californians remained, and in response I planned, 10 years on, a re-run on the neutral ground of New York. The complaint that the results at the Vintners Club had been due to the dominance of 'California palates', was addressed by my choosing a highly qualified but diverse panel, which would have again been nine but for a last minute cancellation by Alexis Lichine. These were: Michael Aaron of the prestigious Manhattan wine merchant Sherry-Lehmann, Alexis Bespaloff of *New York Magazine*, Bartholomew Broadbent son of Michael, Barbara Ensrud of the *New York Daily News*, Robert Finigan, who had been so helpful in selecting the original wines, Georges Lepre' chef sommelier at the Ritz Hotel in Paris, Peter Morrell of Morrell's wine store and Frank Prial of *The New York Times*. The tasting was held appropriately at The French Culinary institute.

Following the criticism of my adding up the scores out of 20 and dividing by the number of tasters in 1976, I asked the judges to give their most preferred wine nine points, down to one point for their least favourite. Writing in his Wine Letter, Robert Finigan remarked that 'to my surprise it was not immediately obvious, apart from the eucalyptus character of Heitz Martha's Vineyard, whether a given wine was French or Californian, but that most of the wines were comparable in both excellence and style'. With eight tasters and nine wines, a perfect score would be 72 and the worst possible score eight. Here are the 1986 scores with their 1976 rankings:

1   Clos du Val 1972 – 57/8
2   Ridge Vineyards Monte Bello 1971 – 54/5
3   Château Montrose 1970 – 45/3
4   Château Léoville-Las Cases 1971 – 43/6
5   Château Mouton Rothschild 1970 – 41/2
6   Stag's Leap Wine Cellars 1973 – 36/1
7   Heitz Martha's Vineyard 1970 – 35/9
8   Mayacamas 1971 – 34/7
9   Château Haut-Brion 1970 – 23/4

With the exception of the Haut-Brion, which was very tired due to poor storage, one might have thought that, while California did well and Bordeaux did not do badly, the Bordelais would be relaxed about this result, but this was not to be the case. The Union des Grand Crus (UGC) was at the same time criss-crossing to the US to promote the excellent 1985 vintage. The fact that four of their top châteaux had been 'beaten' by wines from California received wide coverage and Pierre Tari, President of the UGC and one of the original judges in 1976, accused me directly as having 'personally wrecked their entire campaign'.

Worse was to come: the Bordelais, now distinctly squeamish about Bordeaux-California comparative tastings, raised the objection that such events had now become the favourite diversion of American wine professionals who used them as a marketing tool – a permanent trap for French wines.

Jean-Michel Cazes of Lynch-Bages and Bruno Prats of Cos d'Estournel commented: 'In playing down their losses and bragging about their occasional victories, our California rivals plan to boost their reputation, little by little, to the heights of the great Bordeaux.' They went onto say: 'Neither in price nor in quality do the great wines of the Médoc fear competition. This current challenge is more serious, more pernicious, because it is cultural. In reducing wine to a product that can be measured 'scientifically' these joyless tastings mix the world of taste with that of numbers. The Californians have proved that their wines have body. Have they also a soul?'

California's finest: the Ridge Monte Bello vineyards in the lee of the mist-shrouded Santa Cruz mountains.

Quite plainly, after such bad feeling, I had no intention whatsoever of holding a 20th anniversary re-run. In the August 1996 *Decanter* magazine I wrote: 'Although Château Montelena and Stag's Leap Wine Cellars were catapulted to fame as a result of the 1976 tasting, my feeling is that the event was just as significant for premium California wines as a category. Twenty years ago, California was investing more in research than any other wine region. The recognition of the quality of some of these wines by the French panel was not only a recompense for this, but a spur to further effort. What none of the original critics of the tasting could forsee was the effect on France. After the first shock had worn off, the Napa Valley quickly became a mecca for French producers who began to look further than their local négociant to see what was going on. This interfacing between the Old World and the New World was the single most important result of comparing "apples and oranges" that day in 1976. Twenty years on, there is no reason to hold such a tasting, except for pleasure.'

Nor did I have any intention of re-visiting the Paris Tasting on its 30th anniversary until I was contacted by my old school friend Ben Howkins, who was in charge of Jacob Lord Rothschild's cellars at Waddesdon Manor in Buckinghamshire, with the idea of re-creating the event in England and simultaneously at the food and wine emporium Copia in Napa.

The tasting went ahead as planned – on May 24th 2006, the precise 30th anniversary of the Judgement of Paris.

To correspond as closely as possible to the original format, nine judges were selected for each panel, with one of the 1976 judges present at each of the venues – Michel Dovaz in London and Christian Vanneque in Napa. The tastings were held simultaneously, at 10am in Napa and 6pm in London, and telephone contact was established during the lunch and dinner that followed to formulate the final scores and ranking. Judges were asked to give their top wine one point, their second wine two points down to 10 points for their least-preferred wine.

Freemark Abbey had already admitted that their 1969 was fading back in 1986, but agreed to supply bottles to complete the picture historically. Below are the joint-rankings which appeared on Jancis Robinson's website the following morning. Jancis's marks out of 20 are added first, my own second:

Wine	Combined Ranking	Scores JR/SS
Ridge Vineyards Monte Bello 1971	61	18.5/18.5
Stag's Leap Wine Cellars 1973	79	18/16
Heitz Martha's Vineyard 1970	86	16.5/13
Mayacamus 1971	86	15.5/17.5
Clos du Val Winery 1972	92	17.5/16.5
Château Mouton Rothschild 1970	93	17/17
Château Montrose 1970	106	15/17.5
Château Haut-Brion 1970	116	13/13.5
Château Léoville-Las Cases 1971	132	16/14.5
Freemark Abbey 1969	139	14/11

The judges in London were: Michel Bettane, Michael Broadbent, Michel Dovaz, Hugh Johnson, Matthew Jukes, Jane MacQuitty, Jasper Morris, Jancis Robinson and Brian St Pierre. Those in Napa were: Dan Berger, Stephen Brook, Anthony Dias Blue, Wilfred Jaeger, Peter Marks, Paul Roberts, Andrea Immer Robinson, Jean-Michel Valette and Christian Vanneque.

Under the heading 'California triumphs again at Judgement of Paris re-run' Jancis Robinson stated: 'Last night's re-run of the famous Judgement of Paris 1976 California vs Bordeaux tasting was, much to general surprise, another walkover for California. It was thought that perhaps after all this time the California wines might have fallen off their perch and the famous longevity of red Bordeaux would put the French wines in the ascendant, but this was not the case. There were some lovely wines in this blind tasting and, although I tried to view them completely objectively without trying to second guess their identity, I was aware that some of the wines could only be Californian and were some of the best.'

Both in London and Napa, the panel of judges then went on to taste – not blind this time – a range of much younger wines from comparative vintages. These were:

White Burgundies
Puligny-Montrachet 1er Cru Les Pucelles 2002 Domaine Leflaive
Meursault 1er Cru Les Charmes 2002 Domaine Roulot
Beaune 1er Cru Clos des Mouches 2002 Joseph Drouhin
Chassagne-Montrachet 1er Cru Les Caillerets 2002 Louis Jadot
Bâtard-Montrachet 2002 Louis Latour
Corton-Charlemagne 2003 Domaine Bonneau du Martray

California Chardonnays
Talley Rosemary's Vineayrd 2002 Arroyo Grande Valley
Patz & Hall Hyde Vineyard 2004 Carneros
Ramey Hyde Vineyard 2002 Carneros
Mount Eden Vineyard 2002 Santa Cruz Mountains
Chateau Montelena 2003 Napa Valley
Peter Michael Point Rouge 2003 Sonoma Country

Red Bordeaux
Château Montrose 2000 St-Estèphe
Château Leoville-Las Cases 2001 St-Julien
Château Rauzan-Segla 2000 Margaux
Château Margaux 2000 Margaux
Château Latour 2000 Pauillac
Château Haut-Brion 2000 Pessac-Léognan

California Cabernets
Clos du Val 2000 Reserve Napa Valley
Shafer Hillside Select 2001 Napa Valley
Stag's Leap Wine Cellars Cask 2001 Napa Valley
Joseph Phelps Insignia 2002 Napa Valley
Ridge Monte Bello 2000 Santa Cruz Mountains
Staglin Rutherford 2001 Napa Valley

On her website, Jancis Robinson continued: 'The wines from the original tasting were largely delicious and the experience of tasting them was a huge pleasure. The six young white burgundies and six young California Chardonnays that followed were very much less glorious, many too alcoholic and/or too sweet and not all of these Californian. The final tasting was of six red Bordeaux, mainly 2000s and mainly very impressive, followed by six young California Cabernets, some of which were delicious and some extremely sweet, concentrated and exaggerated. It was in judging these last wines, so different in style to the California Cabernets from the original tasting, that there was the most divergence between the London and the Napa tasters.' I was, of course, very busy making sure it was all going to plan, and can only remember that for my palate the French wines were so much better than those of California. In a later interview I said: 'With the younger vintages, France wiped the floor with California and this just goes to show that in the early 1970s, France was resting on its laurels, but by the early 2000s this was true for California instead.'

I imagined that the story of the Judgement of Paris would have stopped there, but no. In early 2017, Grant Ashton, a financier with a passion for wine, suggested that he could organize a re-run of the Paris Tasting at his members' wine club, 67 Pall Mall, with the same wineries but younger vintages, and could fill the room if it were on May 24th and if I were present. I agreed, and we sat down to assess the modern wines, ranking them on the same 'one mark for the best wine, 10 marks for the worst' system as 10 years before. Here are the results:

Chardonnay

Chalone Vineyard 2011	199
David Bruce Winery 2010	226
Chateau Montelena 2002	230
Meursault 1er Cru Les Charmes 2006 Domaine Roulot	242
Freemark Abbey Winery 2012	266
Beaune 1er Cru Clos des Mouches 2002 Joseph Drouhin	287
Spring Mountain Vineyard 2012	292
Puligny-Montrachet 1er Cru Les Pucelles 2002 Dom Leflaive	302
Veedercrest Ruhl Vineyard 2009	327
Bâtard-Montrachet 2000 Domaine Ramonet	377

Cabernet Sauvignon

Stag's Leap Wine Cellars SLV 2005	233
Château Haut-Brion 2001	242
Ridge Monte Bello 2005	243
Freemark Abbey Bosche Vineyard 2001	250
Château Montrose 2001	271
Château Mouton Rothschild 2001	274
Clos du Val Winery 2001	295
Heitz Martha's Vineyard 2005	301
Château Léoville-Las Cases 2001	310
Mayacamas Vineyards 2002	329

Younger vintages of the white Burgundies would, I think, have shown much better, but I was not allowed to know the vintages as this time my notes were counted. Here my top three were Chalone, Freemark Abbey and Puligny-Montrachet, with the Meursault fourth and Chateau Montelena fifth. For the Cabernets, the vintages were more closely aligned and the results for the top five more tighly ranked. I placed Freemark Abbey first, then Mayacamas, Heitz Martha's Vineyard, with Stag's Leap fourth followed by Clos du Val, showing great support for California.

And that really wrapped up the 40th anniversary.

I would say that if there is one thing that the Judgement of Paris gave to the world of wine it was the creation of a template whereby little-known wines of quality could be tasted blind against known wines of quality and if the tasters were of high quality themselves, the results of these tastings would be respected. This will continue to be the case and both producers and consumers will reap the benefit. 🍂

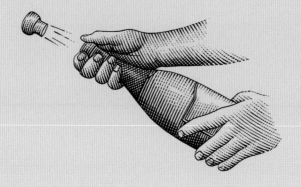

CHAPTER 3

POWER TO THE UNDERDOGS

Notes on a Barbaric Auslese – George Saintsbury (1920)

The Debut of Dom Pérignon – Henry Vizetelly (1879)

'Ah, the Sérinity…' – Randall Grahm (2019)

The English Wine Bubble – Justin Howard-Sneyd MW (2019)

Cyril Ray and the Rise of the *Compleat Imbiber* – Kathleen Burke (2013)

Notes on a Barbaric Auslese

GEORGE SAINTSBURY (1920)

Professor George Saintsbury (1845–1933) was one of the most influential literary historians of the 19th century, and although highly modest, he did once boast that he never gave a second-hand opinion about wine. His wonderfully evocative words on the subject still have a wide following – not least by the wine trade's most exclusive dining club, 'The Saintsbury Club', which still meets twice a year to honour him. In the following paragraphs, Saintbury bemoans the perils of 'barbaric Auslese', and appears to find German wines going though a similar dip post 1870s as they did following the 1970s. However, his grumble doesn't extend to red hock...

German wine has of late naturally shared the unpopularity of German everything – naturally, but not wisely. The true attitude in such matters was long ago put in the 'War Song of Dinas Vawr':

> *His wine and beasts [provide] our feasts,*
> *And his overthrow our chorus.*

Not that hock, as indeed was hinted in a former chapter, has ever ranked with me among the 'first three', or even the first five or six greatest wines. The 'palling' character of its attractions, when at its supposed finest, precludes that. I was once favoured with half a dozen single bottles of the very finest hocks in ordinary commerce – wines, the cheapest of which would have 'stood you in', as the old phrase went, some 10 shillings a bottle at

A charming pen and ink sketch of a street in Bernkastel, in the Middle Mosel, by avowed hock lover Michael Broadbent.

the old prices, and the dearest nearer a sovereign. Except for curiosity's sake, I would much rather have had a similar collection of good second-class claret; and after the first two glasses of each Rhine wine, it would have been no sacrifice in me to leave all the rest to any compotator.

In fact, despite the wonderful first taste of the great Auslese wines, I think both hock and Moselle best as beverage drinks; for in these lower qualities, the overpowering and almost barbaric volume of flavour does not occur, and they are very fresh and pleasant quenchers, going well with most sorts of food. In days when it was still lawful to drink bottles of wine in the plural, I should have said that a bottle of hock at dinner, and a bottle of claret after it, was a decent and moderate allowance, and likely, as one of Scott's people allows of something else, 'to bring a blessing with it'. But for finer purposes I should, once more, regard them as chiefly curiosities; and accordingly, they never figured largely in my wine-lists.[1]

What has been said of hock applies with little change to Moselle. The wines of Ausonius's favourite river have long had a deserved reputation for flowery flavour; unfortunately they have – of late years and even decades – acquired another, also well deserved but much less enviable, as being the most abominably 'faked' of all real or pretended juices of the grape. Whether it was partly due to green unknowing youth or not, I cannot say, but I certainly seem to remember a time when sparkling Moselle, though apt to be a little over-sweet, was

---

[1] Sparkling hock I liked little, and never bought. The 'Cabinet Sekt', which the interesting tenant of Amerongen patronized so strongly, was 'a very German champagne'. [Saintsbury could not resist noting down allusions that only he would understand. This is an example.]

Panoramic view of the vineyards of the Middle Moselle and the town of Bernkastel.

a pleasant and seemed a wholesome liquor. I once, in company with a friend, made a light but agreeable meal at Oxford in the time of fritillaries, on a bottle of it from one of those nice china vases full of ice, which looked like giant conjurors' egg-cups, with some wafers. It also went excellently with a most opposite accompaniment, certain sardine sandwiches, which they then made very well at the 'Mitre'. But after 1870 the general curse of insincerity, overreachingness and fraud, which even such a prophet of prophets of their own as Nietzsche recognized as hanging on Germany, attacked with particular ferocity the banks of the river whose various charms and benefits – its beauty and its variety, its wine and its trout and its grayling – the poet sang fifteen hundred years ago. Sparkling Moselle became a thing to be very carefully chosen or avoided altogether; the 'floweriness' of both sparkling and still had a horrible suspicion of the laboratory; and I once attributed (the faculty not disagreeing) a persistent attack of an unpleasant kind to an unduly prolonged sampling of the lighter sorts. Nor did I ever much affect the loudly-trumpeted Berncastler Doktor [sic]. Still, I own that a really good Scharzhofberg is a very fine wine; and that some of the beverage kinds from Piesporter to Graacher are mighty refreshing. But it may be well to warn those who cellar it that light Moselle, when young, is very apt to cloud, though it should, if good, clear later.

By the way, is there any red Moselle?

For the red hocks, however, I must put in a word, both in justice to them and in charity to my fellow-creatures. They – not merely Assmanshäuser, which certainly is the best, but Walporzheimer, Ober-lngelheimer and others – are specifics for insomnia after a fashion which seems to be very little known, even among the faculty. Many years ago, when I was doing night-work for the press, and even after I had given that up, when I was rather unusually hard run at day-work, I found sleep on the off-nights as well as the others in the former case, and often in the latter, not easy to obtain. I was not such a fool as to take drugs, and I found hot grog or (what is not in itself inefficacious) strong beer, conducive to an uncomfortable mouth, etc, in the morning when taken only a few hours before. But a large claret glass or small tumbler of red hock did the trick admirably, and without deferred discomfort.

Somewhat akin, I suppose, to these red hocks are the still red champagnes, which are very rare in England, but are very nice wines, and quite unsurpassed for what doctors might call neurotic dyspepsia. I think they first came to my knowledge as prescribed for Prosper Mérimée in the illness which preceded his death: and after long looking for them in vain, I was lucky enough, some five-and-thirty years ago, to pick up, at the Army and Navy Stores, some still Red Verzenay of 1868. I have never seen any since in lists.

In the same bin with it once lay some Côte Rôtie – more easily procurable with us, but not very commonly seen on English dinner-tables. Something of what was said in the first of these papers as to Hermitage extends to this, and to Châteauneuf du Pape, and to many other less famous red wines of the south of France. They were, I believe, special favourites with Victor Hugo; and there is a certain Hugonic character about them all, though it never, except in Hermitage itself, rises to anything that suggests the full inspiration of the *Châtiments* or the *Contemplations*. It is more congenial to the novels in prose.

Other oddments of France put themselves forward – Saint-Péray, very pleasing now and then for a change; red sparkling Burgundy, which as noted above, I never found to be a success; while white sparkling Bordeaux is an anti-natural perversity, the invention of which deserved Dante's circle of the fiery rain. Then there is Picardan, the northernmost wine of France and the worst. This I never admitted to my cellar, but I have drunk it… 🦋

Excerpt from Chapter VI 'Hock, Moselle and the Rest' from **Notes on a Cellar Book** *(Macmillan, 1978; first edition 1920). Saintsbury's quote on page 20 published by kind permission of Merlin Holland of the Saintsbury Club.*

THE DEBUT OF DOM PERIGNON

HENRY VIZETELLY (1879)

In his luxuriously bound and illustrated 1879 work Facts about Champagne and other sparkling wines, *English publisher and writer Henry Vizetelly found that the wines of Reims were held by its Burgundian neighbours to be 'irritating to the nerves and conducive to gout'. Fortunately, the winemaking skills of one careful monk changed all this....*

Strong men, we know, lived before Agamemnon; and strong wine was made in the fair province of Champagne long before the days of the sagacious Dom Pérignon, to whom we are indebted for the sparkling vintage known under the now familiar name. The chalky slopes that border the Marne were early recognized as offering special advantages for the culture of the vine. The priests and monks, whose vows of sobriety certainly did not lessen their appreciation of the good things of this life, and the produce of whose vineyards usually enjoyed a higher reputation than that of their lay neighbours, were clever enough to seize upon the most eligible sites, and quick to spread abroad the fame of their wines. Saint Remi, baptizer of Clovis, the first Christian king in France, at the end of the fifth century left by will, to various churches, the vineyards which he owned at Reims and Laon, together with the 'vilains' employed in their cultivation. Some three and a half centuries later we find worthy Bishop Pardulus of Laon[1] imitating Paul's advice to Timothy, and urging Archbishop Hincmar to drink of the wines of Epernay and Reims for his stomach's sake. The crusade-preaching Pope, Urban II, who was born among the vineyards

---

[1] No stranger, we're told, to theological controversy.

Statue of Dom Pérignon – the father of Champagne – in front of the headquarters of Moët & Chandon, Epernay.

of Champagne, dearly loved the wine of Ay; and his energetic appeals to the princes of Europe to take up arms for the deliverance of the Holy Sepulchre may have owed some of their eloquence to his favourite beverage.

The red wine of the Champagne sparkled on the boards of monarchs in the Middle Ages when they sat at meat amidst their mail-clad chivalry, and quaffed mighty beakers to the confusion of the paynim. Henry of Andely[2] has sung in his fabliau of the 'Bataille des Vins' how, when stout Philip Augustus and his chaplain constituted themselves the earliest known wine-jury, the crus of Espernai, Auviler, Chaalons and Reims were amongst those which found most favour in their eyes, though nearly a couple of centuries elapsed before Eustache Deschamps recorded in verse the rival merits of those of Cumières and Ay. King Wenceslaus of Bohemia, a mighty toper, got so royally drunk day after day upon the vintages of the Champagne, that he forgot all about the treaty with Charles VI, which had formed the pretext of his visit to France, and would probably have lingered, goblet in hand, in the old cathedral city till the day of his death, but for the presentation of a little account

---

[2] A Norman troubadour of the 13th century.

for wine consumed, which sobered him to repentance and led to his abrupt departure. Dunois, La Hire, Xaintrailles and their fellows, when they rode with Joan of Arc to the coronation of Charles VII, drank the same generous fluid, through helmets 11 barred, to the speedy expulsion of the detested English from the soil of France.

The vin d'Ay – *vinum Dei* as Dominicus Baudoin punningly styled it – was, according to old Paulmier[3], the ordinary drink of the kings and princes of his day. It fostered bluff King Hal's[4] fits of passion and the 10th Leo's artistic extravagance; consoled Francis I for the field of Pavia, and solaced his great rival in his retirement at St Just. All of them had their commissioners at Ay to secure the best wine for their own consumption. Henri Quatre, whose *vendangeoir* is still shown in the village, held the wine in such honour that he was wont to style himself the Seigneur d'Ay, just as James of Scotland was known as the Gudeman of Ballangeich. When his son, Louis XIII, was crowned, the wines of the Champagne were the only growths allowed to grace the board at the royal banquet. Freely too did they flow at the coronation feast of the Grand Monarque, when the crowd of assembled courtiers, who quaffed them in his honour, hailed them as the finest wines of the day.

But the wines which drew forth all these encomiums were far from resembling the champagne of modern times. They were not, as has been asserted, all as red as burgundy and as flat as port; for at the close of the 16th century some of them were of a *fauve* or yellowish hue, and of the intermediate between red and white which the French call *clairet*, and which our old writers translate as the 'complexion of a cherry' or the 'colour of a partridge's eye'. But, as a rule, the wines of the Champagne up to this period closely resembled those produced in the adjacent province, where Charles the Bold[5] had once held sway; a resemblance, no doubt, having much to do with the great medical controversy regarding their respective merits which arose in 1652. In that year a young medical student, hard pressed for the subject of his inaugural thesis, and in the firm faith that…

> *'None but a clever dialectician*
> *Can hope to become a good physician,*
> *And that logic plays an important part*
> *In the mystery of the healing art.'*

…propounded the theory that the wines of Burgundy were preferable to those of the Champagne, and that the latter were irritating to the nerves and conducive to gout. The

---

[3] The French navigator and explorer Binot Paulmier de Gonneville.
[4] Henry VIII of England.
[5] Charles the Bold was Duke of Burgundy 1467–77.

faculty of medicine at Reims naturally rose in arms at this insolent assertion. They seized their pens and poured forth a deluge of French and Latin in defence of the wines of their province, eulogizing alike their purity, their brilliancy of colour, their exquisite flavour and perfume, their great keeping powers, and, in a word, their general superiority to the Burgundy growths. The partisans of the latter were equally prompt in rallying in their defence, and the faculty of medicine of Beaune, having put their learned periwigs together, enunciated their views and handled their opponents without mercy. The dispute spread to the entire medical profession, and the champions went on pelting each other with pamphlets in prose and tractates in verse, until in 1778 – long after the bones of the original disputants were dust and their lancets rust – the faculty of Paris, to whom the matter was referred, gave a final and formal decision in favour of the wines of the Champagne.

Meanwhile an entirely new kind of wine, which was to carry the name of the province producing it to the uttermost corners of the earth, had been introduced. On the picturesque slopes of the Marne, about 15 miles from Reims, and some four or five miles from Epernay, stands the little hamlet of Hautvillers which, in pre-revolutionary days, was a mere dependency upon a spacious abbey dedicated to Saint Peter. Here the worthy monks of the order of Saint Benedict had lived in peace and prosperity for several hundred years, carefully cultivating the acres of vineland extending around the abbey, and religiously exacting a tithe of all the other wine pressed in their district. The revenue of the community thus depending in no small degree upon the vintage, it was natural that the post of 'celerer' should be one of importance. It happened that about the year 1688 this office was conferred upon a worthy monk named Pérignon. Poets and roasters, we know, are born, and not made, and the monk in question seems to have been a heaven-born cellarman, with a strong head and a discriminating palate. The wine exacted from the neighbouring cultivators was of all qualities – good, bad and indifferent – and with the spirit of a true Benedictine, Dom Pérignon hit upon the idea of 'marrying' the produce of one vineyard with that of another. He had noted that one kind of soil imparted fragrance and another generosity, and discovered that a white wine could be made from the blackest grapes, which would keep good, instead of turning yellow and degenerating like the wine obtained from white ones. Moreover, the happy thought occurred to him that a piece of cork was a much more suitable stopper for a bottle than the flax dipped in oil which had heretofore served that purpose.

The white, or, as it was sometimes styled, 'grey' wine of the Champagne grew famous, and the manufacture spread throughout the province, but that of Hautvillers held the predominance.

To Dom Pérignon the abbey's well-stocked cellar was a far cheerfuller place than the cell. Nothing delighted him more than…

> *'To come down among this brotherhood*
> *Dwelling for ever underground,*
> *Silent, contemplative, round and sound,*
> *Each one old and brown with mould,*
> *But filled to the lips with the ardour of youth,*
> *With the latent power and love of truth,*
> *And with virtues fervent and manifold.'*

Ever busy among his vats and presses, barrels and bottles, Pérignon alighted upon a discovery destined to be most important in its results. He found out the way of making an effervescent wine – a wine that burst out of the bottle and overflowed the glass, which was twice as dainty to the taste, and twice as exhilarating in its effects. It was at the close of the 17th century that this discovery was made – when the glory of the Roi Soleil was on the wane, and with it the splendour of the Court of Versailles. Louis XIV, for whose especial benefit liqueurs had been invented, recovered a gleam of his youthful energy as he sipped the creamy foaming vintage that enlivened his dreary têtes-à-têtes with the widow of Scarron. It found its chief patrons, however, amongst the bands of gay young roysterers, the future *roués* of the Regency, whom the Duc d'Orléans and the Duc de Vendôme had gathered round them, at the Palais Royal and at Anet. It was at one of the famous *soupers* d'Anet that the Marquis de Sillery – who had turned his sword into a pruning-knife, and applied himself to the cultivation of his paternal vineyards on the principles inculcated by the celerer of Saint Peter's – first introduced the sparkling wine bearing his name. The flower-wreathed bottles, which, at a given signal, a dozen of blooming young damsels scantily draped in the guise of Bacchanals placed upon the table, were hailed with rapture, and thenceforth sparkling wine was an indispensable adjunct at all the *petits soupers* of the period. In the highest circles the popping of champagne-corks seemed to ring the knell of sadness, and the victories of Marlborough were in a measure compensated for by this happy discovery.

Why the wine foamed and sparkled was a mystery even to the very makers themselves; for as yet Baumé's aerometer[6] was unknown, and the connection between sugar and carbonic acid undreamt of. The general belief was that the degree of effervescence depended upon the time of year at which the wine was bottled, and that the rising of the sap in the vine had everything to do with it. Certain wiseacres held that it was influenced by the age of the moon at the time of bottling; whilst others thought the effervescence could be best secured by the addition of spirit, alum and various nastinesses. It was this belief in the use and

---

[6] In fact, Baumé's 'hydrometer'. Developed to assess the density of a liquid by Antoine Baumé in 1768, and invaluable to wine growers for measuring the sugars in grape juice, and thus the potential alcohol level of the crop.

English publisher and writer Henry Vizetelly 1820–94.

efficacy of drugs that led to a temporary reaction against the wine about 1715, in which year Dom Pérignon departed this life. In his latter days he had grown blind, but his discriminating taste enabled him to discharge his duties with unabated efficiency to the end. Many of the tall tapering glasses invented by him have been emptied to the memory of the old Benedictine, whose remains repose beneath a black marble slab in the chancel of the archaic abbey church of Hautvillers. 🍃

*Extract taken from Chapter I, 'The Origin of Champagne', in **Facts about Champagne and other sparkling wines** by Henry Vizetelly, Ward Lock (London) 1879.*

AH, THE SÉRINITY…

RANDALL GRAHM (2019)

'California winemaker and founder of Bonny Doon Vineyard, Randall Grahm, is well known for his pioneering exploits with Rhône grape varieties in the hills of Santa Cruz. Here he describes his hot pursuit of the best version of Syrah (the 'genius grape') he can find. Move over Cabernet Sauvignon…

Having been in the wine business now for almost 40 years, I often ask myself what I might still have to contribute before hanging up my spur(-pruner)s. From a career standpoint, clever wine labels, even some clever winemaking have all been well, good and amusing, but in the end, they don't really constitute the kind of contribution I seek to make. I believe that what is most valuable to the world is the creation of original wines and the discovery and expression of singular *terroirs*. Apart from being particularly satisfying for the producer, the creation/discovery of these new elements enrich the world profoundly for those fortunate enough to experience them. The other element of the equation for the discernment of original wine is perhaps the discovery or creation of original grapes, or at least the ability to discern a high degree of congruity or acclimation of a particular grape or set of grapes to a given site. This degree of 'tuned-ness' is what allows the originality of the wine to emerge. Thus, it seems particularly useful to the world for a winemaker to attempt to develop a sort of empathic, I-Thou relationship with a given site instead of unilaterally imposing his or her stylistic vision on the produce of that site. In this way, the winemaker can perhaps express an aspect of Nature's great complexity, far grander than the vision bounded by an individual imagination.

Do we really need more or new grape varieties in this world? Very possibly not, but arguably, we might well benefit from fine-tuning the ones we have, enabling them to be better adapted to the world's changing climatic conditions or better suited to growing sites that are rather different from those of their original provenance.[1] We know that Pinot Noir is capable of producing brilliant wines in Burgundy, but its potential harmony and majesty can often be elusive when it steps out of its historical geographical context. (This is understandable, as there has been ample historical time for producers to note which particular clones, biotypes – even rootstocks for that matter – are best adapted to their sites.) I, for one, am a great fan of Syrah and know that it is capable of producing interesting and complex wines far away from its traditional home in the Northern Rhône. Alas, that's often due to a fair bit of manipulation in the winery to achieve a certain felicitous result. Having said that, it is my core belief that if a 'complete' wine can be made with substantially less winemaking manipulation and vinous *maquillage*, the results are potentially far more dramatic and rewarding than a wine of artifice, and that is the course that I, for one, would prefer to follow. I am intrigued by the idea of trying to craft a unique Syrah wine in the New World with two basic aspirational ideas: (1) Discovery/creation of unique biotypes better suited to the growing conditions of coastal California than that which the extant clonal material currently provides; (2) Utilization of a larger range of distinctive biotypes (or clones) to create enhanced complexity in the wine, with an eye towards a more articulate expression of the unique qualities of the site from where the grapes derive.

Syrah is a genius grape. It can possess a seductive scent that is both hauntingly sophisticated, complex and at the same time expressing a dusky, earthy, animal aspect, in the same way that some great perfumes seamlessly conjoin floral notes with elements of splendid, musky, decadent decay. Like many great wines, Syrah is capable of producing one of wine's great special effects – that of simultaneous weightlessness and great power and persistence. (I think that may be what we mean by 'elegance'.) I wonder sometimes how we mere mortals had the wit to have discovered this brilliant variety. But we did, thank Bacchus. Loving the grape is a necessary but, alas, insufficient criterion for producing a brilliant wine from the variety. What is needed rather more is a greater understanding of and the ability to deliver what the grape truly requires, or, failing that, perhaps the ability to affect changes in the grape itself to attain better congruity to its site. I believe that there are a number of reasons why the prospects of a great Syrah from the New World seem to be a far more manageable proposition than many others I could imagine.[2] But we are beginning from a very different starting point in the New World, in comparison to those who are working from vineyards with long storied histories of greatness, and our methodology in pursuing excellence, however that is understood, must perforce be slightly different.

---

[1] Grape vines can suffer from debilitating viruses as do other species. Viruses are not generally propagated through grape seeds, so sexual replication (via self-crossing), while creating its own challenges, can eliminate at least one major issue.

Two of a kind? Sérine (left) and Syrah grapes.

In the Old World, the traditional way of 'improving' one's vineyard is done through the rather slow and tedious process of *sélection massale*, which is not merely the replacement of sick, moribund or deceased vines with healthy upstarts, but rather actively looking for individual biotypes that might bring a particular character to the overall wine, in some sense enabling the wine to become more complex, balanced, in some ways a more true representation of itself, as far as that constitution is understood. In considering a particular biotype or clone of a given grape variety, one is seeking to capture the purest expression of its Platonic ideal, with the very important caveat that its expression is also caught up in the optimization or idealization of the *terroir* from which it derives. In the New World, we are beginning with a significantly blanker slate, further handicapped by often having but the most rudimentary understanding of the nature of a particular

---

[2] While a great Syrah can certainly be said to be complex and soulful, at the same time it wears some of its unique charms on its sleeve, to wit, its extraordinarily distinctive perfume. While there are certainly other molecules that contribute to its complex aroma, the compound, rotundone seems to be the most important element in contributing to Syrah/Sérine's distinctive fragrance of white pepper. Rotundone can of course be readily detected organoleptically, but an assay for differential rotundone concentrations could easily be set up. As long as other conditions within the vineyard – light exposure, yields, etc – remained static, one could potentially identify the highest rotundone-producing biotypes for warmer sites.

vineyard's *terroir*[3], and working with significantly different environmental and climatic conditions from the Old World paradigm.

Que Syrah *sera*? Modern 'Syrah' appears to be slightly different from what is generally believed to be its varietal antecedent, the variety known in the Côte-Rôtie as Sérine, and in Hermitage as 'la petite Syrah' (a rather different beast than the variety that is similarly named in the New World). There is general agreement that the two varieties are genetically very similar, but phenologically, they do look somewhat different. Compared to Syrah, Sérine produces a smaller, tighter cluster, often more prone to bunch rot and other maladies, and does not grow as robustly as some of the modern Syrah clones. It seems to produce its best work in the coolest sites under generally lower light and more overcast conditions. From a winemaking standpoint, it has been observed in a side by side comparison with Syrah: Sérine's fruit is higher in acidity and varietally more 'typical' – a stronger expression of the characteristic white pepper and bacon fat. It has been opined that Sérine is merely Syrah that has been infected with a particularly felicitous set of viruses.[4] In any event, as I am hoping to discover/create a particular biotype (or biotypes) that will have a particularly intense fragrance under our New World conditions, I've decided to begin with Sérine rather than Syrah.[5, 6]

My plan is to consider the historical variety of Syrah/Sérine in its original context to be in a sense a jumping off point, and rather than attempting to replicate note for note the qualities of an Old World examplar (rather like the famous example posed by Jorge Luis Borges' Pierre Menard)[7], by allowing Syrah vines to self-pollinate or cross with themselves, I am hoping to create alternate variants of the variety; some of them will be

---

[3] Arguably, it would take many, many years for someone to deeply understand the qualities of *terroir* of a relatively new vineyard, if only for the reason that it takes vines a number of years to come into a form of homeostasis or dynamic balance with their surroundings.

[4] Virus-free Sérine is apparently available from French nurseries, but I have no personal knowledge as to whether it is as expressive in its virus-free form as compared to in its wild state. Frankly, it doesn't make much sense to me how the Ur-Syrah, if that's what it is, would be less pristine than its descendants. I'm certain that with more study, this particular mystery will be illuminated.

[5] For one thing, the dryer weather in California should be helpful in obviating many of the fungal issues to which Sérine is susceptible. The higher acidity found in Sérine should also be helpful in a grape that is prone to higher pHs, especially in warmer climates.

[6] It is a pet theory of mine that a clone of Syrah similar if not identical to Sérine already exists in California – the so called 'Estrella River' clone. Putatively imported from Hermitage more than 40 years ago, I've found the Estrella clone to be the most singular of extant Syrah clones in California, albeit only when grown in the coolest sites. It does seem to produce a smaller cluster and a more aromatic wine than everything else out there; I am almost certain that it is the 'petite Syrah' of Hermitage.

[7] In the Borges story, a fictional character, Menard, attempts to rewrite *Don Quixote* word for word, several hundred years after Cervantes, by subjecting himself to experiences analogous to what Cervantes himself might have undergone.

similar, some wildly divergent from their parents. (The differences found from *sélection massale* would tend to be rather minute and subtle.) One would then observe if a particular offspring shows a distinctive personality, expressed in what is a historically new and different *climat* and *terroir*. By creating multiple iterations of the crosses and comparing these biotypes with the parent Syrah/Sérine itself, one can observe telling differences, and the question becomes: What are you actually looking for that might in some sense be more interesting than that which you started with (at least in this new location)?[8, 9] It is not an unreasonable hypothesis that while there may well be one or two particular biotypes of these new Sérine self-crosses that stand out as being 'complete', with the most intense flavour, fragrance and perhaps, if we're lucky, a degree of drought tolerance, it might be the wiser course to select a number of different individuals with somewhat differing qualities – one selected for fragrance (maybe the most important), another for texture or weight, another for acidity, etc. Ideally, we would produce enough vines for a small lot production of these individual lots and then play with creating what we reckon is an appropriately proportionate field blend.[10]

I continue to wrestle with trying to define what makes a particular variety 'great,' and what are the qualities of a particular clone or biotype that make for a superior example of that

---

[8] This methodology is not without some hazard. Because one is performing self-crosses, heterozygous *vinifera* vines will express recessive genes, carrying genetic weakness or defect. A non-trivial percentage of the crosses will be sterile, non-productive, or show other weakness in their phenotypic presentation. Vigorous growth may be a pretty good indicator of a degree of drought tolerance (that's great!), upright growth perhaps is a good indicator of wind tolerance (a plus), and the presentation of smaller bunch size often correlates with greater flavour concentration. Looking for the obvious positive qualities is the relatively easy (if time-consuming) part; discerning the elements of what can produce a great and complex wine from simply tasting the grapes is a bit more challenging.

[9] Owing to many decades of neglect and some misguided human efforts (essentially the restriction of phenotypic variability), the autochthonous varieties, Gaglioppo and Magliocco Dolce, in the Cirò appellation of Calabria had deteriorated significantly but in recent years a group of researchers, sponsored by the Librandi company, launched an initiative to revive or 'improve' these varieties. In other words they were looking to improve qualitative parameters, while at the same time preserving the unique adaptive characteristics of the cultivars to the unique conditions of the region. They employed a similar strategy of allowing self-crosses, beginning with approximately 3,000 accessions, and ending up approximately 20 years later with 22 biotypes. The main difference between their work and the one that I am undertaking is that they are attempting to preserve or return to a sort of historical ideal of these two cultivars, whereas my objective is more open-ended, ie, to attempt to discover vinous beauty in whichever way it will manifest itself.

[10] In the Côte-Rôtie vineyard from whence the Sérine seeds were derived are interplanted Viognier vines. It's not inconceivable that there may be some Sérine/Viognier crosses among the seedlings. It also seems likely that there will be a substantial number of white biotypes produced amongst the seedlings, owing to the parentage of Sérine (the white Mondeuse Blanche and red Dureza). We will look carefully at the aromatic potential of the white biotypes (maybe using Viognier as a 'control') and keep an eagle eye out for pink biotypes (Professor Andy Walker of UC Davis suggests that they very seldom occur), which in my experience also often possess particularly intense aromatic potential.

DEGREES OF ELEGANCE

I would argue that there are certain features that all 'great' varieties share (with the caveat that they are grown in an appropriate location). One crucial feature is the ability of the grape to produce a wine capable of conservation and continued development as it ages. This must certainly be linked to the particular antioxidants found in the grape, but, naturally, every great grape variety solves this problem differently.

The antioxidant profile of Cabernet Sauvignon is rather different from that of Pinot Noir, for example, and the particular profile of antioxidants leads to rather different winemaking protocols, and ultimately to very different wine styles, each with their own merits. What I might propose as another criterion of grape 'quality' is perhaps a bit controversial, and maybe it's more a matter of my own aesthetic predilection rather than an immutable rule. I believe that a 'great' grape variety is one that has enough 'openness' in its structure to allow the expression of soil characteristics to emerge. That is to say that the flavour profile is not so dense or tightly packed with flavour elements as to obscure the expression of soil characteristics. I would argue that certain varieties like Pinot Noir, Nerello Mascalese, Rossese, Cornalin, even Poulsard, can serve as the basis for wines of far greater complexity in comparison to grapes that produce denser, more robust wines, such as Cabernet Sauvignon, Tannat, Mourvèdre, Aglianico, Sagrantino or Charbono. (An interesting corollary to this to this would be the differential concomitant winemaking technique – vigorous, aerative extraction for the latter varietal category versus gentle, less aerative infusion for the former.)

What seems to be key in characterizing the 'openness' of the structure of the wine is the ability of the wine to kaleidoscopically evolve after the bottle is opened, shifting its form and revealing new aspects. Where does one place Syrah on the cool/warm or open or dense continuum? I'd argue that Syrah (or Sérine) grown in cooler sites, such as Côte-Rôtie, has a lot more in common with Pinot Noir in comparison to, say, Cabernet Sauvignon. Analogously, Nebbiolo, grown at higher elevations, in cooler sites, such as in the appellation Carema (in comparison to say, Barolo), is likewise capable of showing rather dramatic finesse and complexity. There will always be wine drinkers who prefer the impact and weight of denser wines, and the eternal Bordeaux vs Burgundy debate is perhaps unresolvable. There are many potential dichotomies at work analyzing the issue of how to achieve success in planting a vineyard in the virgin territory. Knowing where you are in the world at least climatically is helpful, and the Mediterranean vs Continental distinction can be useful. And yet most all of us aspire to be more elegantly Continental (eg, Cary Grant) as opposed to Mediterranean (Anthony Quinn as Zorba the Greek). If your climate is dramatically warm and dry, you are probably best advised to embrace your inner Anthony Quinn and work with sun-loving, drought tolerant varieties. If your site is on the warmer side of cool (and thanks to global climate change, many of us now or will soon find ourselves in this condition), the question might be what steps might you take to bring a degree of elegance and finesse to the wines you're making in a warmer, drier climate that is inexorably pushing them Zorba-ward in the direction of rusticity.

variety. Every interesting grape variety seems to express its worthiness in a different way (*see* left), and its 'quality', with the case of Syrah in large part derives from both its unique texture coupled with its haunting aromatics. Greatness in wine, I suppose, is a bit of a subjective call, but I believe it can only arrive in wines that furnish something like a 'complete' experience, ie, both real complexity as well as a dynamic ability to change and evolve both in the wine glass and in the bottle.[11] Syrah/Sérine certainly meets both of these criteria.

We attempted to germinate almost 8,000 seeds of Sérine in a nursery in the winter of 2017, and achieved excellent success, though did lose a fair number (more than a third) to a late spring frost. We found quite a bit of disparity in the appearance of the seedlings; some were quite vigorous and apparently healthy, others rather puny and etiolated with an odd growth habit. We kept approximately 2,000 of what appeared to be the healthiest ones. When you work with seedlings, the internode distance on the small stalks is very close, and it is very important that you carefully disbud all of the basal bud whorls, lest the seedlings vexatiously shoot suckers from below the surface for the life of the vineyard, which creates a major inconvenience. (We did a reasonable, though not perfect job of disbudding.) The seedlings were then planted out in nursery rows in the spring of 2018 in our vineyard in San Juan Bautista. Nursery rows are very narrow, about a metre between rows and the vines themselves were planted approximately three to four metres apart. In the first year the vines that survived gopher or human blight grew anywhere from a few centimetres to perhaps half a metre in length, and were pruned back to just a couple of buds the following winter. We were blessed by a fairly wet winter/spring in 2018–19, and that contributed to some very impressive growth in the 2019 growing season.

According to Professor Andy Walker of UC Davis, vinifera grape seedlings need to achieve at least two metres of growth (mostly vertical, if possible) before they are able to move out of their juvenile phase and begin to receive the hormonal signal to bear fruit. At UC Davis, where there is deep soil, ample water, lots of heat and very little wind, seedlings generally bear fruit in their third year, whereas in Torino, Italy, it is said to take the order of seven or eight years for the vines to become fruitful. Because San Juan Bautista is generally quite dry (though we did periodically irrigate the young seedlings), not very warm, and exceptionally windy, it was my expectation that we would end up with fruit on a time-table rather more like Torino than Davis. What actually happened is that in this the second year of vine growth, we've observed enormous variability in growth and

---

[11] One might certainly argue that all 'great' wines express some element of soil characteristics, a bit of an ineffable quality, but correlated to identifiable and commonly understood organoleptic clues, included in the vexing concept of 'minerality'. Wines of *terroir* express the quality of dimensionality and a distinctive persistence on the palate.

vigour. Some seedlings are still quite stunted and others have put on truly impressive amounts of growth, well over two metres.

There is an incredible disparity in the appearance of the vines. Not only do they show rather dramatic differences in growth, there are some differences in the shape of the leaves and great differences in the colour of the leaves and stems – every shade between lime green, Kelly green, crimson, even, amazingly, pure black (a rather Goth look). From a practical standpoint, we made the decision to establish a cordon wire at approximately 1.20 metres, and from a cost standpoint, we decided not to use individual stakes for each seedling, but rather attach twine to the wire, anchor it to the base of the seedling and train each vine up the string ladder, as it were. It's of course impossible to predict precisely, but I reckon that maybe we'll see fruit appear on maybe one third or more of our vines next year, which I will regard as something of a miracle.

When Andy Walker came out recently, he counselled us to grub up all of the weak vines, which on its face seemed like sound advice. Sometimes it's clear that the weakness of the vine stems from funny, sub-optimal genetics but often it's not always quite clear whether the problem is a genetic issue or simply the fact that maybe the vine wasn't planted properly or got chomped on early in its life by a critter, or any of the thousand natural shocks that grape vines are heir to. When you train these young seedlings, these are the things that you are doing: making sure that you've removed as many of the suckers (subterranean shoots) as you can locate; disbudding most of the lateral shoots, so as to encourage virtually all growth to the apical tip, ensuring that your vine will grow tall; tying up the vine to the twine every foot or so (the more vertically it is trained, the faster it will grow and the taller it will be. (You're also trying to protect the growing tip from becoming damaged due to abrasion by the wind.[12])

It doesn't really work to stand up between the rows as you will soon need to get back on your knees to do the work, most of which occurs at ground level. I hit upon the clever idea of buying knee pads, such as are used by plumbers and tile people and other folks whose work is highly terrestrial. So, when you have the opportunity to work for several hours on your knees, performing essentially some pretty repetitive tasks, your mind has the opportunity to wander. You begin thinking about how you are going to interpret the vine's

---

[12] I'm not sure if it is entirely due to wind damage that shoots become forked, ie split in two with no dominant apical end. (Might it well be a genetic disposition, such as one finds with the Michet clone of Nebbiolo?) But when it happens, the possibility of achieving the growth you seek is essentially cut in half. One is therefore placed in the Solomonic position of having to decide which of two branching shoots will live, and which will be lopped off. It's not a monumentally difficult decision to make but just a reminder that we are always facing life's forking paths.

The author immersed in his favourite subject.

outward signifiers as indicators of its suitability of purpose. Maybe it's just me but I have a certain tendency to anthropomorphize vines, or perhaps it's a function of inordinate empathy. Will the mesomorph vines – those sturdy, studly, alpha vines really be capable of producing wines with the greatest degree of finesse and elegance?[13] Might it not be the vines that are more moderate and conservative in their growth habit that are better capable of going the distance, ie, not running out of water before the end of the season? Syrah/Sérine possesses the tragic flaw of having very poor stomatal regulation, the ability to conserve moisture under adverse, ie, windy or extremely hot conditions. Very vigorous vegetative growth is often correlated with aggressive rooting capability, as I had previously mentioned, so the ultra vigorous vines might well be the most suitable. Or perhaps not. Stomates that are open all the time will photosynthesize all the time and therefore grow like crazy; maybe it will be the moderate ones that will optimize the water balance. (They may not find as much water in the soil, but won't lose as much through the leaves.) It was

---

[13] And of course I easily succumb to the fantasy that perhaps it is the most misbegotten-looking vine that somehow has the capacity to produce the most flavourful fruit. It's very possible that the big vines will handily overshadow (rather literally) the small vines, but if there's an opportunity to keep some of the smaller vines (at least the ones that are not too anomalous looking), we certainly will, maybe just because 'a vine is a terrible thing to waste'. Small vines do tend to produce small fruit, and all things being equal, small fruit is the most intense. I'm sold now on the concept; we'll retain some small, slower growing vines that do not evidence obvious defect.

Andy's suggestion (and a good one, I believe) to retain the healthiest looking moderate growers as well as the healthiest vigorous ones, and see for ourselves what produces the best result. (It's a bit difficult to work this out *a priori*.)

At the end of the day, we're looking for vines that will produce grapes of extraordinary character under our conditions and at the same time show true sustainability under our conditions, ie, drought and wind tolerance. While a vine that could somehow manage its stomata better than the others would likely appear to be more moderate in its growth habit, until the vines are tested under replicated field conditions, we won't really know. Since the factors governing stomatal regulation are probably located on multiple genes, you probably need an enormous sample size, much bigger than ours, to find an individual with superior regulation. It may well turn out that the best we can determine is which individuals produce the most flavourful and or distinctive character, and pursuing the characteristic of drought tolerance would be a slightly different exercise. I'm thinking that by flying a drone over a large and fairly uniform, unirrigated Syrah/Sérine vineyard – perhaps in Australia, perhaps in southern France or elsewhere – and through remote sensing, most likely the infrared detection of leaf temperatures, seek to detect individual vines with the most functional stomatal regulation (after ground-level confirmation for a few seasons). Perhaps this brilliant water-conserving individual could be crossed with the particularly flavourful Sérine that we've observed, and we'd end up with a great selection of Syrah for a warmer and drier planet.

It could be argued that this project may be a bit of a folly, given that at the moment, in the US at least, Sérine qua Sérine is largely unknown, Syrah is still (rather unfairly) despised and largely misunderstood and perceived as being largely unsaleable.[14] But this project itself will take some years to near completion, and in that intervening time, the fickle public may well come to its senses. Syrah, when grown skilfully in appropriate temperate sites, is certainly capable of producing wines that are at a minimum, soul-satisfying and at best, utterly transformative. May we all find some form of Sérinity. ❧

---

[14] This, owing to the somewhat irrational exuberance of growers planting Syrah in mostly inappropriate areas (way too warm) of California, and perhaps the flooding of the market with certain jaundiced caudal Antipodean examples.

THE ENGLISH WINE BUBBLE

JUSTIN HOWARD-SNEYD MW (2019)

*Justin Howard-Sneyd is a UK-based winemaker, merchant and Master of Wine.
He asks if English sparkling wine's place as the underdog to champagne might
one day undergo a significant shift in perspective.*

In the decades to come, we'll look back at 2018 as the year when English sparkling wine hit adolescence. You know the kind of thing: sudden growth spurts, rebellious behaviour, starting to explore relationships (sometimes with the wrong people), unrealistic expectations, experimentation, arguments… But, how long will it be before it reaches maturity?

The early years were promising. The roots of the modern English industry go back as far as 1951 when Sir Guy Salisbury-Jones re-planted the vineyards at his home in Hambledon, creating the first commercial vineyard in Hampshire (and the UK) for 100 years. But the vines he planted were the modest Seyval Blanc variety. Today's boom in plantings has focussed on the much more marketable champagne grapes, Chardonnay, Pinot Noir and Pinot Meunier, to produce our own English sparkling wine. The change really began in the mid-1990s when the pioneers of *méthode champenoise* wines – Stuart and Sandy Moss at Nyetimber in West Sussex and Mike Roberts at Ridgeview (East Sussex) – began to achieve repeated critical success with their wines.

Since then, the demand for English sparkling wine has grown steadily, and until very recently, the supply has struggled to keep up with demand. This has given rise to a very rare phenomenon in the world of wine: a situation where producers can sell everything they

make to allocated customers, and many buyers are left without the wine they need. (The same thing happened with New Zealand's Cloudy Bay Sauvignon Blanc between 1990 and 2005: demand significantly exceeded supply.)

When there is not enough wine to go round, no producer ever needs to price-promote, and no retailer wants to create a price war for fear of running out of stock. This rather artificial environment trains the customer to pay the full price, and to buy the wine they want immediately, when they see that it is available. But this state of the market can very quickly unravel as soon as supply exceeds demand, even by a small amount. And sadly, it looks as if this is where English Sparkling wine may be headed next.

In any market, when there is a large structural oversupply, things can get messy. When this happens, buyers realize that everyone has wine to sell, and they start to play one producer off against another. Producers who want to make sure that THEY are the ones who hit the volumes in their business plan offer tempting deals to the retailers in return for guaranteed quantity sales. The price spirals downwards.

All of which means we may still have some bumpy adolescent years ahead. So how long before we reach the sunlit uplands of maturity? As Baroness Philippine de Rothschild liked to say: 'Winemaking is easy – only the first 200 years are difficult.'

The great *Grandes Marques* champagne houses were mostly founded between 1740 and 1850 (Veuve Clicquot in 1772, Pol Roger in 1849, Bollinger in 1829, Moët & Chandon in 1743), and while many of the names we know now have survived for two centuries, there were also a number of early names that fell by the wayside. Now, I have no doubt at all that in 200 years time, we'll have our own English *Grandes Marques*, and a number of the names established already will be among them. But, will the current owners' descendants still control their families' businesses, or will the cold winds of commercial reality cause fortunes to be lost, as well as made?

You need deep pockets to set up a winery from scratch, and to keep financing it until any future investment can be funded out of cash flow. To get a return on that original investment takes many more years of generating sufficient profit to pay back the capital. In practice, most successful traditional European wineries have written off the original investment many years ago. But this is not the case with our own wine estates.

Until recently, perhaps the deepest pockets in the English wine business belonged to Eric Heerema, owner of Nyetimber since 2006. It is estimated that that the purchase and

Left: The Nyetimber vineyard, Upper Tillington, and in the background the Sussex Downs.

operation of Nyetimber since he bought this prestigious property have soaked up over £65 million. It has never made a profit, and, in 2018, Nyetimber made a significant loss – admittedly during a phase of considerable investment in further expansion, and while securing further retail and restaurant listings.

Two new players on the scene may have even deeper pockets.

Mark and Sarah Driver founded the Rathfinny Wine Estate near Alfriston in Sussex in 2010, with the stated aim of making a million bottles of wine from 400 acres of land. And just this year, another Mark, Monaco-based businessman Mark Dixon, owner of Provence's second largest producer Château de Berne, is said to be planting 1.25 million vines at several locations, including Kingscote Vineyard in East Grinstead (West Sussex), having purchased the property in 2016. In a good year, Kingscote should start yielding nearly two million bottles.

With all of the other investments in new vineyards, large and small, from new and existing players, we now have enough vines in the ground in the UK to make over 10 million bottles of fizz every year – over 20 million bottles in a generous year. And planting is still on the increase.

But UK sparkling wine sales have yet to exceed an annual four million bottles and only increased by 6% in 2018. So it is hard to see how we are going to drink all we now make.

Both Marks are intelligent businessmen who have taken good advice, and both are prepared to take a long-term view of their investments. And given their net worth, they can both stand several years of losses before their bank managers start to look concerned. But 200 years? Hopefully it won't take that long.

How many more wealthy individuals will be gripped by the fizz-lust? And is English wine beginning to look like a mere bubble?

Here's what I predict for the future of this awkward teenager:

Firstly, there is going to be a short term glut. It may well manifest itself this harvest (2019), if the predicted yields are anything approaching last year's record crop. The price of grapes will collapse, and people will start to question their contracts. New contracts will be signed at lower prices.

Second, the large volume 2018 vintage will start to hit the market in 2020 and 2021. English sparkling wine will push deeper into supermarkets, and the price will drop. More

Pioneer English winemaker: General Sir Guy Salisbury-Jones pictured at his Hambledon, vineyard (Hampshire) in 1969. He planted his first vines in 1951.

wines will become available at under £20. Many more brands – those who have avoided the supermarkets so far – will realize that they won't get close to their volume targets unless they deal with the 'Big Four' (Tesco, Asda, Sainsbury's and Morrisons).

Thirdly, promotional activity will become commonplace, and brands that have established themselves at close to £30 a bottle will be seen price-cutting to around £20 a bottle. For wineries who participate, the resulting sales spikes will become addictive, and their sales above £30 will slow to a trickle.

Then producers who sell through the supermarkets, but who don't participate in promotions will be starved of sales, and their volumes will decrease. They then may lose their listings. There will continue to be success for well-established producers with deep pockets who make the right decisions, keep investing and hold their nerve. They will be investing real marketing money in competing with the champagne houses to buy listings and strike deals with high-profile events partners like Royal Ascot, Wimbledon, the Royal Opera House in Covent Garden etc. But that success will be hard won and expensive. These brave wine companies will not see a profit for a while.

Newcomers will stop establishing huge vineyards, and the rate of planting will slow dramatically as the market slowly catches up with what has already been planted. There will still be a structural oversupply of grapes that will feed a market of supermarket own-labels, and tactical brands that will mostly trade in the £12 to £18 sector of the market, undermining the premium price positioning of English sparkling wine, and possibly eroding the quality perception too.

On the plus side, the quality of the wine from the best producers will continue to improve, and the international reputation of English sparkling wine will become firmly established. Export sales will grow slowly (it is expensive stuff, and this market segment, already dominated by champagne, is not large), and the best brands will become desirable in smart restaurants and wine shops in the likes of Tokyo, New York and Rio de Janeiro.

Those that don't make the grade, or run out of money, will be swallowed up by larger players. Champagne houses who can't plant any more vines in the their own region will seek out ways to expand; many may invest in vineyards in the UK.

Eventually, in 20 to 30 years time, the *Grandes Marques* of England will emerge from the pack as stable, long-term businesses, no longer requiring further injections of cash. Some will do so under their current ownership.

I predict that we will drink as many bottles of English sparkling wine in the UK as we drink bottles of champagne, and our fizz will be talked about in the same breath in opinion-leading markets around the world, not just by journalists and buyers, but by drinkers too.

English sparkling wine will have finally come of age – and paid off the mortgage! ✿

Cyril Ray and the Rise of the 'Compleat Imbiber'

KATHLEEN BURK (2013)

The 16 volumes of the Compleat Imbiber *enjoyed cult status from 1957 to 1992, and today much of their content remains as stimulating to wine lovers as ever. Kathleen Burk charts the unexpected rise of the series and its maverick editor Cyril Ray.*

The *Compleat Imbiber,* published intermittently in Britain from 1957 to 1992, was the quintessential late-evening or bedtime book for those who liked wine. It comprised short essays, both fictional and autobiographical, occasional limericks and poems, and wonderfully drawn illustrations (and less good photographs) from journalist contributors, including wine specialists and a number of the best-known writers of the period. It was beautifully designed. Its readership is less clear; undoubtedly, it included all of the above, their friends, and members of the same cultural and social circles, but it also appealed to members of the public who shared the growing interest in wine that manifested itself in the postwar period. It was often witty, it was easy to read, it was occasionally instructional, and it could give the reader the impression of being part of a literary and gastronomic culture shared by a knowledgeable few. Publication ceased with the death of its longtime editor Cyril Ray.

Presumably the market for such journals had also died, or else a publisher would perhaps have attempted to continue the series. Nevertheless, full sets of the 16 volumes in good shape now command a tidy sum on the secondhand and rare-books market; the combination of wine and good wine writing is still potent. It is a pity that no one has picked up Cyril Ray's torch.

ORIGINAL GIN

In 1953, Philip Youngman Carter, writer, artist and editor of the *Tatler* magazine, helped establish the 'house magazine' of W&A Gilbey Ltd, wine and spirit merchants and distillers of Gilbey's Gin. Called the *Compleat Imbiber*, it was a paperback magazine the size of a glossy magazine, containing, besides advertisements for Gilbey products, a number of stories, essays and doggerel poems about drink. It was a 'heyday of design in Britain', and the pieces were all wittily illustrated.[1] The writers included, along with some then-famous but now-forgotten journalists, a number of the most noted authors of the day: Compton Mackenzie, AP Herbert, Kenneth Tynan (the sometimes ferocious drama critic), Nancy Mitford, John Betjeman (later the poet laureate), Margery Allingham, the very popular crime writer (and wife of Youngman Carter), and George Mikes (author of *How to Be an Alien*). The magazine was enjoyed by its recipients, who were Gilbey's 'friends, rivals and customers, spreading the general idea that life was a lark, and that wines and spirits had something to do with the fact.'[2] By 1956, 12 issues had been published.

This was a period in Britain – as later recalled by John Arlott, dean of cricket commentators and an *amateur du vin* – that saw 'an unparalleled growth in the numbers not only of specialist wine bookshops, but dealers in wine antiques and artefacts, wine prints, tutored tastings' and the happy coexistence of three British wine periodicals.[3] In 1956, to celebrate its centenary, Gilbey's put on a *Compleat Imbiber* exhibition of the drinking customs and paraphernalia of Britain from the Roman period. In addition, Jasper Grinling, then the youngest director of Gilbey's with responsibility for publicity, came up with the idea of publishing a bound volume of selections from the magazine. He had enjoyed a piece of descriptive writing by Cyril Ray in the *Sunday Times* about a visit to the Rhineland, as well as his contributions to their magazine, and he asked Ray to edit the volume.[4]

ENTER THE EDITOR

At this point, Cyril Ray was 48 years old and had already enjoyed a varied career. He was born in 1908 in Lancashire to Jewish immigrant parents from eastern Poland, who, once they had arrived in Britain and settled in Bury, Lancashire, Anglicized their name from

---

[1] Cyril Ray, Introduction to the *Compleat Imbiber 10: an Entertainment* (Hutchinson, London; 1969), p9.
[2] Ibid.
[3] Introduction to the *New Compleat Imbiber* [no 13] (Collins, London; 1986), p11.
[4] Cyril Ray, *In a Glass Lightly* (Methuen, London; 1967), p13.

Rotenberg to Ray.[5] His parents were not well off – his father eventually became a traveling eye-tester for the Co-op – but Ray was well educated, attending Manchester Grammar School and winning an open scholarship to Jesus College, Oxford. After a year, however, through lack of family funds, he left Oxford and took up a succession of jobs, working in a shop, as a teacher and in a riding school. He then took a short-service commission in the Royal Air Force and was posted to an obsolescent observer balloon squadron, soon to be disbanded by the authorities, where he was made adjutant. Here, according to his obituary in *The Times*, 'with his dog and a good selection of books he would be winched up into the heavens. The balloon protected the basket from the elements and there were no duties to distract him.'[6] He then worked as a shop-walker at Lewis's of Liverpool. Moving back to Manchester, he managed an avant garde cinema and then made the breakthrough into his future profession, that of journalism. He got to know staff from the *Manchester Guardian*, and, with their assistance, in 1936 he became a general reporter for the newspaper.

With the coming of World War II, he became a war correspondent for *The Guardian*, first with the Fifth Destroyer Flotilla in the Channel, and then covering the North African landings in 1942 and the Eighth Army's campaign in Italy, where at one point he took over temporary command of a platoon when their officer and senior NCOs had been wounded. (He was mentioned in dispatches.) In 1944, he moved to the BBC and became its correspondent with the American airborne assault on Nijmegen, where he landed in a glider with a number of the soldiers. Ray, who was travelling with the 1939 *Michelin Guide*, 'liberated' the best local hotel himself, and when 'the keen and frightened young American soldiers in camouflage with black on their faces' arrived, he welcomed them with a glass of champagne as he sat on the terrace.[7] He then joined General Patton and the American Third Army when it fought its way into Germany; he was cited by the Americans for bravery at Arnheim.[8] He never denied that he had enjoyed the war tremendously.

After the war, he became the *Daily Express's* correspondent in Rome for a period and then became a freelance journalist. In 1949, he joined the *Sunday Times*, and in 1950 Ian Fleming, then the manager of foreign correspondents, asked Ray if he would like to become that paper's general reporter in Moscow.

On the one hand, bureaucrats and censors made life frustrating, but on the other, he became engaged to Elizabeth Brocklehurst, whom he described as: 'Half my age and twice

---

[5] Information from Cyril Ray's son Jonathan; December 31st 2012.
[6] September 25th 1991, p16.
[7] Katharine Whitehorn, *Selective Memory* (Virago Press, London; 2007), p121.
[8] *The Times*, September 25th 1991, p16. Katharine Whitehorn, 'Socialist With a Nose for Good Champagne,' *The Observer*, September 29th 1991, p22, for 'liberated'.

Man about town – and committed socialist. Cyril Ray pictured in the 1940s by The Picture Post's *Bill Brandt.*

my size.' (Ray was less than 5ft 2in [1.57m] tall.)[9] As a friend later wrote, he 'settled down after 43 years as a bachelor, bon vivant and boulevardier, to live happily ever after with his wife, Liz.'[10] After a couple of years, he returned with relief to Britain, where he enjoyed writing general articles for the newspaper on whatever took his fancy. As noted above, it was one of those articles that brought him to Jasper Grinling's attention.

VOLUMES ONE AND TWO

The contents of the first hardcover volume, also known as the *Compleat Imbiber*, were all taken from pieces that had already appeared in the magazine, with a total of 30 contributors. The cover was by Gerard Hoffnung, known for his cartoons and musical jokes, and the title page replicated the cover of the magazine.[11] To everyone's astonishment, it was a wild success; it ran into a second edition, was published in the USA – an American review referred to it as 'a handsome assembly of distilled serendipity'[12] – and was translated into German as *Der Feuchtfröhliche Geniesser*. The response was such that the publisher Putnam decided that there should be a number two, which was published in 1958.[13]

This was the first volume for which the contributors were chosen by Ray himself.[14] They were an interesting mix. First on the list was Lady Elizabeth Montagu, who wrote an essay on not knowing about wine and wishing that she did. She was the daughter of the Earl of Sandwich, a nurse during the war, and a novelist of whom Graham Greene spoke approvingly: 'She might have gone on writing for many more years but for the alcohol she

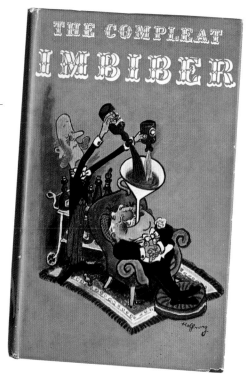

[9] Ibid for the quote. Elizabeth Brocklehurst, after war service in the Wrens, took a degree at the London School of Economics; she had an independent career as a social worker in London and in Kent, where she was a JP, and as the cookery correspondent for the *Observer*, as well as publishing several cookery books. With her husband, she published a food and wine book: Cyril and Elizabeth Ray, *Wine with Food* (Sidgwick & Jackson, London; 1975), 159pp.
[10] Godfrey Smith, the *Sunday Times*, October 13th 1991.
[11] Cyril Ray, ed, the *Compleat Imbiber* (Putnam, London; 1956 [although really 1957]), 256pp.
[12] Kirkus reviews, accessed on December 29th 2012, at www.kirkus reviews.com.
[13] Cyril Ray, ed, the *Compleat Imbiber 2*: an Entertainment (Putnam, London; 1948), 208pp.
[14] For no discernible reason, the volume has a reversible dust jacket: one side is green, the reverse side is pink. Everything else is the same.

felt she needed.'[15] Then came Peter Fleming, an adventurer and travel writer (and elder brother of Ian), who wrote on drinking abroad, lingering on ping – his general term for whatever was locally distilled – reassuring the reader that, no matter what were the immediate effects, it was not normally lethal. There was a theater manager (W MacQueen Pope), a crime writer (PM Hubbard), a broadcaster and crime writer (Edgar Lustgarten), a screenwriter (Paul Dehn, who wrote the screenplays for *Goldfinger*, *The Spy Who Came in from the Cold*, and *Murder on the Orient Express*), a drama critic (Dilys Powell), two art historians (James Laver and John Russell), and a Scottish balladeer (HS MacKintosh). General Sir Guy Salisbury Jones, in 'Hampshire Vigneron', told the story of why and how he had established the first commercial vineyard in England in a century. The moral being, do not open a good bottle of wine at lunch on a beautiful day – it gives you expensive ideas. More famously, Iris Murdoch, Angus Wilson and Kingsley Amis also provided pieces. (To the best of everyone's knowledge, contributors were normally paid in wine, not coin.) An anonymous contributor was Ray himself, who provided a limerick of the kind for which he became widely known (and a number of which were later collected and published as *Lickerish Limericks*).[16] 🍂

Excerpt taken from Kathleen Burk's 'Cyril Ray and The Compleat Imbiber' first published in **The World of Fine Wine**, *Issue 39, 2013. Reprinted here with the kind permission of the author and of Neil Beckett, editor (www.worldoffinewine.com).*

---

[15] Obituary by John Montagu in the *Independent*, January 25th 2006.
[16] Cyril Ray, *Lickerish Limericks with Filthy Pictures by Charles Mozley* (JM Dent, London; 1979), 48pp, including a glossary of all of the drinks mentioned in the text.

CHAPTER 4

WINE TRAVELS

The Wilder Shores of Wine – Hugh Johnson (2019)

A Viking in the Vineyard – Peter Vinding-Diers (2019)

Guisseppe Poggio: Home Winemaking In Piedmont – Simon Loftus (1986)

Out of California's Shadow – Jason Tesauro (2019)

THE WILDER SHORES
OF WINE

HUGH JOHNSON (2019)

Hugh Johnson delves back into the wonderful world of wine pioneer André Jullien (1766–1832) and charts the words and adventures of the young Parisian who laid the foundation stone for today's wine writing.

Nobody has ever followed the vine to the far corners of the earth with quite the energy and thoroughness of a Parisian sommelier called André Jullien. He foreshadowed my own *World Atlas of Wine* by 150 years. I stand in awe of his research, his contacts in the remotest places and his confident opinions. Much of his material on the wilder shores of wine is history now. Australian wine had yet to be invented, and California is covered simply by mentions of the coastal mission stations. But his views on French wine are still cogent, his palate discernible. He stands first among all of us who have tried to give a global view of wine.

Anyone who thinks the French have never looked seriously beyond their own frontiers for anything to drink should read his *Topographie de Tous les Vignobles Connus*, first published in 1816, the result of apparently indefatigable journeys, followed up by more journeys to add new territories to the editions of 1822, 1832 and 1848. By this time Greece, Turkey, Asia, Africa and America had come under his enquiring gaze – though exactly how many vineyards he visited himself it is impossible to say.

When he discourses, however, on the wines of the Caucasus, or even of Persia, he does it with such vivid conviction that you can easily picture the young Parisian, moustached and trim-trousered, no doubt, riding from cellar to cellar, tasting and annotating among the robes, the donkeys and the dust of the Levant. 'The mountain Tartars' he writes, 'who inhabit the highest part of the Caucasus, bring to their city of Kislar stronger and better-flavoured wines than those of Terek; they keep better too, and form the normal drinking of people of means. These Tartars, though Mohammedans, make the wines themselves, and even augment their intoxicating properties by adding the seed-heads of opium poppies to the fermenting juice. Then they drink the wines in public without reserve.'

He traverses the Ottoman Empire with a fine palate for what little was then left of the once famous wines of Anatolia, and especially Cyprus. In Trebizond he finds only raisins, but in Aleppo certain wines faintly reminiscent of Bordeaux, and on Mount Lebanon sweet wines of noble quality, 'Vins d'or', which fetch amazing prices in 'Beyrouth' [Beirut].

On he goes through Damascus and Jerusalem ('strong white wines with an unpleasant sulphurous reek') crossing Arabia with its ambivalent attitudes to liquor but marked taste for palm-wine, until he arrives in Persia with its legendary 'Schiras, the best wine of Persia and the whole Orient.'

'It is hard to imagine a more delicious valley than the surroundings of the town of Schiras [Shiraz]. European fruits grow here in abundance, but they are bigger, more tasty and aromatic. The grapes above all are delicious . . . among them the big red grape they call Damas which produces the celebrated wine.

'[The wine is] red but not dark, with good flavour, body and plenty of vigour, sap and a very pronounced aroma, being neither sweet nor cloying but leaving the mouth fresh and the palate cleansed from whatever you are eating – a sensation of freshness almost like breathing in after a mint pastille.

'The spirit of the wine is completely natural – no *eau de vie* is added. The warmth it produces in the stomach is gentler than most wines recommended for their properties, and although very warm, not at all heady.'

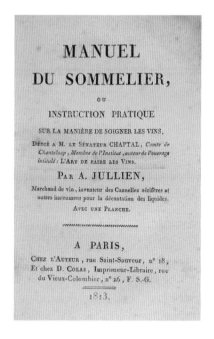

Left: The exceptionally well travelled André Jullien invites his fellow citizens to partake in his worldly wisdom, while his Emperor, Napoleon I, battles the combined armies of Britain, Prussia and Russia.

Jullien goes on to say that he received 50 bottles of 'Schiras' (presumably in Paris) in 1822, varying in size from two to five litres; that he decanted them into smaller bottles, and that they altered only in throwing a tartrate deposit and losing a little colour. If the wine had a fault, it was a slight resinous aroma.

'People of rank in Persia drink Georgian and Schiras wines from bottles of Venetian glass, preferring them to wines imported from Spain, Germany or France. They conceal their drinking, whereas stricter Mohammedans inebriate themselves with opium and cannabis.'

Modern wine-writers rarely, if ever, pursue their researches with Jullien's vigour. True, there are obvious difficulties today in the Muslim world which did not exist in the 16th century. One journey of recent times, following wine to its wildest shores, was made by Warren Winiarski of Stag's Leap Wine Cellars in the Napa Valley and Professor Harold Olmo of UC Davis. Winiarski's interest was in the varieties of fruit which are known to exist in the remote valleys of the Hindu Kush. Ancient strains of plants in great diversity; big juicy walnuts, roses of sumptuous perfume, peaches and apricots unknown in the world outside, have survived who knows how long – and so, of course, have vines.

Hunza, on the Silk Road, the pass through from Pakistan to China, has a tradition of winemaking which suggests the possibility of ancient grape varieties, either indigenous or left behind by 10,000 years and more of traffic. Winiarski's researches were inconclusive. He found less cultivation in Hunza than he had hoped, but nevertheless a variety of apparently wild vines growing wherever some rocky outcrop prevented the goats from browsing them, and sufficient apparently planted vines, either on pergolas and the walls of houses, or trained into trees Italian-style, to produce a substantial crop.

Even in Hunza, a place that sees enough travellers to be less than puritanically Muslim, it was hard to find evidence of winemaking. Plenty of other visitors, though, have tracked down covert supplies of Hunza-water, as it is called. They give it mixed reports. Winiarski took cuttings to plant in the Napa Valley and made a little red wine, which he described as 'interesting on the palate; high acidity, low phenolics', adding later in a letter 'I may have been too hard on the vinifera I made. Along with its high acidity and lack of phenolic depth, it had an intriguing and appetizing flavour suggesting rewards to come.' Some vines he found were definitely *Vitis vinifera*, hermaphrodite, with its characteristic pip-shape. Others were *Vitis sylvestris*. In the middle of a continent, with vines often grown from seed, the chances of finding a challenger to Pinot Noir were slim.

At about the time of Winiarski's journey, I made a start on the vineyards, such as they are, of the border country between the northwest Frontier Province of Pakistan and Afghanistan. Tradition has it that the Kalash, a tribe living in three fertile valleys deep in

Members of the Kalash people of the Hindu Kush– the descendants, it is said, of the army of Alexander the Great, which passed that way in 326 BC.

the Hindu Kush, are not indigenous at all, but the final rear-guard, as it were, of the army of Alexander the Great returning from his Indian campaign. Certainly the Kalash bear no resemblance to their Chitrali neighbours. Many are blonde with high-bridge noses; certainly Causcasian. Nor are there any Muslim constraints; the women wearing bright clothes and not only showing, but painting their faces for hypnotic dances to the beat of haunting drums. Their religion is apparently animist: they worship a rock, a mountain or a tree. In the Elysian landscape of the Bumboret Valley, where the vast silver branches of ancient walnut trees shade rushing irrigation channels, there is much to worship.

Kalash wine, drunk from those little French unbreakable tumblers that start life as mustard pots, was thick, pinky-red, fresh and reasonably clean to taste, with the charm of wild berries but no special character that I can recall. Salty goats' cheese may have hidden its subtleties. Nor did I see anything that could be described as a vineyard. Vines here are on walls and up trees – as indeed they must have been in the Greece of Alexander the Great.

With China becoming wine-conscious, the future of the vine in the East is probably prodigious. New discoveries, new crossings, new *terroirs*... We can only guess. And salute the sommelier who started the investigation.

*The 8th edition of Hugh Johnson's **World Atlas of Wine** was published by Mitchell Beazley, September 2019.*

A Viking in the Vineyard

PETER VINDING-DIERS (2019)

At the start of what proved to be an extraordinary career, Peter Vinding-Diers found himself venturing from Denmark to Bordeaux, then to South Africa in search of wine and adventure. Here, in the first chapter of his memoirs covering his remarkable life in wine, he recalls trying his hand at many things (even parachuting into war-torn Vietnam) before eventually following his heart back to the vineyards of the Cape...

It was the beginning of the 1960s and it was spring time. We had left Geneva that morning and were now on our way south towards Grasse and the Côte d'Azur. The needle on the speedometer hovered in the high 180s, then swung past 200 kilometres an hour, one curve of the road blending into the next. All of a sudden a policeman appeared at the roadside waiving his white staff. I saw the silver glint of his whistle and the arms that tried to waive us down, but we just flew past, leaving him standing, arms flailing like a jumping jack. The owner of the car sat demon-like behind the steering wheel, his wrap-around sunglasses and huge driving gloves emphasizing the drama each time he turned the wheel. Every time we took a corner the whole car shook.

.

At the end of the motorway, we were stopped by another policeman who asked us if we had seen a silver Porsche driving at the speed of lightning. My friend answered with a cool smile that yes we had seen it. It had overtaken us but had stopped further up the road with smoke coming out of the engine.

The Policeman smiled and waived us on.

A life lived to the full: Danish winemaking legend Peter Vinding-Diers.

My friend was Bendt Galatius, a Danish artist who lived in the Congo. He was on a road trip to collect his brand new Triumph TR4 from the factory in England. He had picked it up a week ago and it was one of the very first of its kind, so it was no wonder the policeman couldn't distinguish it from a Porsche.

Bendt and I had met at a vernissage of older Danish art at the Louvre a few days before this, and he had asked me if I wanted a lift to the Côte d'Azur. Why not? I had a small flat in the Rue Saucier Leroy, near the Arc de Triomphe in Paris, from which I was trying to study French literature at the Sorbonne while working as a freelance correspondent for the Danish newspaper *Politiken*. But spring was in the air, and I jumped at the offer of a trip. The plan was to make a detour to the Triumph works in Geneva where the car would be serviced, stop in town overnight, then drive south. Now we were on the road and hopefully on the way to a big adventure.

A change in the landscape took me by surprise. The vineyards of Beaune popped up almost suddenly, the vines standing to attention like small trees. Back then, at the beginning of the 1960s, they were still bush trained and made a wonderful sight. I remember being completely taken-in by the charm of them, and my old dream of becoming a forester suddenly became the stepping-stone to something new. Why not become a vigneron instead? I would still have the charm of the trees, but with the added benefit of tasting and enjoying the fruits of my (and their!) labour. The idea took root quickly, and I somehow imagined I could hear the music of Béla Bartók's *Hungarian Sketches* ringing in my ears as if to serenade it. Something new had begun in my life. It was as if a door in a dream had opened and now, fascinated, I stared through it.

Wine was a by no means unknown in my life back then. At my grandfather's home in Frederiksberg, near Copenhagen, we often had game in the shooting season – he more or less lived for his gun sports as so many of his kind then did. He would often serve a bottle of Pommard with partridge, but when we had duck it was always the wines of Pomerol that were brought to the table – Château Trotanoy was one of his favourites. I remember vividly the slightly smoked taste of those wines.

At home we drank Château Lynch-Bages. My father bought a hogshead every year and had it bottled in Copenhagen. And now, on this spring day in Beaune, I was haunted by the superb taste of cassis from Lynch-Bages and its neighbours Pontet-Canet and Mouton Rothschild – all three of these magnificent reds were famous for their touch of cassis. Then I wondered how it would feel to walk amongst vines of my own that produced these flavours, to drink their wines at my table. It was a good thought, and it became a dream that stayed with me for the rest of that summer.

In the evening we drove over the heights of Grasse where the warm air suddenly hit us, and the sound of the cicadas, like the rapid click of castanets, rattled all around. The scent from the honeysuckle – or was it the flowers of the lemon and orange trees – filled the air with a promise of exotic evenings, and out over the Mediterranean Sea we saw shining stars twinkling like diamonds, lighting up the black night sky. *Bienvenue à Côte d'Azur.* We stopped at Haut de Cagnes, the beautiful medieval hilltop village above Cagnes-sur-Mer, and Bendt told me that this was where Nana Vinding lived. The world was much smaller then, and everybody knew Nana. She was my father's first wife and mother to my brother Nip Andreas Vinding, who was a well known cineaste in France.

It was too late to call on her now, so we went up to the square and had dinner chez Suzy Solidor. Suzy had been one of the most sought after models in France and had sat for nearly all the great painters. Portraits of her lined the walls of the room, and she walked around amongst her guests, still with the pride of her beauty showing. She came over to our table and Bendt immediately began to flirt with her, telling her tales of his life as an artist. But to no avail.

The following day, I met Nana. It wasn't long before a warm feeling of friendship grew between us. She was lively, full of fun and joie de vivre; she and my mother had always got on very well and I could see why. Nana insisted that I stay a while at her home, the old Capitainerie opposite the Grimaldi stronghold (now a museum) that dominated the town. So Bendt and his Triumph went on their way, and I spent the summer in Cagnes. (I was a dreadful student; I never saw the Sorbonne again.)

During my stay with Nana, we supped on noodles with chicken and thyme and a glass of wine every evening. After dinner she would light a cigarette, cross her legs and turn on the television. '*Un grand film chaques soir*' would entertain us before it was bedtime. This proved a great way for me to learn the French language.

Later, Nana helped me rent a small studio further down the mountain. Almost opposite was a small grocer's shop and here I found some unlabelled burgundy that came from the vineyard of one of the grocer's friends. The wine was full of violets, creamy and velvety, and, even better, the bottles were very cheap indeed. I must have drunk most of this stock of heavenly burgundy that summer, and its quality, combined with the sense of well-being it created in me, must have pushed my new-found desire for my own vineyard further forward.

These were great days. My dreams grew, not least because I fell in love with a vineyard in front of a ramshackle farmhouse nearby. Some haystacks and old barrels leant up against its barns, as if the scenery had been taken straight from one of Dunoyer de Segonzac's paintings, with geese, ducks and chickens running everywhere.

Many years later I tried to find this farm and show it to my wife, but it had long since been torn down, giving way to a modern Mediterranean high rise.

My cousin Jacques Renoir came to visit his grandmother, Nana. His mother, my half brother's sister Denise[1], was married to Claude Renoir, also a cineaste, and to top it, Nana's sister was married to Coco Renoir, son of the famous painter Auguste. We all went to see Coco and his wife. They lived in a huge 'loft' in Menton at the Franco-Italian coastal border, filled with paintings by the old master. Everyone called Coco 'Maitre', but in fact he was only a master of spending money... Still, Vindings and Renoirs get on well together, and Jacques became a friend for life. These were great days in a lovely summer that sped by far too fast, until one day I found myself back in my flat in Paris.

Life in Paris was hectic. In those days I had a lot of friends in the artistic community, who neglected their duties as much as I did. In short, we had a great time at a time when you could do so without anyone looking askance. The term 'bons vivants' would certainly have applied. But one afternoon I was reading Evelyn Waugh's book *When The Going Was Good*, and I was caught by an acute dose of travel fever.

Out there was adventure: other civilizations and new challenges awaited me. The urge to throw caution to the wind became too much.

I re-read the book the other day, more than 50 years later, and the same thing happened. The book once again filled me with a longing for adventure and the unknown. Back in 1966 there was no alternative: there were challenges out there that every young man dreamt of facing, and I had no choice but to go and meet them head on.

My lovely Aunt Mutte[2], who had been married to Uncle Bill Cavendish-Bentinck[3], had left me the contents of the Chinese Room at her flat in Hans Crescent. It had been filled with exotic things from huge lacquer vases painted at sea so that not a speck of dust would settle on the wet paint, to some interesting old rolls of beautifully painted landscapes, and pieces of porcelain from the Tsung and Ming periods. Now it was as if she whispered an encouragement in my ear, and most of these lovely things which I had always admired so much, left for the auction rooms. They brought in, even in those far off days, a sum that

---

[1] Our family is full of 'half' brothers and sisters, but we all have the sense that we are full brothers and sisters, which is a nice feeling.
[2] Inger Marie Grantzau-Christensen.
[3] William Cavendish-Bentinck (1925–66, 'Uncle Bill') predeceased his father, Victor, who became the 9th Duke of Portland, and was chairman of the Joint Intelligence Committee during World War II.

could easily carry me around Africa and further if I took care not to overspend. My Mother helped and encouraged me in my preparations, and so one grey winter's day I found myself on the quay in Rotterdam looking up at the black hulk of a freighter from the Holland Africa line. It was simple. I walked up the gangway ready to sail out into the big wide world. Perhaps it was an omen that the first stop was to be Bordeaux?

We sailed up the River Gironde, past all the châteaux sitting along its banks like pearls on a string, straight into the heart of Bordeaux where we anchored up on the quay facing the Place de la Bourse. In those days the town looked like a black hole from the Middle Ages, its white stone all grimey, and I let myself be swallowed up by it. I bought a pair of espadrilles from a shop in a dark alley, had a good lunch at Le Grand Café, then sauntered down onto the Quai des Chartrons where all the famous négociants had their cellars. Their huge doors opened out onto the street and exuded a smell which was an intoxicating mixture of old wine and, strangely enough, brown tobacco.

In one of the houses, where the Danish consul resided, I bought a couple of cases of 'petit châteaux' that I saw brought on-board the evening just before we left. It made me feel like a magnate, and I felt it boded well for the coming trip down the African coast. As the ship turned in the narrow harbour basin, the keel water foamed and the ship's bell chimed. We glided out and away to sea, leaving this mecca of wine behind us. Little did I know then that this would be the place where so many of the big moments in my life would happen. And they would begin less than 10 years later.

It was a wonderful trip. I had the owner's cabin, and was the only passenger on board. Even better, we stopped almost everywhere on the coast of West Africa. Tourism was relatively unknown, so each country still had its own unique flavour. Globalization was thankfully a long way off.

I changed ship in Abidjan, on the Ivory coast, to a modern express boat from the Royal Interocean Line, and sailed further down the coast via Takoradi in Ghana, Lome in Togo, Lagos in Nigeria and the warm Port Harcourt, before we went on to Libreville and Pointe Noir in Congo. Here I met a lovely French girl who had gone fishing on the beach. The white sand, the blue ocean, the avenues of Flamboyants whose falling red flowers covered the streets, and the emerald green lawns in front of crisp white bungalows, made the frame for a romantic time, but then the sound of the ship's siren called me back to reality.

Walvis Bay, in what was then South West Africa, was a Klondyke-like port where the houses were made of wood and the streets were numbered without names. If you were lucky, you could find small rubies in the sand, or even better, diamonds out on Pelican

Island – which was 'no go' land but we visited all the same in the ship's sloop. Somewhere I still have a small button of ruby…

And then the best: the entrance, one early morning a few days later, into Table Bay with its legendary flat topped mountain. Hustle and bustle on the quay-side, where huge cranes rolled up and down, hauling goods from the bellies of the ships. At the shipper's office I found a letter from my mother who tempted me to sail on to the Far East, which would be easy as the boat was scheduled to continue to Hong Kong and the cabin was free.

In the meantime I had a visit from some of my stepfather's relatives, the Diers family, who had emigrated to the Cape three or four generations before. They were very helpful and showed me around the place. We drove to Groot Constantia[4], that beautiful property where the Cloete family once made the fabulous sweet Constantia wine which had been on the tables of all the great and the good nearly 100 years ago. Those wines were made from the Pontac, Frontignan Gris and Frontignan Blanc grapes, and rivalled the great Sauternes and even greater Tokaji wines of the past. Now they were making excellent reds and I bought a case to take on-board. The Cloetes had sold out and the farm now belonged to the state and was under the supervision of the research institute in Stellenbosch. My friend Pieter Bairnsfather Cloete later told me there had been no respect for the legendary vines. Vineyards had been grubbed up and that was the end of it all.

In the evening, as we left that magical farm, I stood dreaming on the deck and wished that one day I could come back to the Cape to learn about growing vines and making wine in this perfect setting. As the ship changed its course and set sail for the Indian Ocean, I saw the Twelve Apostles cliff formation disappear on its port side. It seemed as if the overture from Wagner's *Parcifal* fell to my ear and with its stirring chords my resolution to return strengthened. The music in my imagination was was soon drowned by the reality of the cook's bell as he summoned us for dinner. But before adjourning, I sipped the last of my glass of Syrah from Constantia, little realizing that in the not too distant future I would be offered the post of manager in this very paradise, at that very farm.

The next stop was Port Elizabeth and then Durban where we anchored up for a couple of days. The captain, somewhat red-faced, came and asked me if I would give up my cabin for

---

[4] Groot Constantia is the oldest wine estate in South Africa, granted to governor of the Cape, Simon van der Stel, in 1685. Wine, fruit, vegetables and cattle were farmed and a manor house built. In 1779, it was sold to the Cloete family who made extensive improvements and developed the famous dessert wine, Constantia, which became popular in Europe. In 1885 the estate was purchased by the government for use as an experimental wine and agricultural estate. Happily it is now once more making great sweet wine.

a couple of nights as Mr Dennis Taylor, who owned the stevedoring and shipyard company Taylor Smith in Mauritius, would like a passage with his wife. He hardly need ask; I agreed of course, and I moved into an empty engine room officer's cabin while Dennis and Shelagh Taylor came on-board.

We met in the evening, just as the boat sailed out, and I proposed a glass of champagne to this charming couple. Ahead was Mauritius with its fields of sugarcane and lovely climate, and farther away the Far East with all its spice and magic beckoned. It was enough to lift a glass for. As we were drinking the bubbles Dennis took me aside: 'I see that you like champagne,' he said. 'So do I. Why don't we buy the entire stock on board?' What a devilish idea! And why not indeed. So we did just that.

Some days later, as we sailed past Madagascar, the skipper came back and tugged my sleeve. 'Can I buy back the champagne?' he whispered furtively in my ear. 'I don't really know,' I replied. 'You must ask Mr Taylor.' Dennis agreed, and the Company bought back the stock of champagne for just enough to keep us in free champagne for the trip. Not a dry eye – ours, because the skipper had had to buy back the champagne, and we had a good laugh about it; his, because he was Dutch and had to pay!

Later, Dennis told me that he had seen a telegram on the desk in the Durban office commanding the captain to celebrate the engagement of the Dutch crown princess Beatrix to Mr Claus von Amsberg with a glass of champagne for all on-board. We all had our share of the champagne that evening!

We docked in Mauritius for 24 hours, and the Taylors very kindly asked me for lunch at their home at the Point d'Azur, which was sheer heaven. They were such fun, and many years later we met up again, thanks to my English wine trade friend Robin Byers, who knew them both very well.

Sailing into Singapore harbour in the mid-1960s was like entering an adventure from *One Thousand and One Nights*. As we arrived that evening, with hundreds of lights bobbing up and down on the water outside town, we could have been sailing into of one of those much-loved tales of the Islamic Golden Age. The Sea was full of freighters (slightly out of context with my Arabian dream as these were mostly old World War II Liberty boats), with junks and sampans everywhere in between, waiting for space to unload their wares.

Ours was an express boat so we were able to sail straight in to the port. The warm air of the town was full of the smell of rotten mangroves, diesel spills and decay in general. It is not a completely pleasant aroma, but all the same there is something magical about it. Once you have experienced it, the memory will remain, and every time you breathe it, you will be cast under its spell.

On the hangars along the quays we saw huge black butterflies (or were they moths?) adorning the walls; there were street vendors and hawkers everywhere, selling delicious satays – some of them would skin a live snake, cut it into small pieces, throw it into a hot pan and swish it a couple of times before tossing it into the air for good measure and serving it to you on a small plate.

Singapore then was a far cry from the clean and orderly town it has become today. Then, it was dirty and chaotic, and full of fun. The crew invited me for dinner in China Town – I think it was to thank me for letting them store all the watches and trinkets they had accumulated to sell whenever we docked somewhere. The customs officials always searched everywhere on-board the ship except, for some reason, my cabin. So here their wares were safe. The crew's earnings from this trade surpassed their wages many times over, and I was now treated to real shark fin soup, suckling pig (from which you only eat the skin), Peking duck and goodness knows how many other dishes, as a sign of their gratitude. It was a delicious indulgence and the memory of their kindness has remained with me ever since.

Many years later, I came back to Singapore with my wife and took her to see China Town, but we found – just as we had with the old farm in Haut de Cagnes – that it had vanished forever, replaced by newly built high rises. Here, as on France's Côte d'Azur, building had commenced on a huge scale and the picturesque traditional houses, full of local character, had given way to modernity. New times, but thank goodness I had seen a little of the old world before it was too late.

One year we celebrated Chinese New Year in Singapore with our friends Melina and NK Young, and we all ended up eating from the hawkers' stands under a bridge. The Chinese celebration of New Year is a happy occasion. Another time, we were again the guests of Melina and NK, this time at their own home. We all stood around a big dish with giant chop sticks and tossed the noodles together, smiling and wishing each other a happy and fruitful New Year.

But this is not a travel book, nor a tale of parties gone by. It is a story about the joy of growing vines and making wine. I will therefore skip the rest of a wonderful Grand Tour and go straight to Bangkok where I stayed with the Danish Ambassador, Ebbe Munck, and his wife Birgit.

Ebbe was a Greenland explorer and had been on the famous Pearyland expeditions[5]. He had also been a prominent member of the Danish Resistance during World War II, in which my mother had also played a role. He had been a journalist, and now he was our ambassador. Both Ebbe and Birgit were inspiring and full of life: they each had a gift for getting people involved and enthusiastic, and Ebbe was like a father to me at that point in my life.

One evening, as we were sitting talking on the veranda after dinner, I aired the idea of going to see the war in Vietnam. I was a young man after all, and I was not a coward but it had been a question – as it was for a lot of my generation with 'hero' parents. How would I react in a situation of acute danger? My mother got a DSM (Distinguished Service Medal) for her efforts during the occupation and the whole family was deeply involved in the Resistance. I had grown up with tales of heroism and had an inkling that I should prove myself too. I had hardly finished my sentence before Ebbe had arranged everything, and a few days later I found myself in the office of MACV (Military Assistance Command, Vietnam) where I was asked if I wanted it cold, medium or hot. The answer was easy...

Having done a short stint in the Royal Danish Navy, I wasn't totally untrained in the art of war. And after a few more days and adventures – amongst others, with the Australians who fished bamboo mines off the propellers of boats on the Mekong – I was ready to jump with a section of the 101st Airborne division, The Screaming Eagles.

There was a lot of shooting going on and we came under fire almost immediately, but my parachute was of the old fashioned type and I went down like a stone. The descent was so fast that I felt nothing could hit me. That is before I hit the ground and rolled, just I had done in the officers' mess the previous evening when they taught landing techniques by getting us to jump off the billiard table. Later, I was lying on the jungle floor looking at a column of ants with violet leaves in their beaks, just in front of my nose. They were totally unperturbed by the commotion as if they belonged in another world. There was something positive about this. It calmed the nerves, and it was good to see that life for them at least went on as normal.

I spent a colourful couple of weeks in Vietnam. I did indeed get to see how I fared under duress. But I am afraid that the meaningless slaughter instilled in me a life-long aversion to politicians. Surely there must be other ways to deal with problems than to send young people to their deaths?

---

[5] Pearyland, a northern peninsula of the Greenland landmass, is the most northern ice-free region in the world, and the northernmost point of human settlement. The Danish expeditions of 1947–48, led by Ebbe Munck and Eigil Knuth, established a scientific research station there.

I arrived back in Bangkok just in time for my birthday, and Ebbe gave me his book on the Pearyland expedition and wrote in it the following dedication paraphrasing Robert Frost:

As the old man said to the young blade:
But you have
promises to keep
And miles to walk
Before you sleep
Ebbe Munck, Bankok 3rd June 1966

When I look at the well-thumbed pages now, so many years later, I am reminded of some great times spent with Ebbe and Birgit. Both Susie and I have later enjoyed their friendship, and I had to include the visit to Bangkok here as his dedication became a lodestar for me, shining ever since, and his courage to say what had to be said has been a good example too. God knows that following his lead has cost me from time to time, but I believe it has been worth it. And Birgit, the ideal wife with her wisdom and support. What a couple!

In 1967 I was back in Denmark and did a stint in the cultural department of Danish television. I also moved into a small flat alongside one of the canals near Christianshavn in Copenhagen. Fishing boats floated by my sitting room window where I had installed my library, so sitting reading on the sofa I could lift my head from the book I was reading and contemplate the lively water traffic outside.

At a party in Jutland I had met a young English nurse who worked in the operating theatre in one of the big hospitals. The daughter of a well known GP and obstetrician, she had chosen the medical world as well, and had assisted Professor Roy Calne when he did the first kidney transplants at Addenbrooke's Hospital in Cambridge.[6]

We fell in love and after half a year or so, she moved in. The flat was small, and apart from the big sitting room there was a bedroom, kitchen, a small bathroom and loo. This, incidentally, also became our guest book: you took a pen and drew an outline around one hand on the wall and wrote your name in the middle. A lot of the friends were farmers, and one of them, Mannie Moltke (who farmed two estates in Sealand), drew some very black nails and wrote 'Danish soil under Danish nails'.

There is nothing like being young and in love, and even if we didn't have salt to an egg, it didn't seem to matter. My patient mother helped us every now and then with some food, but if we starved a bit, it never seemed important. We had each other and that was enough. We drove around the country in Susie's green Austin Sprite, often venturing to

Jutland to visit my friend Iver Rantzau[7] who had just taken over the family estate, Rosenvold, by Vejle Fjord.

Here, we helped him remove the wild oats that had been allowed to grow everywhere, and saw him transform that lovely old property into one of the best-run in the country. He didn't have salt to an egg either. But we ate well and cheaply. We would go down to the fjord to collect mussels, then manage to find a bottle of local plonk over which we'd talk and laugh our way through the evenings after work.

Iver's future was secure, or more or less, and we talked about my idea of growing vines and making wine. Nobody thought it strange and I got all the encouragement I needed from both my friends and family. But the benediction I really needed came from Susie, and throughout it all she stood by me.

So how to get a foot in?

A good friend had a brother-in-law who was in the wine business, and who by chance imported the wines from the KWV[8] in South Africa. He wrote to them but I got a negative answer back. I knew deep-down that this was where I wanted to go, so this rejection presented me with an extra challenge. Constantia was still playing in my head – the lovely old farms, the green vineyards and clement climate drew me in much more than those of France, where both my father and grandfather were well-known personalities with far too many contacts for a young man who was everything but his father's son.

So one evening at Rosenvold Susie and I decided to get married and set off for South Africa anyway. Susie wrote to the Groote Schuur Hospital in Cape Town and got a job immediately, so we had something to fall back on. The visas and permits took a few months to sort out, but one day a package from the legation in Stockholm dropped through the letterbox. 'Best wishes for a happy and successful future,' it said.

We got married in the Old Navy church at Holmens Kirke in Copenhagen. The church was full of friends. Iver Rantzau was best man. Susie's parents sadly could not get out of

---

[6] This was in 1966. Over 3,500 kidney transplants have been performed at Addenbrooke's since then.
[7] Iver is my oldest and best friend in Denmark. His family estate is in Vejle, Jutland, which is where I live too when visiting home. It is a place I love, with views over the fjord to Fyen, the 'middle island', where Iver owns another estate called Krengerup – this is where Churchill stayed during his visit to Denmark.
[8] The Koöperatieve Wijnbouwers Vereniging was established as a small coop in 1918 and is now one of the largest wine and spirit producers in South Africa.

England as Wilson's £50-pound annual travel allowance[9] had already been spent. Afterwards, my mother gave a reception at home. She was wonderful and always supported the idea of our marriage and travels. There was time for a visit to Ebbe and Birgit Munck before we left. (He had now been appointed head of court for the Crown Princess of Denmark, and had moved back to Copenhagen.) Ebbe and Birgit encouraged us too, which was a tremendous help. Good moral support often pushes you half way there.

Following the wedding, we spent a few days in the country at a house near the sea which a friend had lent us. While we were there, we dreamt of a future amongst the vines in South Africa... 🌿

*This is Peter's own translation of Chapter One of his memoirs, published in Danish under the title **A Handful of Olives and a Glass of Wine**, Lindhardt & Ringhof (Copenhagen) 2016.*

And a personal note from Hugh Johnson: 'This is the prologue to one of the most original and varied careers in wine. I met Peter in Bordeaux in the 1960s; we've been friends ever since. His trajectory since then has sparked new thinking and made wonderful wines in France, Italy, Hungary and now Sicily. He and Susie, creative and uninhibited, have an amazing story to tell.'

Right: A dream come true: Groot Constantia (right), the oldest wine producing estate in South Africa.

---

[9] 1967–68: Harold Wilson's government imposed a £50 per adult spending limit on British citizens travelling abroad.

Giuseppe Poggio: Home Winemaking In Piedmont

SIMON LOFTUS (1986)

Simon Loftus is a wine writer, restaurateur and merchant, known for his influential tenure at Adnams brewery in Southwold. Simon's enthusiasm for Italian wines was awakened during a family holiday on a tiny farm in Piedmont. He says: 'Every day I drank the farmer's own wine, a simple Dolcetto, and learnt to relish the touch of bitterness which gave such appetizing definition to the flavour of ripe damsons and black chocolate. As I began to explore the diversity of Italian grapes I was determined to find the perfect Dolcetto, a search that ended in the tiny cellars of Giuseppe Poggio. The 'Riserva Speciale Adnams' that Giuseppe bottled especially for my customers remains the finest example I have ever tasted. This tribute was written in celebration of a wonderful man and his delicious wines, in 1986. A year or two later Poggio died and his vineyard was abandoned by his heirs.'

Autumn in Piedmont is a marvelous time. The days are bright, the air is crisp and the vintage brings a feeling of satisfying activity. From early morning you come across piles of empty baskets or plastic boxes stacked beside the road, and groups of strong and cheerful women, ready to set to work. Later in the day the boxes (filled with grapes) will be lying in the shade of the vines, waiting to be loaded onto trucks and trailers, even the occasional ox-cart, and taken to the *cantina*. This may be a large

cooperative, modern and well equipped, or the modest cellar of an individual grower. It seems that every farm has a barn with a few vats of fermenting must and on the back streets of every village the doors of these barns stand open. As you peer from the bright sunshine into the cool darkness of these unsuspected cellars you can smell the fresh grape juice and watch the operations of primitive winemaking, essentially unchanged since medieval times.

On one such street in the hill village of Rocca Grimalda, high above Ovada, the pavement was blocked by a small old-fashioned basket press. Three elderly men were enjoying the sun as they squeezed the last juice out of the red grapes, following the fermentation. Noticing my interest they invited me into the tiny cellar, brought out a bottle of the previous year's wine (with a handwritten label) and insisted that I taste the stuff. The labourer paused in his work at the press and the *padrone* and his friend beamed proudly as I muttered a wholly unmerited compliment on their homemade wine.

It was an entertaining and picturesque scene but it has to be admitted that the end result was almost undrinkable. There was little difference in scale, and none in basic technique, between their winemaking and that of the man I had come to see, whose equally simple cellar lay a few doors up the street. Yet their Dolcetto was the worst I have ever tasted, while his is by far the best.

Giuseppe Poggio is a perfectionist with the air of a village grocer. In his stained brown coat he's the sort of man you'd expect to find behind the counter of an old fashioned shop, selling everything from vegetables to horse liniment; the kindly old fellow who wraps up

your bit of cheese with the smiling and courteous deference of one who knows that you won't find better quality in any of the fancy shops or flashy supermarkets.

But this modest man is, in his local way, quite famous. Anyone in the village will direct you to his house, and he carries off the most coveted prizes at the Asti wine fair. He is one of those small growers whose name, for enthusiasts of his region's wines, far exceeds his very limited production. 'My preoccupation is to make a good wine, not a lot of wine.' He points to the end of the little cellar: 'Look at this wall of bottles – all my production is there – it's a nice wall, eh?' He makes no more than 700 cases of wine a year, almost all of them Dolcetto.

This, the 'little sweet', is a grape that appears to originate in Piedmont; one of the three varieties that produce all the notable red wine of this region. Nebbiolo makes the grand Barolo and the slightly less grand Barbaresco: wines that have a rich, autumnal complexity, a hint of tar and the capacity for long life. Barbera, much prized locally, is the red equivalent of Bourgogne Aligoté – appetizing but sometimes too astringent to the non-Italian palate. Dolcetto makes the quaffing wine, the Italian Beaujolais. It is normally drunk within a year or two of the vintage when you can relish its delicious immediacy, its mouthfilling flavour of ripe fruit which has a refreshing bitterness at the finish.

Autumn in Piedmont: the Castello di Grinzane stands proudly amid one of the region's most famous winemaking areas.

In Poggio's hands this grape is transformed to make a wine that has an extraordinary depth of character, a rich, almost chocolatey density of fruit, great length of flavour and the stamina to last well in bottle. He attributes a great deal of the quality to the situation of his vines on the Trionzo hill. 'The wine there is special, it's something in the ground.' He has two vineyards on this rock, one facing south, the other northwest, covering a total of three hectares. The combination of grapes from both sides of the hill produces, he believes, a better balanced wine.

There is nothing unusual about the vinification of Poggio's Dolcetto unless you count his perfectionism and the fact that the miniature cement *cuves* in which he ferments the wine are painted to resemble wooden *botte*; the large casks that are the source of Italy's vinous woes. The interesting thing is the maturation, which takes place in an extraordinary group of small oak casks, too miscellaneous in origin to be dignified with the title '*barriques*'.

The question of '*barrique* versus *botte*' is a subject of much dispute in Italy. There is debate as to whether the small French-style cask is better than the big Germanic barrel, sometimes made of chestnut, sometimes oak. There is a considerable argument as to whether the smell and taste of new oak is a desirable ingredient in wine and there is a historical dispute: some growers, Poggio included, argue that prior to this century the Italians always used small casks for maturing the wine and that *botte* were only employed for fermentation. Above all, there are claims and counter claims as to who, among the present generation of winemakers, was the first to experiment with *barrique* ageing.

Guiseppe Poggio is not one of the fashionable candidates in this contest but we may as well record that he bought his first *barrique* (actually a 200-litre cask of Slovenian oak) in Yugoslavia, in 1970. He's not a fan of new oak, much preferring the effect of second-hand casks, which he buys all over the place. The most unlikely item in his collection is a Scotch whisky cask, formerly a sherry hogshead, that he found in Genoa. It took him ages to get rid of the smell of whisky. He steamed the cask, rinsed it repeatedly with hot and cold water, and finally cured it with wine: Dolcetto, Malvoisie, Moscato and Barbera. It took over three weeks of continuous labour.

Most good winemakers have a few eccentric habits and Giuseppe Poggio is no exception. He thinks things out for himself, adapts the old traditions, and delights in astonishing the world with the results. Many well-qualified oenologists would refuse to believe that anything good could come out of such scruffy cellars and I have heard an American taster, furious at Poggio's haphazard indifference to hygenic theory, mutter crossly about residual sugar. But the fact of the matter is that he produces the best Dolcetto wine in Italy. His 'normal' quality was my idea of perfection until I realized that in exceptional vintages he produces minute quantities of something even more remarkable, his 'Riserva Speciale'.

Having always thought that Dolcetto was his only love, it came as a slight shock to discover that he also plays around with Barbera. His version is dark in colour, with a slight prickle of gas, and has greater generosity than most specimens of this dour grape. Poggio's secret is to leave the lees of his Dolcetto in the vat and to ferment the Barbera on top. He claims this softens its natural astringency.

Guiseppe likes surprises. On my last visit he greeted me like a conjuror about to produce a wholly unexpected treat. We went upstairs to his house to sample the new vintage of Dolcetto, to munch a few grissini and to haggle about prices. There on the table, the focus of all attention, was his little baby. 'I am not the only producer in the world of this wine.' Guisseppe Poggio untied the cunningly knotted string that held the cork in place and poured the bottle carefully, so as not to disturb the sediment at the bottom, into half a dozen mismatched glasses. With the attentive air of a proud father he waited for our reaction.

It was delicious: green-gold in colour, scented of honey and elderflowers, gently effervescent. The mouthfilling flavour of ripe greengages was given life and definition by a fresh acidity and a marvelously invigorating bitterness at the finish. Poggio was delighted at our enthusiasm. A smile and a nod, a little clearing of the throat. As he topped up our glasses it was clear that this bottle-fermented sparkler had not been disgorged, for there was sediment at the bottom of the bottle and the wine was now slightly cloudy. Realizing that we liked it, Poggio became voluble with enthusiasm.

He explained its history. Years ago, this *spumante* was something of a local speciality made by most of the local growers. Production gradually died out and even the name of the grape variety was forgotten. Only an obscure nickname survived: *Kari-ja L'Osü*, 'the ass's burden'.

That is Piemontese dialect. The Italian translation, Carica L'Asino, is what appears on the hand-drawn, photocopied label that adorns Guiseppe's bottle, together with the words 'Vino Raro'.

Rare indeed. Poggio has only been making the wine since 1981 and he is the last producer, working from a few unreliable scraps of the old traditions and using a great deal of his own winemaking intuition. He has at least managed to find a few rows of the old vines but they don't yield much. There's just enough juice to fill a small cask, sufficient to make 200 bottles if all goes well. He sells a few bottles locally but essentially it's home-made wine for enjoying with his friends.

There are moments when I wish I lived in one of those quiet, sunny streets of Rocca Grimalda, perched on its cliff in a remote corner of Piedmont. There is a timeless restfulness about the place and the local food is delicious: some of the best pasta in Italy, and, in the winter, the pungent magic of the white truffle. There would be the constant delight of being able to drop in on Guiseppe Poggio for a glass of Dolcetto, or Barbera, or of Carica L'Asino, the rarest wine in the world. Then I realize that it would also be necessary, from time to time, to take a glass of wine with his neighbours; and the memory of what *they* produce is sufficiently awful to cause me to rejoice in the bleak reality of a February day in east Suffolk. Winemaking, on the whole, is best left to professionals. 🍃

Simon Loftus joined Adnams in 1968, became chairman in 1995 and retired in 2006.

OUT OF CALIFORNIA'S SHADOW

JASON TESAURO (2019)

What time is it, dear oenophile? In Virginia, it's striking wine o'clock. Jason Tesauro, sommelier, writer and photojournalist, tells the story of America's fifth largest wine producing state as it emerges from California's shadow. Now's the time to try its wines...

During a 2014 residency of The Chef's Penthouse at Jumeirah's Grosvenor House Suites in Mayfair, London, Michelin-starred chefs Robert Wiedmaier (Washington, DC) and Simon Hulstone (Torquay, Devon) collaborated on a series of 10-course meals mirroring the US/UK partnership at the new American Embassy at Nine Elms. While they manned the salt, I manned the cellar. Alongside classics from familiar regions like Champagne, Piedmont, Kamptal and Central Otago, I poured delicious obscurities from Crozet, Purcellville, Middleburg and Barboursville, important hamlets in Virginia (VA) wine country. *Decanter, Foodepedia* and *Great British Chefs* were all there. And they were blown away. The Virginia wine clock, for them, started that day, but let's trace it back.

EARLY HISTORY

A book published in 2018, *Virginia Wine* (by Andrew A Painter, George Mason University Press), touts an impressive-sounding byline: 'Four Centuries of Change.' Does the clock really start at the time of James I? The chronology of VA viticulture indeed includes Sir Thomas Dale, who arrived at Jamestown in 1611, a year before Capuchin friars founded Austria's famed Domaine Weinbach. Sir Thomas served as acting governor and planted a modest vineyard along the James River not far from Virginia's modern capital, Richmond,

MONTICELLO, THE EAST PORTICO.

Monticello – Virginia residence of wine-loving Founding Father Thomas Jefferson.

so-named for a scenic bend in the James that uncannily mimics Richmond Hill's vista in Richmond-upon-Thames. Sadly, the fruits of Dale's labours – along with a third of his people – were lost when Native Americans, rightfully fearing an invasion, massacred the colonists in 1622. Virginia vineyards weren't mentioned again until French Huguenots crafted in 1702, according to a prominent Colonial historian, a 'noble, strong-bodied Claret, of good flavour'. Perhaps the VA wine clock more accurately begins then?

But the French had switched to reliably profitable tobacco by 1715, so never mind. Maybe the clock kicks-off in 1759 when the Virginia General Assembly went seemingly all-in, appropriating lands for a public vineyard and funds for a chief winemaker. By 1777, though, VA turned from wine to war, shifting its treasury and human resources to the fight for independence from Great Britain. Still, something happened in the brief window from 1771–1807 that changed Virginia forever. Thomas Jefferson and George Washington, with vital contributions from Italian viticulturist-cum-statesman Filippo Mazzei, imported *Vitis vinifera* cuttings and planted thousands of European vines. Promoted to Minister Plenipotentiary to France in 1785, Jefferson visited Aix-en-Provence, Condrieu, the Côte

Portrait of Filippo Mazzei by the French painter Jacques-Louis David (c1790).

d'Or, Bordeaux and crossed into northern Italy's Piedmont and Liguria. Later, he'd go into debt to the tune of $10,000 ($200,000/£155,000+ in today's money) stocking his cellar as third president of the United States. Regarded as the Father of American Wine, Jefferson visited noble houses and set his sights on bringing the craft and lifestyle to fruition in Virginia. Nearly all of that early work was for naught, however, due to the arrival of the ruthless pest phylloxera, but while the plants themselves died, the planted idea of European vines in America firmly took root.

For many, the Virginia wine clock first ticks at that moment, and then it stalls yet again. Mazzei returns to Italy, the vines perish, Jefferson passes, and nothing notable happens in stateside wine culture until Dr Daniel Norton hybridizes French and Native American varieties in the 1820s. By the American Civil War in 1861, Virginia's Norton grape is the second-most planted variety in the country. For the next several decades, native and hybridized grapes make a big splash until economics, politics, vineyard diseases and environmental pressures ostensibly kill off Virginia viticulture and convert the Commonwealth to a one-fruit state: apples. Throw in Prohibition (when America foolishly teetotaled from 1919–33), the Great Depression, World War II, a liquor-is-quicker generation of martini and highball consumption, and the entire American wine industry essentially dries up.

TURNING POINTS

And then came 1976. One hundred and fifty years after Jefferson's death, another Italian brought Mazzei's dreams to life. Gianni Zonin, the visionary patriarch of a family wine company founded in 1821, purchased an historic, 700-acre sheep farm once owned by VA Governor James Barbour. Zonin signed the deed on April 13th, Jefferson's birthday, and immediately installed an ambitious Italian polymath, Gabriele Rausse, to oversee the launch of Barboursville Vineyards.

The clock restarts; this time for good. In 1978, Barboursville produces Virginia's first commercial vintage of vinifera wine. In 1980, the VA Farm Winery Act passes, providing a slew of tax advantages to incentivize planting and experimentation. Fees and taxes are reinvested into education, marketing and oenology research. In 1984, Virginia establishes the Monticello AVA (American Viticultural Area). By 1990, the number of VA wineries tops 40 and an alphabet soup of intrepid producers – Farfelu, Horton, Ingleside, Jefferson, Linden, Meredyth, Chateau Morrisette, Oakencroft, Oasis, Piedmont, Prince Michel, Rapidan River, Shenandoah – find their footing. Ten years later, the number crosses 100. Now, it's over 300 and Virginia is the fifth-largest wine-producing state in America. Studies in perseverance, many of those original vanguards are still in operation today.

It's romantic to think of Virginia wine as 400 years old, yet even counting only the 150 years since Jefferson is misleading. For we oenophiles of the world, wine here essentially began in the 1990s. That's when her winegrowers really dug their boots into the soil and asked not 'What do I want to drink?' but rather 'What does my land want to grow?' Knowledge grew, technology evolved, experimentation flourished. Producers started cracking the code on everything from clonal selection to rootstock, trellising to pruning, fermentation to cooperage. In 1998, Virginia's long and winding road to legitimacy hit pay-dirt: a gorgeous vintage. More than that, grape growers understood by then how to harness that sunshine, and winemakers knew how to express it. It was that vintage which made me quit a sterling wine job in Atlanta in 2002 and move – against all sommelier colleagues' advice – to join this burgeoning movement in Virginia. That same 1998 vintage also moved Michael Broadbent to first break the VA wine story internationally in *Decanter* in 2003 with a serendipitous discovery and glowing review: 'By any standards, superb,' he wrote: '…a four-star-plus rating.'

As we all know, Broadbent's now-famous 'Tasting Note 387: States' Evidence: Virginia 1, California 0' led to a cavalcade of ebullient critics huzzahing Virginia like a Greek chorus. The talk of the town, Virginia surpassed Oregon and Washington in domestic hipness and the Commonwealth's own citizens flocked to VA wine-flush retailers and restaurants with pride. Coast to coast, consumers shifted their drinking and buying habits away from oaky opulence to minerally finesse. The American wine press embraced this emerging region which bridged Old World approaches with New World approachability and the rest is history. Except, sadly, apart from Tasting Note 387, NONE of that actually happened. Yes, top somms and tastemakers in the US adore acid, ageability, artisanship and elegance, but the plonk-swilling masses are still blindly seduced with billboard marketing and chain store discounts. In short, one of the main reasons Virginia wine continues to be niche is that Americans don't yet truly know or trust their own palates. And with the rise of millennials, who prefer spirits and craft beer over wine, I worry that Virginia wine, like Grand Cru Chablis, will be revered by connoisseurs and the curious, but relegated to the fringes of popular wine culture. Whatever the recent trends suggest, our Old Dominion rolls onward.

YOUNG, BUT MATURING

In the convening years since her breakout vintage, three tiers of VA producers have emerged. There are the Hobbyists: affluent thrill-seekers with second careers and third homes marching forth into VA wine with contracted growers and high-priced consulting vintners as their ante-up into 'the game'. There are the Showpieces: savvy developers with luxe event spaces and wedding venues flanked with a few scenic vines but oceans of juice to be exclusively poured at those parties. And then there are the Artisans: ranging from tiny family enterprises like Ankida Ridge Vineyards, with its single-digit acreage and triple-digit case production of the state's finest Pinot Noir, to The Williamsburg Winery, a massive operation with 40,000 cases and 45 wines.

So what exactly is in those artisan bottles and why should anyone care? Virginia is banking her name on evocative Viognier rivalling the Rhône Valley and beguiling dry Petit Manseng that will make you google Jurançon. She's got Chinon-besting Cabernet Franc, category-redefining Petit Verdot and Tannat, and Bordeaux-busting blends that don't demand a king's ransom or a generation of patience. Lean, green whites like Vermentino and Albariño, and razor sharp *blancs de blancs* from steely Chardonnay evince Virginia's grasp on crop management, maceration and precision between crush pad and tank. Proprietary reds like Adagio (Williamsburg), Eluvium (Early Mountain), Hardscrabble (Linden), Lost Mountain (RdV) and Octagon (Barboursville) illuminate

Right: The new 'Golden State'? Vineyards near Hillsboro, Virginia.

the blender's art and gleaned wisdom from decades of tinkering in the cellar. You don't have to take my word for it, though. Besides Broadbent, Jancis Robinson MW, Steven Spurrier and Oz Clarke all tasted enough during past London Wine Fairs that they each made subsequent journeys to Virginia. Those early accolades from overseas helped galvanize American critics, while also inspiring grit at a time of uncertainty.

Scores of VA winemakers have foreign accents. They come from Italy, France, Portugal, Spain, South Africa, England, New Zealand, and their releases of Nebbiolo, Meritage and Touriga National reflect a respect for heritage. Industrious successes with sweet wines, orange wines, rosés, pétillant naturels and lesser-known grapes, on the other hand, demonstrate an exuberant liberation from strict tradition. They are fearless in the face of vintage variation yet humble in the wake of a mercurial, sometimes heartbreaking, climate. And the wines show this. Like magnificent sculptures emerging from a rough block of stone, Virginia's iconic wines are world-class masterpieces hewed from soil and toil. Her unearthed *terroir* is coming into focus: we know the Monticello AVA's silky clay and Middleburg AVA's rocky slopes, but viticultural literacy in the limestone skeins of Shenandoah Valley AVA or the sandy soils of the Eastern Shore AVA is half-fluent at best. How exciting it is to think that Virginia's best wines have yet to be bottled, or that her most defining varietal has yet to be planted?

WINE SHOPPING, NAME DROPPING

Virginia is doing her part. The Old Dominion's old guard has pushed experimentation, collaboration and camaraderie into the 21st century. It's led to booms in agro-tourism and the kinds of vino-hued day-tripping and vertical-centric collecting that Old World oenophiles have practised for generations. There's a Winemaker Research Exchange, a dedicated VA Wine Month (October), and more producers to add to the canon of consistently terrific Virginia wineries: Blenheim, Boxwood, Chatham, Chrysalis, Delaplane, Keswick, Michael Shaps, Rosemont, Stinson, Veritas, Walsh Family – the wines from several of which can be found in the UK. How long has it been since your last Virginia wine? I've named over 20. Now it's your turn. Start the clock. 🍃

CHAPTER 5

THE MISCHIEF OF TEA

A Nice Cup of Tea – George Orwell (1946)
Tea Works its Mischief Slowly – Cecil Torr (1918)
Tea vs Bollinger – PG Wodehouse (1964)

A NICE CUP OF TEA

GEORGE ORWELL (1946)

*Prolific journalist and author, George Orwell, famed for his iconic
20th-century novels* Animal Farm *and* Nineteen Eighty-Four, *sets out
the 11 rules he regards as 'golden' in the art of making tea.*

If you look up 'tea' in the first cookery book that comes to hand you will probably find that it is unmentioned; or at most you will find a few lines of sketchy instructions which give no ruling on several of the most important points.

This is curious, not only because tea is one of the mainstays of civilization in this country, as well as in Eire, Australia and New Zealand, but because the best manner of making it is the subject of violent disputes.

When I look through my own recipe for the perfect cup of tea, I find no fewer than 11 outstanding points. On perhaps two of them there would be pretty general agreement, but at least four others are acutely controversial. Here are my own 11 rules, every one of which I regard as golden:

First of all, one should use Indian or Ceylonese tea. China tea has virtues which are not to be despised nowadays – it is economical, and one can drink it without milk – but there is not much stimulation in it. One does not feel wiser, braver or more optimistic after drinking it. Anyone who uses that comforting phrase 'a nice cup of tea' invariably means Indian tea. Secondly, tea should be made in small quantities that is, in a teapot. Tea out of an urn is always tasteless, while army tea, made in a cauldron, tastes of grease and

whitewash. The teapot should be made of china or earthenware. Silver or Britannia-ware pots produce inferior tea and enamel pots are worse: though curiously enough a pewter teapot (a rarity nowadays) is not so bad. Thirdly, the pot should be warmed beforehand. This is better done by placing it on the hob than by the usual method of swilling it out with hot water. Fourthly, the tea should be strong. For a pot holding a quart, if you are going to fill it nearly to the brim, six heaped teaspoons would be about right. In a time of rationing this is not an idea that can be realized on every day of the week, but I maintain that one strong cup of tea is better than 20 weak ones. All true tea-lovers not only like their tea strong, but like it a little stronger with each year that passes, a fact which is recognized in the extra ration issued to old-age pensioners.*

Fifthly, the tea should be put straight into the pot. No strainers, muslin bags or other devices to imprison the tea. In some countries teapots are fitted with little dangling baskets under the spout to catch the stray leaves, which are supposed to be harmful. Actually one can swallow tea-leaves in considerable quantities without ill effect, and if the tea is not loose in the pot it never infuses properly. Sixthly, one should take the teapot to the kettle and not the other way about. The water should be actually boiling at the moment of impact, which means that one should keep it on the flame while one pours. Some people add that one should only use water that has been freshly brought to the boil, but I have never noticed that this makes any difference. Seventhly, after making the tea,

---

* Wartime rationing was still in force in 1946.

one should stir it, or better, give the pot a good shake afterwards allowing the leaves to settle. Eighthly, one should drink out of a breakfast cup – that is the cylindrical type of cup, not the flat, shallow type. The breakfast cup holds more, and with the other kind one's tea is always half cold before one has well started on it. Ninthly, one should pour the cream off the milk before using it for tea. Milk that is too creamy always gives tea a sickly taste. Tenthly, one should pour tea into the cup first. This is one of the most controversial points of all; indeed in every family in Britain there are probably two schools of thought on the subject. The milk-first school can bring forward some fairly strong arguments, but I maintain that my own argument is unanswerable. This is that, by putting the tea in first and then stirring as one pours, one can exactly regulate the amount of milk whereas one is liable to put in too much milk if one does it the other way round.

Lastly, tea – unless one is drinking it in the Russian style – should be drunk without sugar. I know very well that I am in a minority here. But still, how can you call yourself a true tea-lover if you destroy the flavour of your tea by putting sugar in it? It would be equally reasonable to put in pepper or salt. Tea is meant to be bitter, just as beer is meant to be bitter. If you sweeten it, you are no longer tasting the tea, you are merely tasting the sugar; you could make a very similar drink by dissolving sugar in plain hot water.

Some people would answer that they don't like tea in itself, that they only drink it in order to be warmed and stimulated, and they need sugar to take the taste away. To those misguided people I would say: Try drinking tea without sugar for, say, a fortnight and it is very unlikely that you will ever want to ruin your tea by sweetening it again.

These are not the only controversial points that arise in connection with tea-drinking, but they are sufficient to show how subtilized the whole business has become. There is also the mysterious social etiquette surrounding the teapot (why is it considered vulgar to drink out of your saucer, for instance?) and much might be written about the subsidiary uses of tea-leaves, such as telling fortunes, predicting the arrival of visitors, feeding rabbits, healing burns and sweeping the carpet. It is worth paying attention to such details as warming the pot and using water that is really boiling, so as to make quite sure of wringing out of one's ration the 20 good, strong cups that two ounces, properly handled, ought to represent. 🍃

*First published in the **Evening Standard** (London) January 1946.*

TEA WORKS ITS MISCHIEF SLOWLY

CECIL TORR (1918)

Cecil Torr, lawyer, antiquarian and amateur scholar, decided in 1916 that the folklore of his village on Dartmoor was too precious to be lost. What began as a simple set of notes quickly got out of hand and went, as Torr apologized, 'much further than I meant'. Three volumes of Small Talk at Wreyland were published, in 1918, 1921 and 1923, and were a welcome relief to the constant drone of war news. Here he has some careful thoughts about a drink we know and love... (So, if cider is better for us than tea, then surely wine is too?)

On the whole, less harm is done by cider than by tea; but cider gets more blame, as its ill effects are visible at once, whereas tea works its mischief slowly. Nobody says anything against tea-drinking now; but Parson Davy in his *System of Divinity*, vol xix, page 235, which he printed at Lustleigh in 1803, spoke with indignation of 'the immeasurable use of that too fashionable and pernicious plant, which weakens the stomach, unbraces the nerves, and drains the very vitals of our national wealth; to which nevertheless our children are as early and as carefully enured, from the very breast, as if the daily use of it were an indispensable duty which they owed to God and their country.' And in his *Letter to a Friend Concerning Tea*, published in 1748, John Wesley spoke of tea drinking as tea-drinkers speak of drinking alcohol now: 'wasteful, unhealthy self-indulgence';—'no other than a slow poison';—'abhor it as a deadly poison, and renounce it from this very hour'. ☙

*Excerpt from **Small Talk at Wreyland**, Cecil Torr (1857–1928), First Series, 1918.*

Tea vs Bollinger

PG WODEHOUSE (1964)

In his tale of mistaken identity, young love and general mayhem, Galahad at Blandings, *PG Wodehouse offers the genteel evidence that drinking champagne rather than tea is better for us.*

A moment later, Lord Emsworth bustled in, wreathed in smiles. 'Ah, here you are, Mr Whipple,' he said. 'Capital, capital. I will ring for tea.' 'Tea?' said Gally. 'You don't want tea. Filthy stuff. Look what it did to poor Buffy Struggles.'

'Did I ever tell you about Buffy? Someone lured him into one of those temperance lectures illustrated with coloured slides and there was one showing the liver of the drinker of alcohol. He called on me next day, his face ashen. "Gally," he said, "what would you say the procedure was when a fellow wants to buy tea?" "Tea?" I said. "What do you want tea for?" "To drink," he said. I told him to pull himself together. "You're talking wildly," I said. "You can't drink tea. Have a drop of brandy." He shook his head. "No more alcohol for me," he said. "It makes your liver look like a Turner sunset."

'Well, I begged him with tears in my eyes not to do anything rash, but I couldn't move him. He ordered in ten pounds of the muck and was dead two weeks later. Got run over by a hansom cab in Piccadilly. Obviously if his system hadn't been weakened by tea, he'd have been able to dodge the vehicle. Summon Beach and tell him to bring a bottle of champagne. I can see from Whipple's face that he needs a bracer.'

'Perhaps you are right,' said Lord Emsworth.

'I know I'm right. The only safe way to get through life is to pickle your system thoroughly in alcohol. Look at Freddie Potts and his brother Eustace the time they ate the hedgehog.'

'Ate what?'

'The hedgehog. Freddie and Eustace were living on the Riviera at the time and they had a French chef, one of whose jobs was to go to market and buy supplies. On the way to Grasse that day, as he trotted off with the money in his pocket, he saw a dead hedgehog lying by the side of the road. Now this chef was a thrifty sort of chap and he saw immediately that if he refrained from buying the chicken he'd been sent to buy and stuck to the money, he'd be that much up, and he knew that with the aid of a few sauces he could pass that hedgehog off as chicken all right, so he picked it up and went home with it and served it up next day *en casserole*. Both brothers ate heartily, and here's the point of the story. Eustace, who was a teetotaller, nearly died, but Freddie, who had lived mostly on whisky since early boyhood, showed no ill effects whatsoever. I think there is a lesson in this for all of us, so press that bell, Clarence.'

Lord Emsworth pressed it, and Beach, resting in his pantry from the labours of the afternoon, was stirred to activity. Heaving himself up from his easy chair in a manner which would certainly have led Huxley Winkworth, had he seen him, to renew those offensive comparisons of his between him and Empress of Blandings rising from her couch, he put on the boots which for greater comfort he had removed and started laboriously up the stairs. His face as he went was careworn, his manner preoccupied.

In the 19 years during which he had served Lord Emsworth in the capacity of major-domo it had always been with mixed feelings that Beach found himself regarding the weekly ceremony of Visitors' Day at Blandings Castle. It had its good points, and it had its drawbacks. On the one hand, it gratified his sense of importance to conduct a flock of human sheep about the premises and watch their awe-struck faces as he pointed out the various objects of interest: on the other all that walking up and down stairs and along corridors and in and out of rooms hurt his feet. It was a fact not generally known, for his stout boots hid their secret well, that he suffered from corns.

On the whole, however, the bright side may be said to have predominated over the dark side, the spiritual's pros to have outweighed the physical cons, and as a general rule he performed his task with a high heart and in an equable frame of mind. But not today. A butler who has been robbed of his silver watch can hardly be expected to be the same rollicking cicerone as a butler who has undergone no such deprivation. He had woken with his loss heavy on his mind, and as he led his mob of followers about the castle he was still brooding on it and blaming himself for not having kept a sharper eye on that fellow with whom he had collided in the entrance of the Emsworth Arms bar. He might have known that no good was to be expected from a man with a twisted ear.

On his departure for America to take up his duties in the offices of Donaldson's Dog Joy Inc of Long Island City, the country's leading purveyors of biscuits to the American dog, Freddie Threepwood, Lord Emsworth's younger son, had bequeathed to Beach his collection of mystery thrillers, said to be the finest in Shropshire, and in three out of every 10 of these the criminal, when unmasked, had proved to be a man with a twisted ear. It should have warned him, Beach felt, but unfortunately it had not, and it was with a feeling of dull depression that he entered the study.

The next moment, this dull depression had left him and he was tingling from head to foot as if electrified. For there, apparently on the best of terms with his lordship and Mr Galahad, sat the miscreant in person. His head was bent as he scanned some photographs which Lord Emsworth was showing him, but that ear was unmistakable.

It is probable that if Beach had not been a butler a startled cry would at this point have echoed through the room, but butlers do not utter startled cries. All he said was: 'You rang, m'lord?'

'Eh? Ah. Oh yes. Bring us a bottle of Bollinger, will you Beach.'

'Very good, m'lord.'

'And while it is coming, Mr Whipple,' said Lord Emsworth, 'there are some photographs of the Empress in the library I would like you to see.' ✿

*Excerpt from Chapter Eight of **Galahad at Blandings**, Barrie & Jenkins (London) 1964.*

CHAPTER 6

SHOULD PORT BE FORTIFIED?

A Call to Ban Port's Fortification – Cyrus Redding (1833)

The Best of Both Worlds? – Dirk Niepoort (2019)

The Scandal of Elderberries – H Warner Allen (1951)

The Port Trials – Ben Howkins (2019)

A Call to Ban Port's Fortification

CYRUS REDDING (1833)

Cyrus Redding was a Cornish journalist and free-market thinker vociferous in his condemnation of wine tariffs and government-supported monopolies. In his book A History and Description of Modern Wines *(published in 1833) his praise of the wines of Romanée-Conti, Lafite and Montrachet is as glowing as it would be from today's wine writers 187 years later, but his firm views on the fortification of port and the power wielded by the Douro Wine Company (founded 1756) are far more controversial...*

Never was there more sophistry displayed than in the laboured answer made by the company at Oporto to the charges brought against them; they published utter nonsense in their defense. The grounds upon which they rested their arguments, and the arguments themselves, were insulting to the understanding of all who knew anything about wine in this country. An eminent wine merchant of London observed 'that it seemed as if the Oporto people were fools enough to imagine that no one knew anything about wine but themselves, and that there were no other growths than those of Oporto in the world'.

Why Englishmen should not have the benefit of the best wines of the Cima do Douro in a pure state, without adventitious mixtures, no rational answer can be given . . .

The powers allowed to this company were of the most despotic character. As all competition was swept away, and they were the sole dictators, so they found the usual evils of arbitrary power recoil upon themselves. They set bounds to the vine country: 'so far shalt thou grow and no farther', was the mandate to the possessor of the soil. The consequence was excessive smuggling. Smuggling, as it naturally does when prohibition is overdone, demanded injurious and tyrannical power over the agrarian population to repress it, but in vain. The next step was to crave military aid of an arbitrary government for the purpose, and military interference was followed as usual by waste and ruin to the inhabitants without removing the evils; those evils which were the pretences for the establishment of the monopoly of the company, and the removal of which they urged as most necessary for the interest of the trade, but which they renewed immediately, and systematized for their own advantage.

Having monopolized the wine and brandy trade, and even the taxation upon them and the brandy imported into Portugal, they purchased inferior wines to dispose of as port, or mingle with the stronger kinds, to all which they affixed the price, and for ever barred the improvement which could only be effected by greater remuneration from the merchant to the grower, and in consequence by a larger rate of payment from the consumer. One class of wine alone, differing a little in strength and taste, was most beneficial to the company's monopoly, and they were determined to have as much as they could obtain at the smallest cost, because it was attended with the largest profit. They levelled the superior growths known before that pernicious interference, and amalgamated the white wines into the common hotch-potch which composed the company's favourite and unique species.

The mischief was long accomplished before a sort of modification of the company's charter took place in 1823, in consequence of the injury to agriculture and commerce arising out of the existence of this sordid body, even in the view of so obtuse a government as that of Portugal. Their power had been too long absolute . . .

Trade must be free as air. The folly of the interference of the government of a country with its manufactures, either directly or through the grant of a monopoly, does not now need any effort of the pen to expose. The wines of Portugal, left to the emulation and spirit of individuals, would have risen in estimation. They would have been divided into classes, each grower being emulative to attain the highest. High prices would have purchased wine of proportionate worth, and England would not have had to pay dearly for one inferior article. The coarse vines of Portugal would have been succeeded by those of a better and choicer character. The grower would have been enriched, and the British public, who were forced to purchase under a most specious and impolitic treaty, would have had a less love for ardent-spirited wine, decidedly injurious to health.

Accustomed as we now are to these wines, the improvement of them is to be greatly desired and will some day no doubt be effected. Now it is only occasionally that a glass of very fine unadulterated port is to be met with, which seems to have got into England like the fly into amber. A worthy wine in such instances it is found to be. In the richest country in the world, it is mortifying to discover that every inn or tavern, where enormous prices are demanded for a bottle of wine, nothing is met with still, from the Lands End to Caithness, but a coarse brandied product of the Oporto company, which in any other region but this would be flung into the still.

It is now fitting that something should be said of the districts and vineyards, the farmers and proprietors of which have been thus weighed down, and the wines of which have been so sunk below their real merits by the pressure of the foregoing monopoly.

The wine country of the Douro extends along the banks of that river about 14 leagues [about 48 miles] from the city of Oporto. The vine is very generally cultivated in Portugal; but it is from vineyards of the Douro alone that its wines have derived a celebrity in England, by the injudicious financial measure to which allusion has been already made. The best wine of this district was capable of great improvement had competition been suffered to exist, and the market remained open. The wines of Portugal are now inferior to the wines of Spain, the sherries of which country have continued to improve, and to approach much nearer to the first class of wines than formerly. This arises not from any fault in the soil or climate of Portugal, which is admirably adapted for the growth of the vine, but from the sordid monopoly already dwelt upon.

The wine country of the Douro is called the district of the Cima do Douro, or the Higher Douro, and that is again subdivided with respect to product into, first, Factory wines, *Fritorie*, and secondly, Branch wines, *Bamo*. The sites which it affords are excellent, and the powerful sun of the south renders the failure of the crops a matter of rarity. The vine training is of the low kind of the French, and the vineyards are on the slopes of schistous hills, of most favourable aspect. No less than 67 varieties of vine have been reckoned in Portugal; but in the wines made for the Company, no nicety of choice has been exemplified, the favourite species is the product of a vine, which gives out the greatest abundance of a black fruit: they are exceedingly coarse, rough and deeply serrated. The species called Donzelinho, Alvarelhão and Souzão are in much request; but whatever are the varieties, they are mingled together, and the wine is sweet or harsh as by accident one particular species of grape may predominate. It is evident, therefore, that no justice has been done to the wines of the Douro, nor have their 'capabilities' been fairly put to the proof.

The grapes are trodden in vats in a slovenly way with the stalks, and while the process of fermentation proceeds this uncouth operation is repeated. The time of fermentation varies, but it rarely exceeds 75 hours. The wines are then removed into tuns, containing upwards of a dozen pipes each. The wine is racked after the great wine sale in February, and carried to the cellars of the Company, or of the purchasers. It is generally exported at the end of the year from the vintage, during which period it is twice brandied, the taint of which it holds until age ameliorates the wine at the expense of its natural vinous flavour and perfume. It is an effect of the admixture of the spirit, that in order to drink the wine of Oporto, with the real virtues of the grape, it must be swallowed in a fiery state from brandy, or if the consumer wishes to avoid the ardent nature of the combination, and cause less injury to his stomach, he must wait until the better vinous properties are deteriorated, and the little flavour and aroma of the wine are utterly destroyed.

No valid excuse has ever been made for the practice of adding such a quantity of brandy to the wines of Oporto in the extraordinary manner which has been the custom. The quality of Portuguese brandy is for the most part execrable. It is frequently distilled from figs and raisins, of which no other use can be made. They even once tried to make it from locust pods, but that scheme failed, and they were obliged to resort to importation for the extra quantity they wanted. That the wines will keep and bear a sea-voyage without the addition of brandy to such an extravagant excess, there can be no doubt. A couple of bottles of good brandy to a pipe when put on board ship, would, if such an assertion were true, answer every purpose of preservation. In some years 27,000 tuns of port wine have been imported into Great Britain, in every one of which, besides the portion of spirit in the wine, no less than six gallons 162,000 gallons of ardent spirit.

To get rid of this liquid fire, the wine must be kept a dozen years, and ruined in flavour, when it might be drank in half the time by omitting the brandy. If the Oporto charge made against the English taste were true, how comes it that even down to 1754 the admixture was censured as flagitious and abominable, even by the merchants themselves? Port wine had then been drank in England for nearly 60 years, and the wines were found warm enough for the taste of Englishmen. The truth is, that quantity being the great desideratum, because a good deal of middling wine is more profitable than a small quantity at a high price, brandy aids in making all the growths equal, after being kept a longer or shorter time, for the inclination of the inferior qualities always is to descend in the market, even below their worth, as the better increase. The mischief is thus easily explained. By this practice, and the ease with which the mass of any people is cajoled, a taste in wine of a most extraordinary kind has prevailed in this country, among the bulk of those in the middling classes who drink wine, and who seem to prefer the juice of the grape the more it resembles the product of the still rather than of simple fermentation, the very excellence of which consists in the slight interference of artificial effort for completing its product, after the earth and sun have done their part. 🍇

*Excerpt from **A History and Description of Modern Wines** by Cyrus Redding, Whittaker, Treacher & Arnot (London) 1833.*

THE BEST OF BOTH WORLDS?

DIRK NIEPOORT (2019)

Dirk Niepoort is a Douro Valley maverick. His family have been port merchants in the Douro Valley since 1842 and today Dirk's Colheita and vintage ports are amongst the finest made. But Dirk is also a strong believer in the qualities that the Douro's native grapes show as table wines. So what does he say to Cyrus Redding's 1833 cry against their fortification (pages 124–27)?

What Cyrus Redding has to say is fascinating to me. To think back in time; to realize his thoughts at such an interesting historic moment – when Portugal was in its decline and England the richest country in the world – is intriguing. It is difficult to imagine what would have happened if Cyrus Redding had succeeded in his mission to stop the 'adulteration' of Douro wines. It seems to me that the 'Company' would have had an overwhelming influence on the matter. The monopoly held by the Douro Wine Company was all-pervading: it controlled every aspect of port production, from the vineyards to the market. Port could only have been prohibited from fortification if there had never been such a monopoly. IF…

But *if* there hadn't, maybe Portugal's wines would have followed the greatness of the French – and the German wines for that matter. I would want to believe that Colares and Bucelas, which made incredible ageworthy wines around and before 1900, and Dão, which was the most famous area of Portugal for a long time, would today be reference points in the world of wine. The Douro would have been there too, with its own identity, standing next to areas like Bordeaux and Burgundy.

Continuing the family tradition – master port-maker Dirk Niepoort.

In reality it was the British clients, merchants and drinkers who liked the fortified versions of the Douro wine. It was for them that the producers fortified it in the first place – probably to help the wines survive their shipment to the UK. And because it became a big business, the Company interfered and took control of it all.

But some people, like Cyrus Redding, were afraid the adulteration would destroy the character of the real Douro wines. Another influential person who felt the same way was Baron Forrester, who was one of the pioneers of the port industry in the 19th century. Eleven years after Cyrus Redding's writing, in 1844, Forrester wrote an anonymous booklet called *A Word or Two on Port Wine*, in which he promoted reforms to the way port was made and regulated. He also created the detailed maps of the River Douro and its properties – from Spain through to Oporto – that enabled the accurate demarcation of the region (the Douro was the the first classified wine area in the world).

Forrester was a very important and influential person in his time. He had the same opinion as Cyrus and was against the fortification of the Douro wines. He wanted to regulate against it and tried hard to stop it. But the English merchants were too strong, and fortified port was too successful.

My feeling is that it was stupid to fight about it. Why not have both? Table wines and port should have been made side by side. It is a ridiculous discussion that we still have today. Only as recently as 1986, when Portugal joined the EU, were we allowed to sell our wines direct from the estate. Before this, they all had to go to Vila Nova de Gaia to be matured and sold as port. All the focus was on fortified wines. When the EU lifted this crazy rule, we were able to make different wine styles that could be appreciated for their own merits.

Port still has many rules controlling its vineyards and production, and some people compare me to 'Barão' Forrester in that I don't want to live by those rules.

When I started working with my father in 1987 there was only one priority here. Everyone made port. There were very few exceptions. My theory at that time was that we should start to get to know the Douro better and find out more about the first demarcated wine area in the world. After all, it is huge – 45,000 hectares – with vines growing from 80-metre elevations to 800, all sorts of exposures and 85 different varieties (18 more than the 67 Cyrus mentions).

There are many reasons for planting a mix of different varieties. The major one was to avoid having big problems with disease. By planting many grapes we would have avoided a monoculture where if one variety succumbed to a virus, the whole crop would be lost. So I think we should be celebrating these grapes more, getting to know their flavours and their wines. We know the ones that work for port, but what about all the others? What characters do they have to offer?

I feel that we should have two priorities now, not just one. In the Douro we should have our minds and logistics organized so that we can do both wines, fortified and unfortified, at the same time.

The port houses are still obsessed with their companies wanting to sell more and more. But the reality is that they are in great danger of banalizing the image of port. It's time to think about the future of the Douro and not just of port.

I have respect for fortified port, for all its beauty and tradition, and for its great past. It is still the essence of the Douro. But I also have respect for the unfortified wines. The best vineyards for port are not the best for red and white wine. So we can create table wines separately. We can create strong brands, but parallel to that some 'boutique' wines too. These small scale, high quality wines will make the point that Douro wines can be as outstanding as any in the world. We should respect the beauty of the Douro and open it to tourism – not mass truism.

I love port and without a doubt it is one of the great wines of the world – even being fortified. But it's as true now as it was in Cyrus' day, if we think in a brighter and broader way and don't limit ourselves with unnecessary monopolies and restricting laws, the Douro has a great future. 🌿

THE SCANDAL OF
ELDERBERRIES

H WARNER ALLEN (1951)

*An entertaining voice from the 1950s, wine author H Warner Allen delves even
further back and finds a fascinating document written by one John Croft in
1788. Croft throws some amusing sidelights on the port trade of his day,
complaining that the wines are not so rich and mellow as they used to be and
do not keep as well ('an Englishman of any descent, condition or circumstances,
cannot dispense with it after his good dinner, in the same manner as he uses a
piece of Cheshire cheese for pretended digestion-sake'). Allen explores why.*

Before port could become popular across the seas, it had to be fortified with brandy
to check its fermentation and retain in the wine sufficient sugar, for the wine of the
Douro, if it is allowed to ferment out, is horribly harsh and dry. This expedient was
discovered and put into use between 1725 and 1750, but more was needed. Wine and
alcohol shut up in the narrow limits of a bottle need time for amalgamation and for the
throwing off of impurities, and if wine is to keep, bottles must be binned on their sides.
The early port bottle was a picturesque, bulbous receptacle, and a good many years passed
before its shape was so modified that it would lie comfortably on its side. Evidently this
difficulty had been overcome when Mr Croft wrote, for he says that red port 'bottled and
laid upon its side, will only bark, or tinge, and stick close to the bottle in November and
December'. He was in favour of bottling the wine four years after the vintage and keeping
it for two before use. Elsewhere, he complains that the Oporto factory 'were obliged to keep
their wines so long in their warehouses, as they were not demanded on sale in England of
so considerable a time, it having become the fashion there to use none but the oldest wines.'

The evolution of the port bottle during the 18th century.

Nonetheless, wines did not keep as long as they used, partly on account of poor vintages and partly, it would seem, for another unexpected reason.

On my first glance at the Treatise, I was completely stumped as to the inward meaning of a Latin quotation on the title page: *Sensi ego, quum insidiis pallida vina bibi*: 'I marked him, when I drank the wine pale with treachery.' It comes from an elegy by Propertius telling how, after her funeral, the ghost of his mistress, Cynthia, visited him and reproached him and all his household with neglect and treachery. A servant must be tortured with red-hot irons, because he had given her the 'pale wine', which presumably poisoned her. Why the worthy John Croft should start off an essay on port with a reference to pale wine defeated me, and the dictionary suggestion that the '*pallida vina*' were wines that made people pale, on the analogy of pale death, did not make matters much clearer. Then, when I read the Treatise, I found that there was a sly, malicious point in the Latin reference, though it was the author's port that was rich red by treachery, not pale in colour like Cynthia's wine. The treachery was, in point of fact, that ancient skeleton in the port cupboard, the elderberry. Now elderberries have no business to find their way into wine, but I think I should prefer a stray elderberry giving colour to my port to elder flower producing a Muscatelle flavour.

According to the worthy Croft, port in its early days had to compete with Florence wine, a very highly coloured and inferior form of Chianti. The public taste demanded colour, and port at that time was pale, 'because the red and white grapes were squeezed and jumbled together, as they promiscuously grew in the vineyards... A liquor nearly the same as red and white port being mixed.' 'A Mr Peter Bearsley, an Englishman, who resided at Viana as a factor, was the first who went to Oporto in the view, and for the purpose of speculating in the Port Wines; and on the road to the Wine country, at an Inn, he met with an Elder tree, whose juice he expressed, and mixed with the ordinary wine, and found it had the effect of heightening and improving its colour.'

I am afraid that Mr Croft was not so shocked by the strange meeting between Mr Bearsley and an Elder tree as he should have been; for he writes: 'When too great a quantity of rain falls at the vintage, the red grape will be almost the colour of the white, and even requires the juice of the Elder to give it a proper red, though now all such sophistication of the wine is not only strictly forbidden in Portugal, but attended even with capital punishment and confiscation of the wine. ...By the law of the General Company of the Douro, if an Elder tree is found in or about a vineyard, the penalty of 40 shillings shall be incurred; and if any of the berries, or expressed juice (which they term *Baga*) is found or discovered in any lodge or repository of wine, the owner or proprietor is liable to be imprisoned at the mercy of the King. This I knew put into execution, and several gentlemen of family and high rank in the Wine Country were sent to prison on suspicion only, some Elder berries having been unluckily strewed in the pathway of their lodges, which might have been done through an evil design. The Portuguese, not being allowed to add the Elder juice to their wines, is the reason why the port wines either come over of late years so deficient in colour, or lose it so soon, that they will not keep properly in bottles above five years, without become pale and tawny. This, and the very small portion of brandy afforded to put in them, owing to the exorbitant price it is held up at by the Company, the sole vendors of it, is a very sufficient argument against the port wines being so long kept, as well as that the vintages, for many years past, have not afforded so rich or mellow wines as they formerly possessed.'

I have allowed Mr Croft to tell his story in his own words, for the sake of reading between the lines. Black-strap he wanted, and had done a fine trade in the *Baga* wines. He was no purist, and quite unable to share the gratitude of the modern wine-drinker to the Portuguese monopoly, which put an embargo on the elderberry and compelled wine-grower and winemaker to improve their wines and vinification in order to produce such wines as the British public demanded, without fraud or adulteration.

*Excerpt from **A Contemplation of Wine** by H Warner Allen, Michael Joseph (London) 1951.*

THE PORT TRIALS

BEN HOWKINS (2019)

'Fascinating reading...' says port enthusiast, author and export director, Ben Howkins, of these three heartfelt articles about port and the wines of the Douro, but does he agree that port took a turn in the wrong direction 200 years ago?

Cyrus Redding was a man with a mission. He did not like monopolies. He fought for free trade. I sympathize, but cannot agree with his arguments. Douro wines had to be fortified if they were ever going to arrive in England in any state of drinkability. The state monopoly may not have been perfect, but the alternative might well have been more unstable – and by that I mean both the wines and the body that governed them.

As with that other Iberian fortified wine – sherry – the ups and downs in quality do not belie the fact that the English of that period, the 18th and early 19th centuries, needed their own customized central heating during the cold, bitter winter months. This came in the form of a bottle, or several, of port or sherry. Quality wines they were not all the time, but by George, they were welcome in the home and on the hunting field.

H Warner Allen was a bit of a snob. He delves into all kinds of related issues from the pros and cons of drinking hot chocolate or mulled port on an August morning to using Cheshire cheese as a 'pretended digestion' for gentlemen. He correctly identifies farmers who blended white grapes and red grapes to produce greater quantities of rather inferior wines. These same chaps then added in '*Baga*' (elderberries) to raise the demanded colour profile. The Douro monopoly, about whom Mr Redding is so rude, even imprisoned those who dared to have an Elder tree in their vineyard. My own view is that, of course, this is

A traditional Rabelo – a sailing vessel for transporting casks of port – on the River Douro in Oporto.

politically correct EU policy thinking, but I wonder how many of us have thoroughly enjoyed a glass of matured vintage port that might just have had a soupcon of elder in it, by mistake of course?

During the later part of the 19th century and for most of the 20th century, vintage port was the only 'fine wine' coming from the Douro Valley. It is only since the dawn of the 21st century that all port producers have upped their game to focus on the outstanding merits of vintage, Colheita and old tawny ports, and as Dirk Niepoort says, they have begun to branch out into table wines too.

The other factor is that until the motorway carved its way into the steep banks of the Douro, the vineyards and the town of Oporto were two different 'islands', connected only by river; the twain only ever communicated at harvest time. From the 21st century you could commute, so better technology, better quality control and better understanding betwixt town and country could be achieved.

Dirk Niepoort is an avowed maverick. Every wine region should have a Dirk. He knows more about the ins and outs of producing intriguing wines in the Douro than anyone. But I am not sure his hypothesis that Douro wines could have followed the greatness of the French stands up, if by those he means Bordeaux and burgundy. The pure simplicity of the dominance of the Cabernet Sauvignon in the former and the solo Pinot Noir in the latter, hewn into perfect *terroir*, make these wines trade royalty. The sheer complexity of the grape blend in the Douro, to this day, precludes this comparison.

However, I fully and completely support Dirk's plea for equal opportunities for producing both port and table wines in the Douro. IVDP (Instituto dos Vinhos do Douro e Porto) please note. This refers to a more equal pricing policy allowed for port and table wine grape production.

Port is becoming more branded, which is correct for its market place, whereas Douro wines are much more *terroir* and variety driven, which makes them exciting for the producer and consumer alike.

Currently two-thirds of the Douro's revenue comes from port and one-third comes from table wine. The future does look good for the Douro. Tourists are welcomed; port is making a profit, and Douro table wines are becoming mainstream. 🍇

Ben Howkins is author of **Sherry – Maligned, Misunderstood, Magnificent!** *published by the Académie du Vin Library in September 2019. He is also a specialist in port and has written two books on the subject:* **Rich, Rare and Red** *(now in its fourth edition) and* **Real Men Drink Port… and Ladies do too!**

CHAPTER 7

To the Table
At Last

To Decant or Not to Decant? – Jane MacQuitty (2019)

Beyond the Banyan Tree – Hugh Johnson (1980)

Wine on Wine – Gerald Asher (1996)

Memorable Menus – Steven Spurrier (2018)

To Decant or Not to Decant?

JANE MacQUITTY (2019)

Wine critic for The Times, *Jane MacQuitty, explores the myths and fallacies that surround the decanting process. Is shifting our most precious vintages from the bottle that's been their safe home for years really necessary? Or is this piece of showmanship an essential part of serving our finest wine? How should we best prepare our wine for the table?*

To decant, or not to decant? So much bunkum and balderdash is regurgitated on decanting, it's time to set the record straight. Wine does not have lungs and it does not breathe. There is no scientific evidence to support the theory, still bandied about in contemporary wine manuals, that decanting somehow 'reduces the concentration of certain acids and tannins, making wine taste smoother'. All that happens when you remove cork from bottle is that the wine within starts to oxidize and deteriorate.

Of course any wine that has thrown a deposit, particularly venerable claret and port, needs its bitter, gritty and often tea leaf-flaky sediment to be removed. Skip decanting both and you'll end up with an off-putting, muddy, earthy glass of wine and unbecoming black bits stuck in your teeth. To avoid unnecessary oxidation, I always decant old bottles as close to a meal as possible, expecting to lose up to two-thirds of a glass to sediment-tainted wine. With very frail, old vintages, including the 1905 Château Latour, bought by my mother and drunk in honour of my father's 85th birthday, there is only a minute or two of ethereal perfection in the glass before the wine keels over. The solution is to shift ancient bottles into a decanting cradle, let the sediment settle horizontally for at least 24 hours, before pouring the wine swiftly into everyone's glasses.

Back when I was a baby wine writer, there was a cheapskate ruse doing the rounds that if you left a low-life Argentinian or Spanish red 24, or even 48, hours in a decanter before dining, somehow it will have turned into a distinguished, mature *cru classé* claret by the time you sat down to eat. What rot. By the time the decanter was broached, the wine within had turned into a horrid, oxidized and often vinegary mouthful. The only similarities it had with ancient claret was that it was dead-as-a-dodo.

I am not alone in my anti-decanting stance. Experience has taught me that the best route to fine wine appreciation, due to the variables of glass, vintage and temperature, is to allow the wines served at my table to develop slowly in my guests' glasses over the course of a meal; any tight, buttoned-up wines just need an extra twirl or two in the glass to open up. Young wines need more twirls than old wines but it's fun over several hours at the table to see how both evolve and marry with food. Most wine merchants concur. Adam Brett-Smith, Corney & Barrow's managing director, like me, is a passionate anti-decanter, citing two of his most prestigious producers, the late Gianfranco Soldera from Brunello di Montalcino and Aubert de Villaine from Domaine de la Romanée-Conti. The former instructed Adam 'NEVER to decant his wine, young or old'. The charming, circumspect Aubert was equally adamant on this point: 'We do not decant in Burgundy…remember, Adam, the sediment in our wines is their heart, it is delicious to drink.'

One insightful oenophile who disagrees is Doug Wregg from Les Caves de Pyrene who maintains there is a difference between carafing, 'pouring a wine into a carafe', and decanting. He claims that the 'overall effect of aeration seems to bring wines, particularly natural and skin contact wines, into greater aromatic focus'. Hum.

Aesthetics play a part too. I was given a pair of handsome Waterford Irish crystal decanters as a wedding present and rather like the look of mature, blood-red wines glinting at me on a dinner party night. Then again, with those beguiling bottles of 1982 Château Cos d'Estournel we bought long of – care of generous wedding cheques – I merely double decanted the wine off its sediment and poured it back into the bottle as the labels are amongst the prettiest in Bordeaux.

Perhaps the last word on the subject should come from the late, great, Cyril Ray's *Compleat Imbiber No 16* where he quoted Queen Victoria's chief cook, Charles Elmé Francatelli, and the sound advice he gave in *The Modern Cook*, published in 1862: 'Let it be remembered that all possible care should be taken in removing the bottles from their bins, and afterwards also, in handling them for the purpose of drawing the corks, and decanting the wines, not to disturb any deposit that may exist in the bottles, for that deposit, if shaken, destroys not only the brilliancy of the wine, but impairs its flavour and bouquet'. Quite. 🌿

Beyond the
Banyan Tree

HUGH JOHNSON (1980)

Hugh Johnson remembers a meeting of the Zinfandel Club convened by 'the man with the million dollar palate', Harry Waugh. Guests of honour were Joe and Alice Heitz, creators of one of the first great Cabernet Sauvignons of the Napa Valley, 'Martha's Vineyard' – a successful combatant in Steven Spurrier's 1976 blind tasting vs the Bordeaux First Growths.

The informality of the Zinfandel Club has not inhibited a steady stream of Californian luminaries from accepting its invitations to dinner. Robert Mondavi, his brother Timothy, the Davies' of Schramsberg, Janet Trefethen, the pace setters of California have all checked in, dined, taught us a lot – and I am sure have learned a little themselves. The cement that holds together this genial group is of course the presidency of Harry Waugh.[1] I have served under banyan tree presidents (in their shade, nobody flourishes). Harry is – forgive me, Harry – the alder that enriches the ground it covers. Small wonder the princes of the vine travelled so far to draw corks with his clubbable friends. This said, it was still a faintly improbable night when Joe and Alice Heitz came to Brook's[2], St James's Street, on their first trip to England (and that, I have the feeling, only because it is so handy for Ireland).

---

[1] Harry Waugh (1904–2001), prolific merchant, writer, journalist, connoisseur and celebrated figure in the wine world. Harry was one of wine's great innovators, and in later years became a passionate advocate of California wines.
[2] One of the oldest gentleman's clubs in London. Established 1764 by Messrs Boothby and James in response to their being blackballed by Whites's (est 1693), an even more exclusive club then in Mayfair.

Joe Heitz started making (or more strictly, at first, buying and maturing) Napa and Sonoma wines in about 1960 – long before it was fashionable or, most thought, even sensible. They were the days of Vision and Grit. Somehow the mature Heitz keeps a boy scout glint in his eye, though he quickly dispatches any such cosy notions with his conversation. Joe doesn't suffer fools, and is apt not to hear questions he sees no reason to answer. A Zin Club member asked him how much he paid for the grapes in one of the wines we were drinking. Most Californians would have discoursed learnedly on prices and trends. From Heitz the answer was 'How do you like the wines?'

The answer was very much indeed. The limelight has been so steadily on Heitz Cabernets, and Martha's Vineyard in particular, that it came as a surprise to many members that Joe is as much a master of white wines as of red. Our aperitif was a glass of his 1979 Johannisberg Riesling, a classic California 'JR' of the old dry style, broad in the beam by modern standards, a totally different kettle of fish from today's fashionable mouthful of chilled fruit. Its smoky, oily, somehow immensely adult taste reminded me of an actress's husky voice. I find it sad that the consensus has moved away from dry Rieslings in California (where, oddly enough, I have heard people express a positive dislike for Alsace Riesling). The facile Fumé I fear has taken its place – at least while the current fashion lasts. Even Joe Heitz has not made a 'JR' since 1979.

Chardonnay is another matter. The first great Heitz wine I ever tasted was a Chardonnay he brought from the Hanzell Vineyard in 1960 or thereabouts. He has refined his style a little since then, but retains his singular sense of balance, and taste for austerity, that makes his Chardonnays taste more like white burgundies than most Napa wines. The 1978 vintage made a perfect match for an excellent piece of turbot with sauce hollandaise, tasting fresher and younger even than many white burgundies of the same splendid year.

Three Cabernets made the set-piece of the dinner, served in quick succession with a saddle of lamb (for which the chef at Brooks's deserves special commendation). Heitz Cellars 'regular' Cabernet Sauvignon 1978 was an impressive introduction, not for its force but for its clean, clarety flavour; nothing overblown, no over-emphasis on oak but an eminently appetizing equilibrium. It seemed to me very much in the same state of development as many middle-ranking Médocs would show from the same vintage.

Second to be poured was 'Bella Oaks' 1977 Cabernet, from the vineyard at Rutherford belonging to Belle and Bernard Rhodes. In recent vintages Bella Oaks has been capturing clients from the longer-established and more famous Martha's Vineyard. The 1977 'Martha's' was poured third. I suspect opinion among members was pretty evenly divided on the competing merits of two remarkably good wines.

Bella Oaks was the winner for elegance and charm, harmony and the range of flavours it displayed. Altogether a suave and expensive-tasting production, at or very near its peak of development.

The universal reaction was wonder at the totally different style of Martha's Vineyard, from vines grown on the same celebrated 'Rutherford Bench', the central western slopes of the Napa Valley, within a mile or so of each other. Nobody seems to have fathomed a simple physical reason for the fact that Martha's is as burly as Bella's is elegant. The 1977 Martha's seemed almost brutal, packed with flavour, intensely aromatic with a singular gum-tree fragrance that marks it out. At Brooks's that night I preferred the more urbane of the two. Perhaps in the Napa Valley my vote would go the other way. Either way, Joe Heitz is in the unusual position of the maker of two outstanding wines (in fact I would go as far as three) from the same grape variety and the same district.[3]

With our cheese soufflé – again, *chapeau*, chef – we drank the first Heitz Zinfandel I have ever tasted, and I believe the first he has made – his 1981. If only more Zinfandels were as deftly judged as this, gentle and round, lightish but lively and tangy enough to drink with cheese. It made no pretence at being a great wine – but after the Cabernets, a pretentious Zin would have been futile.

The applause for Joe Heitz at the end of dinner was not just for the winemaker whose genius gave California its first first growth, but for a wine man whose independent spirit goes on finding new ways to express itself. 🌿

---

[3] *See* pages 40–48 for Martha's Vineyard's scores at Steven Spurrier's 1976 'Judgement of Paris', and subsequent rematches.

WINE ON WINE

GERALD ASHER (1996)

*California-based author Gerald Asher questions the setting in which
our most treasured wines should be presented at dinner – the wines
that precede them being of equal importance to the food with which
they're served. Or maybe even more so?*

It was a deliciously uncomplicated dinner at the home of London friends: mussel soup, boiled beef with young carrots and parsnips, salad and some English and Irish cheeses. We drank a glass of champagne before sitting down to a 1982 Meursault Genevrières. Then a duo of red wines made from Bordeaux grape varieties – Coleraine 1985 from the Te Mata Estate in New Zealand's Hawke's Bay, and a Dominus 1985, from the Napanook Vineyard at Rutherford in Napa Valley (I rarely see either of these wines, and had never before had an opportunity to taste them together) – led two Pauillacs, a 1961 Château Grand-Puy-Lacoste and a Château Latour of the same year. Finally, with a plain almond cake, we had a disconcertingly unfamiliar sweet white wine that turned out to be a late-picked and slightly botrytized 1991 Chardonnay from Mâcon-Clessé. Our hosts had smiled discreetly as their guests – all of us professionally involved with wine in one way or another – tripped over themselves trying to guess what it might be. None of us came close.

Not that we'd shone at guessing the other wines. Almost inevitably, when one of us would take a really strong stand about what a wine could not possibly be – part of the process of arriving at a wine's identity, after all, is to close off options – he or she would regret having spoken. Once we'd decided the two Pauillac wines were about 30 years old (having been told they were of the same vintage), one of us lost no time in eliminating what turned out to be the correct year, and another, when we'd concluded they were Médoc rather than Graves or Saint-Emilion, in saying: 'Well, at least they're not Pauillacs, that's for sure.'

Fortunately, with hindsight, it was easier to guess why those particular four wines had been brought together. The Coleraine had probably been chosen as a compliment to John Buck, Te Mata's owner, who was visiting from New Zealand, and I expect the Dominus was to help me feel at home, as I'd arrived only a few days before from California. But neither wine was presented as a mere courtesy; each was also a foil for the other (the tight and slightly angular New Zealand wine in bright contrast to the more somber Dominus), and both helped us appreciate more fully the 1961 Pauillacs that appeared with the cheese – they, too, having been chosen to set each other off as well as for our delight.

It's customary to use a young (or at least younger) wine to bring out the complexity of an older one, and the ploy works – provided, of course, that the one is neither so youthfully vigorous nor so massive as to make the other seem weary or flimsy rather than delicate and polished. It might have been less risky for our hosts to use other red Bordeaux to show off those 1961s: a couple of 1984s, for example, might have made an interesting though perhaps not very agreeable introduction to the older wines. In both 1961 and 1984, a wet spring caused the Merlot vines, ever capricious, to drop their blossom rather than set fruit, so the Médoc production in both years was almost pure Cabernet Sauvignon instead of the usual Bordeaux mix of grape varieties. But in 1961 a glorious summer followed that wet spring and it gave one of the great vintages of the last 50 years, whereas in 1984 a cold, wet September scotched the grapes' final ripening, leaving them low in sugar and tough with unripe tannins.

Our hosts, taking seriously their responsibility for our happiness while under their roof, had spared us that particular exercise, electing to take a chance instead. But not too much of a chance: the two 1985s (both, remember, produced from traditional Bordeaux grape varieties) had enough in common with the two Pauillacs to point up their greater maturity, while, to my surprise and pleasure, throwing into relief their distinctively French measure and harmony. So clear was the distinction between the two pairs of wines, in fact, that the Pauillacs seemed at first more similar to each other than was really the case. Only when New Zealand and California had ceased to linger, figuratively, on our palates, were we able to focus our attention on the older wines for themselves alone and notice how the silky restraint of the Grand-Puy-Lacoste underlined the almost opulent breadth of the Latour, which in turn allowed us to appreciate more fully the Grand-Puy-Lacoste's subtle charm.

It is difficult to put even two wines together, let alone four, free of all hazard: no wine can be relied on to perform exactly as expected. The longer it's been in bottle, the more likely it is to have deviated from the accepted norm for that growth of that year. 'One cannot talk of wines, only of bottles'; is an old saying we sometimes dismiss too quickly as folklore.

Perfect partners – or gastronomic adversdaries?

Each of the four wines served to us in London would have tasted different in a changed context because our perception of any wine is always affected by others. If one is very tannic, another will seem less so, allowing us to notice in the latter a quality we might otherwise have missed. A wine that's aromatic but a little thin will be remarked on for its fragrance rather than its lack of body if it's preceded by a glass of something light and fairly neutral. With this in mind, we begin to understand how we can use one wine to enhance another by emphasizing its advantages.

The key to a full appreciation of any wine is to choose a suitable foil. That's more important than embarking on a quest for the holy grail of the perfect food match.

There is no perfect food match when wine is a meal's focus, but within the abundance of possibilities the simplest fare – such as our boiled beef in London – is most often the best and the least distracting. (Simple should not mean penitential, however. A few years ago, when I was a guest at a wine luncheon in a restored monastery in the Loire Valley, our host had the genial idea of serving us the meal 14th-century monks assembled in that same refectory might have eaten: raw fava beans as an appetizer, then plain boiled tripe followed by cheese curds. He had gone to great trouble to have wheat roughly milled so that we could eat – or choke on – bread that resembled chaff cakes. Spiritually and physically, it must have done us a world of good; but the exceptional wines he had chosen for us to drink, though not really diminished by the truly depressing food, were certainly not enhanced by it either.)

Ideally, the first of two wines should establish a frame of reference for the second, even introduce, if possible and need be, any stylistic imperfection that might divert attention from the qualities of the older, finer wine that follows. For example, suppose one wanted to show off a 1979 Château Pichon-Longueville Comtesse de Lalande. The 1979s (of which this was one of the best) were aromatic and elegant rather than massive. I could precede the 1979 with a more modest Médoc wine – from Listrac, say, or Moulis, or even the château's own second wine, de la Comtesse – from a vintage like 1987, a year in which the wines were agreeably balanced but lacked concentration. The 1987 would establish a base from which the 1979 would soar.

If I were concerned, however, that the 1979 might now lack sufficient power to hold centre stage with a main course, even something as low-key as a leg of lamb, I could serve it after the main course – as is more often the case with the finest wine offered at dinner at any of the great Bordeaux châteaux. In that case it would provide a graceful epilogue to some livelier wine, but one with less finesse, served before it. Because of its place in the order of things, that wine would have to have more character than a 1987, and I would probably choose a 1988 of a good *cru bourgeois* like Chasse-Spleen or Sociando-Mallet. The 1988s have a density that remains somewhat unyielding, and, because they are still quite brisk, I would probably prefer to serve this wine with a rack of lamb or even duck breast – in any case, a slightly richer meat – before bringing on the 1979. For the relationship between the two wines to work, I must not get carried away and decide on a 1988 that is too distinguished. If I were to show Château Pichon Longueville Comtesse de Lalande's own 1988, for instance, it would overwhelm the 1979 rather than confirm its stature.

Any wine – a Bordeaux, a mature Chianti, a California Cabernet Sauvignon – can be improved for having been properly introduced in this manner. I remember how a 1967 Léoville-Barton was used several years ago at a dinner in San Francisco to prepare the way for a fading Langoa-Barton 1937. The 1967 was softly agreeable – just substantial enough yet with little to catch on to. Its very quiescence, however, allowed us to enjoy the flavour and bouquet of that 1937 (which none of us is ever likely to taste again), when most other wines would have made it seem feeble at best.

Even the most sumptuous wine needs a setting to be enjoyed to the full. On one of the few occasions when I tasted the 1961 Petrus, Jean-Pierre Moueix, the château's co-proprietor, served before it his extraordinary 1962 Trotanoy to emphasize – if indeed emphasis were needed – how even more extraordinary the Petrus was.

TASTING NOTES FROM THE MASTER

Michael Broadbent is known for his eloquent tasting notes. Over 6,000 of them have been published, each describing the wines he tasted in intricate (if occasionally florid) detail. Here are a selection of his 2002 views on seven wines described by Gerald Asher.

1

1961 Château Grand-Puy Lacoste
A first-rate classic though understated Pauillac. Still tannic. Plenty of life left in 1992.

2

1961 Château Latour
Immensely impressive, beautifully balanced but, not surprisingly, 'still severe' when first tasted in the autumn of 1968. Its great depth of colour, concentrated magnificence, richness and length noted thoughout the 1970s – but slow to evolve. On two occasions in the 1980s, I gave it 6 stars, 4 for its impressiveness, 2 for future splendor. Of the eight recent notes, its depth of colour is the first thing one notices, and its nose, rather like Lafite's, is a bit slow to open up. Surprisingly sweet too yet a very tannic finish (in 1994) . . . despite its extraordinary sweet, nose-filling bouquet, a mammoth wine, all the component parts excessively represented. Last tasted Jan 2000 ****(**). Another half century of life.

3

1979 Château Pichon-Longueville Comtesse de Lalande
Over a dozen mainly admiring notes, full of crisp fresh fruit, and excitement, from cask to the early 1990s. Two recent more studied notes . . . an imperial in 1994: very deep, still youthful looking; nose hard to get to grips with; sweet enough flavour relatively (after the 1985) lean and tannic. At a masterclass in 1995: palate more interesting than nose but lack of balance. At best ****. Drink soon.

4

1988 Château Pichon-Lalande
Although Lalande was not at first as immediately impressive as [its neighbour Pichon-] Baron, my most recent three notes have been consistently complimentary, each one ending 'a good '88'. . . .richly coloured; good fruit, a whiff of lavender and 'sea breeze'; mouthfilling, sweet, masked tannin. Two recent notes: mahogany-rimmed maturity; sweet, fleshy. A good ripe 1988. 'Delicious now'. ****

TASTING NOTES FROM THE MASTER (cont'd)

5

1961 Château Petrus

For some time, and understandably, one of the stars of the saleroom. Though I first tasted it in 1967, I only awoke to its magnificent, amazing fruit and velvety richness in 1978 and made eight glowing notes through the 1980s. Colour 'black as Egypt's night', opulent, 'rich, rich, rich', spicy, even peppery (alcohol), chunky yet velvety, with soft ripe mulberry-like fruit, fleshy, 'almost cloying', a 'railroad chairman's wine' – which sounded a rather old-fashioned expression: well, an oil-rich potentate or tycoon's wine, for the reason that you do not have to be an expert to appreciate this wine, you wallow in it; and you have to have that sort of wealth to have it in your cellar, let alone to order it in a restaurant. But I must stop being condescending. It is a superb, almost unbeatable mouthful . . . Back to 1994 for a superb bottle, sweet, exceedingly full – body and fruit. A luscious mountain of a wine. ***** *and no end in sight.*

6

1981 Heitz Bella Oaks Cabernet Sauvignon.

Hot growing season with the earliest harvest – mid-August – in living memory. *Medium-deep, lovely colour: fabulous scent; fairly sweet, delicate fruit, delicious. May 2000* ****

7

1970 Beaulieu Vineyard, Georges de Latour Cabernet Sauvignon

Small crop, one third of normal, the result of 28 nights of frost and severe summer heat. *I first went to the Napa Valley in the early 1970s, and thereafter I visited regularly . . . This was the first Beaulieu Vineyard I tasted in cask (100% oak), in 1972: deep purple, full of fruit, stalky. I was able to follow its progress over the years. By the end of the 1970s, though deep and tannic, it was rich and harmonious. By 1985 it was still struggling to get out of its shell, concentrated, tarry, 'silky' (texture), 'yet leathery' (tannins). I have half a dozen notes since: intense, meaty (1997), and two years later no fewer than five ... by now it was medium-deep, crisp, fragrant, very sweet on the palate, rich but with very dry, edgy finish, but showing well ... Like all red wines of this ilk, the Beaulieu Vineyard 1970 proved a perfect accompaniment to 'Confit of Duck'.*

Ratings at a glance
***** Outstanding
**** Very good
*** Good

When selecting a wine to precede a California Cabernet Sauvignon, it is wiser to take the Petrus rather than the Langoa-Barton approach. California Cabernet Sauvignons remain vigorous for longer than their French counterparts and therefore rarely need especially gentle introductions. What would one use if they did? Even young Cabernet Sauvignons from California's less successful years are rarely as retiring as Bordeaux wines of vintages like 1980 and 1987, and so they cannot be relied on to perform in the same way. I have found that a young, not-too-muscular, and fairly low-profile Merlot – Kenwood Vineyards' Sonoma County 1990, for example, or Hanna Winery's Alexander Valley 1990 – provides better preparation for a fine, mature California Cabernet Sauvignon like Heitz Cellars' Bella Oaks 1981, Beaulieu Vineyards' Georges de Latour Private Reserve 1970 or Joseph Phelps' superb 1975 (all legendary wines) than practically any young Cabernet Sauvignon would do.

Alternatively, California Cabernet Francs, growing in number, are usually svelte enough for the purpose, provided they're not too aromatically varietal (which would raise irrelevant expectations). One of the best I've tasted is the elegantly discreet 1991 Moon Mountain Vineyard Cabernet Franc from the Carmenet Vineyard in Sonoma Valley. That wine would be a worthy prelude to any mature California Cabernet Sauvignon. But then, on second thoughts, perhaps not all of them. It really is so fine, it could make quite a few I can think of seem as rough as grizzly bears. ✤

First published in **Vineyard Tales, Reflections on Wine** *by Gerald Asher, Chronicle Books (San Francisco) 1996.*

Tasting Notes reprinted by kind permission of Michael Broadbent.

Memorable Menus

STEVEN SPURRIER (2019)

As long as the wine trade has bottles in its cellars, lunches and dinners that serve its vinous treasures will be a fact of life. Steven Spurrier recalls a few of the many dining events he has been fortunate enough to attend, and the wines he has enjoyed.

O ver more than five decades I could have filled a whole filing cabinet with memorable menus annotated with details of the marvellous wines that accompanied them. And sifting through three bulging folders to select just a handful reminded me once again that one of the core characteristics of wine people is their generosity and pleasure in sharing their best bottles. The earliest notes I found were from a few days spent at Château Langoa-Barton in late September 1968, when the youngest wine served was a white Domaine de Chevalier 1958, the oldest a Léoville-Barton 1928 that out-classed the impressive 1934 Beychevelle that had come before. The latest were from the Shortest Day Lunch, always at the Garrick Club, appropriately on December 21st 2017. There are many in between that were so impressive in terms of the wines served, but here are notes on a handful where I was more personally involved.

May 19th 2005, Dinner at the Vintners' Hall
hosted by John Avery as Master

The Vintners' Company was created in 1363 and is one of the 12 Great Livery Companies of the City of London. It still maintains its historic premises on the north bank of the River Thames, and this makes a wonderful venue for fine dining and wine trade celebrations. Each year a long-serving Vintner will be named Master and host a personal dinner for wine trade colleagues and friends.

A Whist–er at Boodles – or a –
choice peice of double milled Yorkshire Broad cloth –

Pub.ª July 1820 by Fores Panton S.t Hay market

J.R. Cruikshank fect.

Evidently well lunched: an early 19th century denizen of St James's arrives at his club.

Champagne, Avery's Special Cuvée

Seared salmon with chive and beurre blanc frisée
Fletcher Vineyard Chardonnay 2002 Villa Maria, Marlborough, New Zealand
Puligny-Montrachet 1er Cru Les Referts 1995 Remoissenet Père & Fils

Roasted Veal stuffed with spinach wrapped in Parma ham, roasted Parmentier potatoes
Bin 707 Kalimna Cabernet Sauvignon 1986 Penfolds, Coonawarra, Australia
Château Figeac 1986 1er Grand Cru Classé St-Emilion
Domaine de Chevalier 1982 Cru Classé de Graves in double magnums

Quail's eggs benedict.
Château Rausan-Segla 1961 Margaux

Summer pudding millefeuille
Schloss Vollrads Riesling Auslese 2000, Rheingau

Coffee and Swan chocolates with Avery's 1963 vintage port

(John's father Ronald purchased six 'pipes' (equal to 660 bottles) of port – three
Sandeman, two Fonseca and one Taylor – to make his personal blend. Once bottling
vintage port in the Douro became obligatory, such idiosyncratic blends were forbidden.)

October 2nd 2008, The Garrick welcomes the Boodle's Wine Committee

Boodle's, my club in St James's Street (founded 1762), gets on well with Brooks's (founded
1764) right opposite, and the respective wine committees welcome each other on alternate
years to a 'bring your own' dinner. We attempted such an arrangement with The Garrick
(founded 1831) in Covent Garden, but its wines proved too grand for us to keep up with:

Cuan native oysters and smoked salmon
Champagne Krug Grande Cuvée

Paupiette of sole with shellfish chowder and baby leeks
Chassagne-Montrachet 1er Cru Morgeot 1999 Domaine Ramonet
Puligny-Montrachet 1er Cru Clavoillon 1999 Domaine Leflaive

*Roast Grey Leg partridge with foie gras, new season's ceps and chestnuts, game chips, celeriac
purée and braised red cabbage*

Château Haut-Brion 1983 Grand Cru Classé de Graves in jeroboam
Château La Fleur-Petrus 1979 Pomerol in imperial

Fougeru cheese with truffles and Poilâne bread
Taylor's 1966 port

The Cellarmen

This was a dining club founded by Dr Louis Hughes in the 1980s to which I was admitted in the late 1990s, actually bringing the average age down a little. The bi-monthly dinners were held at the Savile Club in Mayfair, whose motto *Sodalitas Convivium* (convivial companionship) summed up our meetings. Each member brought his best bottle to follow the theme chosen at the end of the previous dinner, usually 10 to 12 attending. The menu never changed from Louis' choice of:
Cold sea trout mayonnaise
Roast rack of lamb, Parisienne potatoes and buttered French beans
A French and an English cheese
Coffee and mints

Here are two examples of the bottles we enjoyed. The final dinner, in memory of members John Avery, Bill Baker, John Boys and Louis Hughes took place on April 16th 2012.

February 6th 2006 – Northern Rhône
White
Condrieu 2003 Alain Perret
Hermitage 1999 Jean-Louis Chave
Red
Côte-Rôtie La Landonne 2001 Guigal
Hermitage La Chapelle 1990 Jaboulet Aîné
Hermitage La Chapelle 1988 Jaboulet Aîné
Hermitage La Chapelle 1986 Jaboulet Aîné
Hermitage La Chapelle 1983 Jaboulet Aîné
Hermitage 1983 Jean-Louis Chave
Crozes-Hermitage Domaine de Thalabert 1978 Jaboulet Aîné
Hermitage 1978 Guigal
Hermitage 1978 Jean-Louis Chave
Hermitage La Chapelle 1978 Jaboulet Aîné
Hermitage La Chapelle 1961 Jaboulet Aîné
And then: Fonseca's 1963 port and Aszú Eszencia 1995 Royal Tokji Wine Company

Premier Cru: Château Mouton Rothschild en route à table.

December 14th 2009 – Burgundy
White
Chablis Grand Cru Les Clos 2000 Billaud-Simon
Chablis Grand Cru Les Clos 1990 René Dauvissat
Puligny-Montrachet 1988 Louis Carillon
Montrachet 1985 Baron Thénard
Red
Corton Perrières 1998 Vincent Girardin
Morey St-Denis 1er Cru 1990 Hubert Lignier
Echézeaux 1989 René Engel
Clos de Vougeot 1988 Méo-Camuzet
Gevrey-Chambertin 1985 Domaine de Varoilles
Chambertin 1985 Armand Rousseau
Nuits St-Georges 1er Cru Les Cailles 1923 Morin
Chambolle-Musigny 1er Cru Les Amoureuses 1921 ex Dr Barolet

And then: Fonseca's 1963 port and Schloss Johannisberg 2002 Eiswein

May 8th 2012, The Bordeaux Club at Brooks's
hosted by Michael Broadbent

The Bordeaux Club was founded in Cambridge by the great historian Sir John Plumb and has only six members, each of whom are allowed to bring a guest to the single annual dinner. I am now a member, but will not be able to match Michael Broadbent's selection:

Champagne Pol Roger 2000
Champagne Dom Pérignon 1996

Mock turtle soup
Sercial Madeira 1937 Pereira d'Oliveiras, bottled in 1997

Roast rack of lamb, leaf spinach and gratin dauphinois
Château Lafite Rothschild 1990 1er Cru Classé Pauillac in magnum
Château Mouton Rothschild 1990 1er Cru Classé Pauillac in magnum
Château Mouton Rothschild 1975 2ème Cru Classé Pauillac in magnum

Rhubarb and stem ginger fool
Rivesaltes 1927 Domaine Borg
Tokaji Eszencia 1927

Colston Bassett Stilton and Vignotte
Sandeman's 1927 port (1927 was Michael's birth year)

And then: Vieil Armagnac de Goudoulin

December 21st 2017, Shortest Day Lunch at The Garrick
in memory of Tim Stanley-Clarke

The idea of the 'Shortest Day Lunch', always held at his beloved Garrick Club as near as possible to the shortest day of the year, came from Tim Stanley-Clarke. Tim was an expert in port and fortified wines, known for his ebullience, charm and fond love of a practical joke. He aimed to convene 18 wine trade chums, each bringing along a bottle or two, with the intention not to leave the table until it was dark outside. Tim died in June 2017. His and other losses that year had reduced our numbers to 13, but we made up for it in their memory:

Blanc de Blancs 2014 Bride Valley Vineyard, Dorset
Champagne Pol Roger 2006 in magnum
Champagne Gosset Grand Rosé NV in magnum

Roast Devon scallops with bacon, Jerusalem artichoke and apple purée
Bernkasteler Badstube Riesling Kabinett 2014 Erben Thanisch, Mosel, Germany
Meursault 2015 Les Caves de Colombe
Pouilly-Fuissé 'Les Vieux Murs' 1996 in magnum

Roast pheasant with apples and bacon, game chips, root vegetables and red cabbage
Gran Coronas Cabernet Sauvignon 2013 Torres, Penedès, Spain
Morey St-Denis 2010 Hubert Lignier
Nuits St-Georges 1ᵉʳ Cru Clos de la Maréchale 2004 Frédéric Mugneret in magnum
'Les Asteries' Jonathan Malthus 2005 St-Emilion in magnum

Selection of farmhouse British and Irish cheese
Château Léoville-Barton 2008 St-Julien
Château Léoville-Barton 1988 St-Julien

Mince pies and clotted cream
Gould Campbell's 1977 port (From the Symington stable, Tim's employers, still excellent.)
Delaforce's 1963 port

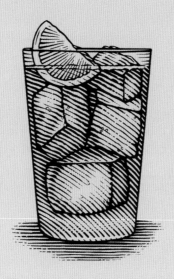

CHAPTER 8

SOMETHING A LITTLE DIFFERENT

Sting Like a Bea – Dan Keeling (2019)

Mint Julep, a Cocktail to Crave – Jonathan Miles (2008)

Sting Like a Bea

DAN KEELING (2019)

Dan Keeling weighs up the pros and cons of rich, high-alcohol wines, finding one from Italy that he's prepared to make an exception for. Enter Paolo Bea's Sagrantino di Montefalco 'Pagliaro'.

D o you shy away from high-alcohol Napa Cabernet in the interest of self-preservation? Does the mere mention of Châteauneuf-du-Pape's ABV summon ghosts of hangover anxieties dormant within your bones? Do you pass on port, avoid Amarone, and would you rather swim an ocean than swallow Aussie Shiraz? If the answer is yes to any of the above, then you may be suffering from 'rich-wine neurosis' – a phenomenon defined by Andrew Jefford in *Decanter* magazine, who cites historic *terroirs* such as Priorat and Maury as examples of how those embracing the zeitgeist for lower-alcohol styles are missing out.

I agree, at least in part. Just because a wine is high in alcohol doesn't mean it isn't harmonious or delicious (Brunello di Montalcino, Vin Jaune and Madeira spring to mind), and with the planet's temperatures rising, balance is one of the most important winemaking challenges of our times. The trouble, however, is that I like drinking wine – and lots of it – which rich styles do not permit. I love copious flavour and manifold aromas and sensations – not feeling as if I've been repeatedly hit over the head with a large rubber truncheon. Indeed, there are few wines I'd like to drink less over a four-course meal than a super-ripe, 15% ABV modern Bordeaux. Whose body wouldn't thank them for its restrained 1980s predecessors instead? But, of course, there are some vinous heavyweights I'd be happy to go the distance with, then suck up the pain. If, as Jefford suggests, 'Those suffering from "rich-wine neurosis" should seek a cure', then Paolo Bea Sagrantino di Montefalco 'Pagliaro' is the big and beautiful wine I self-prescribe.

Dark and structured, yet graceful and fresh, 'Pagliaro' is the liquid embodiment of 'Float like a butterfly, sting like a bee'. Made from 100% Sagrantino grapes grown in the 400m altitude 'Pagliaro' vineyard in Montefalco – a 12th century town midway between Perugia and Spoleto in Umbria – it incorporates aromas of graphite, exotic spices, fruit and flowers with a prickle of balsamic vinegar and a refreshing bitter finish. At circa 15% ABV, it is a serious wine that takes no prisoners, and like old-school reds from Italian greats such as Soldera, Conterno and Quintarelli, demands long ageing in large oak barrels to develop complexity and round its edges; in this case, Sagrantino's notoriously fierce tannins.

Indeed, until 40 years ago, Sagrantino was made only as a sweet passito wine, using the *appassimento* technique whereby grapes are dried on rush mats before being pressed. Today, it's also been reinvented as a full-bodied, dry wine with DOCG status by a handful of producers including Giampiero Bea, the youthful 62-year old visionary behind the Paolo Bea estate.

Bea's family roots go back hundreds of years in Montefalco – one of the few wine towns I've visited where your ears pop on the way in and out because of the high altitude – although grape growing is traditionally only one part of the local polyculture. His father Paolo's principal business has always been farming Chianina cows, the white Tuscan cattle breed used for *bistecca alla Fiorentina*. It was only when Giampiero left to study architecture at Rome University in 1980 that he began lobbying his dad to plant more vineyards and start bottling wine. 'Slowly, slowly' – a phrase Giampiero repeatedly uses to convey their gradual development – they refined their Sagrantino wines alongside smaller plantings of Sangiovese, Montepulciano and Trebbiano Spoletino, although it soon became apparent that they had very different ideas.

'I wanted to produce a dry Sagrantino wine, but my father wanted to stick to making the traditional sweet style,' Giampiero says. 'The first time I tried making it, he didn't speak to me for three months!' Because of a lack of experience in producing the dry style, the first vintages oxidized after a few years in bottle, so in 1984 Giampiero started using long maceration to draw out more tannin. Today, the wines spend between one and two months on the skins, followed by a year in steel tank, and a further three maturing in large Slavonian oak barrels. 'We argued a lot about winemaking at the time,' he says, laughing. 'Then my American importer introduced me to some like-minded producers and I began to absorb ideas. I met Guiseppe Quintarelli in 1993, who was very helpful and became almost like a second father. Then Stanko Radikon, with whom I started ViniVeri, an association of Italian natural wine producers. And I got to know Josko Gravner, who was the first natural wine producer in Italy. It was amazing to be able to speak to such a pioneer.'

'Nothing added and nothing taken away' is how Giampiero describes his simple winemaking philosophy – a simplicity that is, in fact, fiendishly difficult to get right. He adds only very minimal sulphur and never filters his wines, as proven by the delicious, jewel-like skins and pips often found at the bottom of his bottles. While other domaines in Montefalco use flavour-manipulating techniques and new oak *barriques*, Giampiero gently tames the small-berried, thick-skinned Sagrantino, resulting in authentic, characterful wines.

'Conventional producers get rid of the skin and kill the universe of elements involved in wine. My idea is to use the natural process as a closed circle – this soil, these grapes, these yeasts, which are different in every vineyard.' While the annual production of 'Pagliaro' rarely exceeds 20,000 bottles, Bea makes another rarer, even more powerful and monolithic Sagrantino from the three hectare 'Cerrete' vineyard located 50 metres above (this is 'the Romanée-Conti of Montefalco'). I admire its stylish red and white label and ask myself: 'Can my head take it?' Never mind 'rich-wine neurosis' – you've got to do what you've got to do. 🍂

Written by Dan Keeling and reproduced by kind permission of **Noble Rot** *magazine; first published in the June 2019 edition (www.noblerot.co.uk).*

Packing an autumnal punch: Montefalco vineyards, Umbria, Italy.

Mint Julep, a Cocktail to Crave

JONATHAN MILES (2008)

For solace on a hot summer's afternoon, or simply reviving the soul after a working day (even a Tuesday), American journalist and author Jonathan Miles finds a cocktail that's cool at any hour.

Aside from the martini, the Mint Julep may be the most iconic cocktail in America. There's not a citizen alive who hasn't heard of it, which is more than you can say for the Manhattan, the Cosmopolitan, the Sidecar and the Negroni, all of which outsell Mint Juleps by a staggeringly wide margin. And that, mind you, is if you can even locate the rare bartender willing to fix you one.

So here's the saloon riddle for the day: If we know and adore Mint Juleps – 'the very dream of drinks,' as a Kentucky newspaperman named J Soule Smith wrote, accurately, in the 1890s – so damn much, then why don't we *drink* them? Allow me to cut you off before you tell me about your last Derby Day party: sorry, that don't count. A drink this sublime – 'the zenith of man's pleasure,' Mr Smith went on – shouldn't need to be relegated to sipping just one day a year, like a fruitcake waiting for Christmas. It does not require, as a garnish, a televised horse race and a bunch of Yankees doing Foghorn Leghorn imitations. Nor will I brook the claim that Juleps are hard to make. They're no more difficult than all the Mojitos that have been creeping their way north from Miami for the last half-decade or so. They're easier, in fact, since they don't require a giant sack of limes. No, our weird resistance to drinking Mint Juleps – let's cue up Mr Smith one more time, before we call him a cab: 'He who has not tasted one has lived in vain' – is owing to something else.

King of Cool: a classic Mint Julep.

Here's my theory: The Mint Julep has become too iconic to merely drink. It's like the communion wafer of cocktails. For one, there's all the back-and-forth scuffling among historians and professional 'alcohologists' (to crib H L Mencken's great term[1]) about the inscrutable origins of the drink and the proper and properly authentic way to mix a Julep – do you leave the mint in or remove it? Must the ice be crushed? And was the actual cause of the Civil War, as the author Irvin S Cobb posited in 1936, an obnoxious Northerner adding nutmeg to a Mint Julep? (Uh, no.) Then there are those silver Julep cups that tradition dictates using. They're intimidating. And it feels downright silly drinking out of one those while you're watching the Braves[2] on TV with your other hand nestled in a bowl of Ruffles. (I have a vast collection of those cups, all of them awarded to me for playing the groomsman role in various Southern weddings. In fact, there's one on my desk as I type this. I keep pens in it.) Owing to all this pomp and kerfuffle, drinking a Mint Julep, to some folks, can feel too much like an affectation, akin to rechristening the porch the verandah, or yourself 'the Colonel'. That's way too much cultural pressure when you're just trying to cool yourself off on a summer afternoon. Makes you want to reach for a Bud and be done with it.

---

[1] HL Mencken, 1880–1956, 'The Sage of Baltimore', an American journalist and cultural critic renowned for saying: 'A politician is an animal which can sit on a fence and yet keep both ears to the ground.'
[2] Atlanta Braves, an American baseball team.

Don't. The Mint Julep may be sacred in the South, but so is college football, and that doesn't stop us from enjoying it. It's not a tuxedo, requiring a special occasion. It's a drink, a splendid and simple drink, the ideal analgesic to a tough day at work, and the perfect – yes, perfect – counter to the redlining mercury of a hot Southern day. Its central ingredients – mint, bourbon, sugar – do not suffer from clumsy commingling, nor demand engraved vessels. (They will, however, violently boil over if you add nutmeg.) Citizens, it's high time to reclaim the Mint Julep from the curators, the purists, the tsk-tsking authenticators and frowning archbishops of Southern culture. Think of it like the blues: it's swell that all these archivists are preserving it, and it's great that a microtonal analysis of Robert Johnson's 'Drunken Hearted Man' demonstrates Robert's debt to Lonnie Johnson, but, really, shouldn't we all be dancing?

Mint Julep

'Sip it and dream – it is a dream itself,' wrote our friend J Soule Smith. (Weren't we calling him a cab?) 'Sip it and say there is no solace for the soul,' he went on, 'no tonic for the body like old Bourbon whiskey'. Oh, to hell with the cab. I'll have what he's having.

15g (½ oz) caster sugar
30ml (1 oz) hot water
8 mint leaves, plus one mint sprig
60ml (2 oz) bourbon

Dissolve the sugar in the water in an Old Fashioned glass (or Julep cup, of course). Add the mint leaves and press them lightly with a spoon – you want to seduce the oil from the mint leaves, not beat it out of them. Add the bourbon, fill the glass with cracked ice, and stir. Plant the mint sprig in the ice alongside a short straw and serve.

Yield: 1 serving 🍃

*First published by **Gun & Garden** magazine (Charleston, US), May/June 2008.*

CHAPTER 9

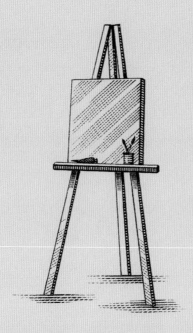

WINE AND ART

Art, Wine and Me – Andrew Caillard MW (2019)
Is Wine Art? – Elin McCoy (2018)
Best Dressed and Bottled at Home – Joan Littlewood/Philippe de Rothschild (1984)
For a Piece of the Glamour – Tony Aspler (1997)

Art, Wine and Me

ANDREW CAILLARD MW (2019)

Andrew Caillard is an Australia-based Master of Wine, author and painter. The palate and the palette have been the tools of his trade for over 40 years. He explores here the fascinating similarities between making wine and the creation of art.

Art and wine have been interconnected for thousands of years. When the archaeologist Howard Carter entered the tomb of King Tutankhamen (1332–1323 BC) in 1922 he discovered ideograms on ancient amphora jars which still contained residue from red wine. Even before Christ, grapes became a symbol of resurrection as depicted by 'a vine leading to the nose of Osiris' in the Nakht papyrus held at the British Museum. In Western Thebes a vine symbolizing rebirth of the dead is painted on the ceiling in Sennefer's tomb. The Greeks designed their drinking cups with dancing figures, warriors, gods or mythical scenes. 'Black-figure' amphorae and craters were also intricately decorated showing the importance of wine in ancient times.

At the *symposion* (symposium), the rich would get drunk on spiced yet watered down wine while talking, singing or being entertained. The Romans drank at *conviviums* where they would get drunk on wine. It was considered the height of bad manners to drink full strength wine, yet there are plenty of beautiful works of art on wine vessels that depict men (and women) in vinous reveries. Other terracotta pottery from Classical Antiquity (8th century BC to 6th century AD) depict games, domestic scenes, imagined battles, animals, gods, and gestures of love and bravery. The methods of production of these art objects or accoutrements to wine drinking have been intricately studied by academics throughout the ages, although the published research does not always give an insight into the artist's emotions, designs or beliefs.

For thousands of years the lives of people and the values of society have been explored through the art and craft of their times. In western culture wine is a surviving symbol of civilization, despite the anti-alcohol lobby, prohibition and temperance movements that punctuate the ages. It has even fended off periods of decline, substitution and existential threats like phylloxera and the gin epidemic of the 18th Century. The Romans marched on wine to avoid drinking contaminated water. The French army were unable to function without their daily ration of *pinard*, even though most of it came from Spain. And the United States Navy was banned from consuming it because of wowsers[1] in the highest levels of government. On the other hand, the health benefits of wine have been championed by the King of Thailand and the Chinese Communist Party. It boosts immune systems, works as an antioxidant, increases bone density, lowers cholesterol and combats type two diabetes. This magical substance which weaves through civilization at every juncture is symbolic of the blood of Christ, western culture, exaggerated truths and the arc of life.

Like a child, wine develops a character of its own yet is imbued with the place it was born. Some have a strict upbringing and others are left alone. After being bottled it is sent into the larger world to be consumed, collected, abused or deified. Some get popped off before their time while others are stacked away and forgotten. The greatest are celebrated and remembered through the times, like Shedeh, Dénthis, Falernum, Constantia, Corton-Charlemagne, Romanée-Conti, Lafite, Opus One and Penfolds Grange, while the ordinary are bundled into 'BOGOFs'[2] or 'Receipt Offers'. Wine mirrors the sweep, mystery and mundanity of life. It comforts, inspires, offends and ruins in equal parts. Art does the same, although an art addiction does not damage the organs, unless the artist uses turpentine in the wrong way.

Cyrus Redding's *History and Description of Modern Wines*, which was first published in 1833, records the most famous wines of the early 19th Century. Romanée-Conti, Chambertin, Richbourg, Clos Vougeot, Romanée-St Vivant, La Tâche, St Georges and Corton were 'the first and most delicate wines in the world'. Châteaux Lafite, Latour, Margaux and Haut Brion – 'of fine colour and perfume' – were also recognized 'Wines of The First Class'. But so was Contnar – a luscious sweet wine from Moldavia – and Constantia from the Cape of Good Hope (South Africa).

A remarkable transformation took place between the 1830s and 1860s as a consequence of the political, social and economic developments and reforms of those times. Industrialization and rapid transmission, aided by the steam engine, accelerated

---

[1] Australian expression for those individuals who seek to deprive others of something they consider wrong or sinful.
[2] Buy One Get One Free.

standards of living, hygiene and life expectations. One must not forget, also, that this generation was obsessed by developing a modern nobility based on wealth and power. The wine industry benefited hugely from the agricultural reforms of these times although it was hampered by the arrival of pests and diseases from the New World. The concept of *'terroir'* and the power of the land began to take hold just at a time when substitution and adulteration were becoming a massive problem. When Napoleon III ordered a Classification of Bordeaux wines to be drawn up for the Paris Exhibition of 1855, he established an imperial aristocracy of fine wine. It began a movement that would eventually result in an international fine wine trade steeped in pretensions of grandness based on vineyard site, quality and price.

When Baron Philippe de Rothschild commissioned the French designer Jean Carlu to create a label for Château Mouton Rothschild for the 1924 vintage, he foreshadowed a closer relationship between art and modern wine. When the 1945 *'Année de Victoire'* was released, the label incorporated a 'V for Victory' motif by Phillipe Jullien. This remarkable gesture was further enhanced by the wine's reputation as one of the greatest vintages of the 20th century. Using the label iconography immortalized by Britain's wartime prime minister, Christie's wine auctioneer Michael Broadbent famously described 1945 Mouton Rothschild as a 'Churchill of a wine'. Its legendary status is undiminished and by all accounts its freakish longevity continues.

In 1973 a perceived injustice of leaving Mouton Rothschild out as a First Growth in 1855 was repaired by France's Minister of Agriculture (later President) Jacques Chirac. Baron Philippe de Rothschild's enlightened and aesthetic view of wine and wine culture played no small part in deeming the significance of Château Mouton Rothschild to a wider world. The label art by Jean Cocteau, Marie Laurencin, Georges Braque, Wassily Kandinsky, Jean Miro and Marc Chagall, prior to this momentous elevation to First Growth status, gave the wines an extra level of richness, meaning, intrigue and worldliness and enhanced the estate's reputation. There is something extremely beautiful about combining the imagination of an artist with the character, quality and experience of the wine itself. The underlying transaction that takes place is full of optimism, emotion and generosity of spirit; the three elements that make Mouton Rothschild so exceptional in the first place.

Many wine estates have followed the example of Château Mouton Rothschild in the modern era. The world of wine is full of sculpture parks, wine museums and label art, reflecting the increasing traffic of fine wine around the world. At home, Leeuwin Estate successfully built a reputation for its Art Label Chardonnay, combining exceptional detail in the wine with images by both indigenous and non-indigenous artists. Further back in Australia's modern wine history the Woodley's Treasure Chest Series (1949–56) combined post-colonial visions with Coonawarra 'Claret'. These ground-breaking label

'Belle Isle'. Painting has illuminated Andrew Caillard's career in wine...

...giving him a wide range of perspectives to draw from. 'Dying Lilies.'

'At home in Leichhardt, Sydney': Andrew is stimulated by his natural surroundings....

...and the living environment he experiences day to day. 'King Parrots.'

designs by the Adelaide-based designer Wytt Morro helped shape Australia's modern fine wine aspirations. The sculpture park and architecture at Paddy McKillen's Château La Coste in Provence, comprising works by Tadao Ando, Louise Bourgeois, Alexander Calder, Tracey Emin, Frank Gehry, Jean Nouvel, Renzo Piano, Sean Scully and Ai Weiwei, illustrate a grand and inclusive vision that is mind-blowing in its scale and modesty. These estates, and many others like them, exemplify a genuine love for the creative, imaginative and expressive spirit.

The dialogue between art and wine has been a feature of my personal and professional life for over 40 years. The palette and the palate are tools of trade. Mixing colour, creating images, tasting and blending (or writing about) wine are my daily bread. Painting has illuminated and foiled my career in wine. It has given me perspectives that are probably quite different to those of many of my colleagues.

At Roseworthy Agricultural College in South Australia, I was trained to taste wine with a strong emphasis on identifying grape varietal definition and technical faults. During the early 1990s I embarked on the Master of Wine programme. The experience of learning to analyse and identify wine through trial and error, failure and triumph (I took the exam three times) was of immeasurable value. It is a discipline, formed by memory, that underpins every wine encounter, whether it is reviewing, blending or drinking for pleasure. Like painting there are many different genres, but there are natural laws that cannot be interfered with. Stability in wine, which relates to oxidation, elemental instability and microbial spoilage, is something that can be monitored and governed by the logarithmic pH scale. Stability and longevity in paintings is governed by a myriad of things including the quality of the surface and the way the paint itself interacts with it. Faults can be found in both wine and paintings from both a technical or aesthetic point of view. Sometimes wine or art – damned by one generation – can be praised by another, such is the fickle nature of fashion and opinion.

Ambition, gesture, composition and identity are the most compelling similarities between wine and art. These elements interact in very different ways depending on the raw materials (as Max Schubert would say) and the personality of the winemaker or artist. While researching Australian wine history for the book *Penfolds, The Rewards of Patience* (Hardie Grant, Melbourne 2013), I was inspired by the stories of old timers who spoke about the magical qualities of the colonial vine Mataro from the legendary Quarry Vineyard, at Auldana near Adelaide, which was pulled out during the 1970s. Their nostalgic memories were so compelling that I ended up wanting to produce my own wine.

The intention, based on my knowledge of Mataro, was to make wine that was recognizably classic, with attractive fruit definition, moderate alcohol, medium body, underlying new oak and long, slinky tannins. The ambition was never to make a *Grand Vin* or cult-like wine but something that was fine drinking and not overly expensive. Although I am experienced in making much larger blends, the options for a small brand like Caillard Mataro and Shiraz are extremely limited. The fruit sourcing and wine needs to be pretty good in the first place and the fidelity of winemaking and oak maturation all have to be exemplary. I have observed that unforced, naturally balanced wines (without the overlayering effects of oak embellishment, tannin or acid adjustment) often have a spatial quality. With age the elements of acidity, tannin, oak, flavour compounds etc fold into or lay over each other building complexity and richness and further strengthening the intrinsic identity and beauty of the wine.

Every artist has a favourite medium and I have used Australian-made Artist Spectrum oils for around 30 years. They come in various opaquenesses and transparencies. In addition to classic European colours, Artist Spectrum has developed unique Australian colours that reflect our bush, rocks, foliage and sky. Some are transparencies like Australian Green Gold. When thinly applied it is gold, when more thickly painted it is iridescent green. Some are opaque like Tasman Blue or Australian Grey. For many artists these types of colour are useful in establishing an identity of place built on the inherent colours of Australian *terroir*.

In painting I have always been fascinated by Western colour theory; how primary, secondary and tertiary colours interact. The opposite to blue is yellow. If the two are placed together on the same field each colour becomes more intense and vibrant. If blue and yellow are mixed it becomes green. If crimson red is placed over a field of Siena Brown, the intensity of the red increases. If green is placed over yellow an impression of sunlight through grass can be achieved. By using white, grey or black, colours can be tinted, toned or shaded. A 'cartoon' of Chromium Green on white canvas will often harmonize the colours placed upon it.

Many of the concepts that surround colour theory are mirrored by wine and winemaking. Each grape variety could be a colour with a different chromatic profile. Riesling, Pinot Noir, Grenache and Nebbiolo are transparent whereas Cabernet, Tempranillo and Shiraz are opaque. The impact of acid, tannin, residual sugar and oak will vary like tints, tones or shades depending on the volume, density and richness of the wine. If the winemaker is clumsy or cold hearted, inevitably the wine will be lumbering or overly precise. UK wine personality Robert Joseph cleverly said that 'if Viognier was a colour it would be orange'. He is so right on many levels. Both orange and Viognier are secondary colours and when overt can offend.

Blending wine also works in a similar way to painting. Envisaging the final composition and style is always the first thing that comes to mind. Every new vintage is a blank canvas

'Les Alpilles, Provence.' When opposing colours are placed together they become more vibrant.

'Pearl Beach Garden.' For Australia Andrew uses a palette of colours unique to its 'terroir'.

'Pittwater – from Pearl Beach': its beautiful bay is a frequent subject for Andrew's paintings.

And vines, too, make a regular appearance: 'Red Vine Dragonfly'.

and every painting has its challenges. Despite being vastly different to each other there are rules, determined by nature and science, that cannot be ignored. The inherent characters and limitations of grape varieties and paint colours have to be respected. Yet there are collective perceptions and traditional thinking that can and should be challenged by individuals. The people who succeed in changing the world with new meaningful, different and lasting visions, are remembered for their foresight, individual gestures and genius. Nonetheless, art and the memory of artists endures well beyond the oldest surviving wines and recollection of winemakers.

Revolutionary ideas are often seeded, derived or evolved from the philosophies, inventions and efforts of other cultures, places and people. The development of Penfolds Grange, for instance, was ground-breaking but based on observations of winemaking in Bordeaux, the Australian discovery of the relationship between pH and wine stability and adaptation of resources. Science, new technologies and generations of effort have brought wine at every level to new standards. Yet at the same time there is significant pushback from new thinkers and natural winemakers who offer wine drinkers an alternative experience steeped in concepts of sustainability and authenticity. Every generation, through discovery, participation and adventure, finds a voice. Nostalgia sometimes brings old aesthetics back into fashion again. But technology, new inventions and contemporary perspectives always improve or refine the present even if it might seem regressive at the time.

The label art associated with Caillard Wine was a consequence of happenstance rather than design. Separate to my wine project, I have always been fascinated by Impressionist and post-Impressionist painters especially Claude Monet, John Peter Russell (who was Australian), Pierre Bonnard, Vincent Van Gogh and Paul Gauguin. The Australian artists Arthur Streeton, Charles Condor, Fred Williams – who did the label painting for the Hunter Valley's Rothbury Estate in the 1970s – William Robinson and Cressida Campbell are also painters who have belonged with or borrowed from these late 19th century movements. All of the above were inspired or aware of the Japanese woodcut artists of the mid-1800s. Utagawa Hiroshige was probably the most important Japanese artist of the 19th Century. Although he was prolific during the early- to mid-1800s (exactly the same time as the Australian wine industry was getting underway) his international fame was achieved after his death with the opening up of trade links with Japan during the 1860s. 'Japonism' emerged as a massively important influence on Western Art. For instance, both Claude Monet and Vincent Van Gogh were captivated by Hiroshige's compositions and viewpoints. During the late 1860s the Impressionism movement took hold, aided by the invention of portable oil paint tubes which enabled *en-plein air* paintings and rapid completion of works.

The Japanese were masterful at distilling complex landscapes or bustling village life into simple compositions. Using concepts of negative spaces and juxtapositions familiar to all those who understand colour theory, these wonderful woodcut depictions of Japanese culture and life inspired many European artists to abandon classical or traditional forms of painting. When I appropriated a woodcut image by Utagawa Hiroshige entitled *Four Seasons* (with added-in Australian Waratahs), I became fascinated by the simplicity yet intricacy of his compositions.

The Caillard Wine labels borrow from Japanese aesthetics but mostly depict Australian landscapes, fauna and flora with the exception of the 2008 and 2011 vintages which are both heavily 'hommaged' to Hiroshige. The paintings (not woodcuts) are detailed with a warmness and richness that can only be achieved through multi-layering of colours and painstaking cutting-in with a paint brush. The use of vertical lines, usually in downward rhythmic brush stokes, is also a technique that gives a richness, resonance and movement to negative spaces or background fields. When I paint landscapes, I am stimulated by the natural or living environment around me. Our gardens at Pearl Beach and Leichhardt are frequent subject matters as are still life compositions, particularly flowers, the beautiful expanse of Pittwater, the New South Wales coast line, the Barossa Valley, and occasional European subjects. Recently, we were in Belle Ile en Mer, where Monet, Renoir and Russell painted. When I finished one of my drawings of Port Goulphar I was astonished to see how the shadows and forms corresponded almost exactly to Monet's completed work of the same subject. I must have been positioned exactly where he was painting over 120 years before. It felt like walking in the footsteps of a giant.

It would be pretentious to suggest there is any meaning to my paintings other than it is a medium that allows personal expression on another plane. Although there is a purpose and challenge to every canvas, I paint for myself rather than others. After quite a successful exhibition in 2004, I realized that making a living as an artist creates pressures that could destroy the optimism and carefree enjoyment of painting pictures. In some respects, making wine and needing to sell it has created that same scenario. The anxiety of maintaining decent reviews and then finding support within the wine trade, is probably widespread. The wine business has become transactional with buyers distant to the challenges of grape growing and winemaking. Many come from buying baked beans or knickers and are ingrained into the fast-moving consumer goods culture. Wine writers have increasingly become brands rather than the journalists they once were. Greed is rampant across the fine wine world where prices in some way deify reputations and remove the magic of drinking great wine. The late Australian winemaker and surgeon Dr Max Lake described this state as 'the crisis of expectations'. The same has also happened in the art world, but at least the images can be consumed by everyone. And like winemaking there is great pleasure to be had out of a simple, well executed painting with no ambition behind it other than portraying a personal feeling of place. 🖋

IS WINE ART?

ELIN McCOY (2018)

*When Elin McCoy tasted Domaine de la Romanée-Conti's 1945 La Tâche
30-odd years ago, she had one of those transporting 'aha' moments familiar to
all serious wine lovers – when a wine seems as deep and layered as a great
painting, with ethereal aromas and flavours that evoke hidden associations and
strong emotions. But does that make it art?*

Every time a wine speaks to you and seems to express the very idea of beauty through sheer sensual pleasure, it stays in your memory like Proust's madeleine. But is it art? I'm not so sure. Philosophers, critics and drinkers have batted the question around for centuries, and doubtless way before that, given that wine's history goes back thousands of years. It's the kind of topic to contemplate while indulging in a great old port in front of the fire, or to discuss passionately with wine-inclined friends while you're snowed in at a remote ski cabin with nothing to do but raid the cellar and talk.

In truth, there are arguments for and against whether wine is art, and – spoiler alert – I can't seem to come down firmly on one side or the other. Instead, I'm going to try to sketch out some of the myriad links between them.

So, let's start with obvious: wine is a uniquely complex beverage in terms of taste and the environmental, historical and cultural factors that influence its production. Its creation is part of the rise of civilization and evidence of what it means to be human. Like great art, it can be beautiful, linger in your memory, communicate visceral sensations and embody ideas and spiritual connotations, all of it worth describing in high-flown language. The big word is 'can'. Only fine wine fits this profile. Most vino is commercial drink, crafted more or less well, like any industrial product. As with art, intention matters.

Art, maybe – but once it's drunk it's gone.

WINE AND PERMANENCE

One factor that counts against wine as art is that to appreciate a particular wine, you have to destroy it. Much of what we think of as art – Greco-Roman sculptures, Leonardo's Mona Lisa, Shakespeare's plays – is nearly indifferent to time. We're confident that these artworks will retain all they have to offer for generations to come. True artistic experiences, like a great theatrical or musical performance, are unique and can't be repeated (we'll never hear Callas singing Tosca again, alas), but the play itself, the score itself, allows a similar experience to be brought to life again and again. The same is the case with great gastronomic experiences: the recipes can be realized over and over in any number of contexts.

The key thing that distinguishes fine wine is that some bottlings approach a kind of permanence that also allows us to revisit their taste. Well, sort of. A superb wine – let's say a first growth Bordeaux from a great vintage – is an ever-evolving masterpiece. It has a lifespan, from an impressive barrel sample that only hints at what it will eventually become, to a plateau of splendid maturity where year after year it exhibits all its complexity, but inevitably it fades into a graceful, autumnal decline in which, hopefully, we can still perceive the echoes of what it once was.

Experiencing a specific wine doesn't have to be a one-off. It can be a repetitive exercise, encapsulated in numerous (or not so numerous) bottles waiting to be uncorked. Think of Michael Broadbent's tasting notes on, say, 1945 Mouton Rothschild, documenting his impressions of the wine over the years and demonstrating its slow, almost time-defiant march. Great wines stimulate the kind of effusive note-taking in which critics love to indulge. Still, unlike looking at the Mona Lisa, there's a time limit to repeating the experience of a great wine. Each time you open a bottle of it, the wine is slightly different, not just because of bottle differences or the context of tasting it, but because it's a bit older – or a lot older. An unopened bottle stored in a cellar, no matter how superb, will not last forever. It has to be opened and savoured to be appreciated.

Can it still be art? As Bill Harlan once pointed out, the fact that wine doesn't last forever 'doesn't make wine inferior to other art forms, just different. . . We may treasure the moment more because it's time-limited'. I see a parallel with installation art like Christo's Wrapped Reichstag, which now remains only as notes, photographs, diagrams. (That's why some of us, like me, hold on to particularly memorable empty bottles.) Maybe fine wine is at least closer to art than anything else we can put in our mouths.

THE PHILOSOPHERS' TAKE

When it comes to declaring something as art, philosophers have long prized seeing and hearing over touching, tasting and smelling, though you could argue that smell and taste are the most intimate and human of our five senses.

That's partly why many philosophers have been skeptical as to whether food and wine belong in the category of fine arts. Take Kant. While he observed that both aesthetic appreciation and 'mouth taste' were based on an individual's experience of pleasure, he claimed that mouth taste doesn't include the kind of contemplation and imaginative involvement that art does. In effect, this contemplation is the aftermath of sensual experience. Experiencing paintings or music goes beyond mere subjective pleasure but also taps our cognitive capacity of understanding.

But let's remember that central to most philosophical definitions of art is the idea that it can be judged critically, something wine lovers have no trouble applying to fine wine. Barry Smith, a British philosophy professor at the Institute of Advanced Studies at the University of London, points out in *Questions of Taste: The Philosophy of Wine* that 'there are standards by which we can judge a wine, or a musical score, or a painting to be better than another, and these reflect discernible properties of those objects, though it may take practice and experience to recognize them'. In other words, being a fine-wine critic is very similar to being a fine-art critic.

That idea works for wine – mostly. Even though scientific research has shown that biological perceptions of smell and taste are very individual, not all judgments are simply subjective. There's a difference between preferences – I like this style of wine – and having the experience and knowledge that some wines (like some paintings) are generally recognized as more worthy of our attention than others, and therefore superior.

Just look at this year's Liv-Ex survey of experts, merchants and critics, as to the best wine of the 2018 vintage in Bordeaux. I was happy to see that most of them agreed with my assessment that it was Château Lafite Rothschild.

And finally, there's the question of art as something that has 'meaning' to an observer, a notion that Sir Roger Scruton sees as part of its definition. Wine doesn't seem to suggest meaning the way a painting does, but it may still embody a meaning – the idea of *terroir*, or a philosophy of winemaking or the customs and rituals that surround it.

WINE AND THE CREATIVE PROCESS

In an interview on winesearcher.com, Edouard Moueix – whose family owns Bordeaux châteaux in Pomerol and Saint-Emilion, as well as an impressive art collection – said he disagreed with the idea of wine as art. 'We are farmers, artisans, interpreters of nature,' he said. 'We don't create anything.'

But winemakers don't just channel grapes; they're constantly making choices in the vineyard and cellar that partly determine what results in the bottle, starting with the choice of the site itself. Wine may be a natural product, but it is not a pure expression of elemental nature the way birds, trees or rocks are. It's formed by human intention and actions. It owes its existence, at least in part, to the human mind, fulfilling Kant's idea that art is an activity of making something according to a preceding notion.

Yet the process for wine is different from making art. Randall Grahm put it this way in a conversation with Dwight Furrow, a professor of philosophy who writes the fascinating Edible Arts blog: 'You can't simply dial up elegance, harmony, et cetera. Typically these features spontaneously arise from great *terroirs* that are farmed thoughtfully. You can compose a wine by blending (through trial and error and some intuition) with the intention of creating (or better, discovering) some of these aesthetic elements, but a blended or composed wine will very seldom have the same degree of integrity and seamlessness as a wine that is naturally complex without artifice. Again, this is not something that one can reliably produce through one's winemaking efforts.'

IS DRINKING WINE AN AESTHETIC EXPERIENCE?

How we think and talk about wine and the way it influences us suggests that it is worthy of aesthetic appreciation in the same way art is. This is why I put in a call to Terry Theise, the author of *What Makes a Wine Worth Drinking*. His book is filled with thoughts about the beauty and 'soul' of wine.

To my surprise, he came down firmly on the side of wine as not art. 'Wine is a being of beauty, and it's common to link art and beauty. But if you extend the definition of art to

The Blue Hat, Closerie des Lilas by John Duncan Fergusson, oil on canvas (Fergusson Gallery, Perth, Scotland).

anything beautiful, then there's nowhere to draw the line,' he said in a phone call. 'It suffices for wine to be beautiful. You don't have to elevate it to art.'

He prefers to talk about aesthetic experience and 'the pleasure factor'. In his view, a wine is worth drinking if it's honest and authentic and delivers pleasure. But it's only worth paying serious attention to if it offers something more. Theise outlined two kinds of aesthetic judgements. One is, hey, when you've emptied the bottle of wine. The other is deconstructing a wine's aroma and flavour sensations, its complexity, its temperament, asking yourself whether it refers to anything beyond itself.

He points out that some wines, though, 'are so haunting and stirring that they bypass our entire analytical faculty and fill us with image and feeling. We glean the larger purpose of wine, and of beauty, and of life.'

That's what happened when I drank the 1945 La Tâche. 'That kind of experience is a purely aesthetic moment without narrative,' he explains. 'This is the ultimate attraction of wine – elusive, incandescent moments of meaning, the sense that truth is being revealed.'

A surprising number of California winemakers have a background in philosophy and think deeply about the meaning of wine, and like philosophers everywhere, they have their own strong views. Just to check off a few: Randall Grahm, Paul Draper and former professor of philosophy Abe Schoener of the Scholium Project, who has become a kind of sage of experimental California wine. Naturally, he has plenty of thoughts on the aesthetics of wine. After several years of making wine, he began to ask himself whether a wine could actually be tragic.

'Wine can be like opera – not necessarily in the sense that it is an artistic creation on the same scale or worthy of the same admiration,' he emailed, 'but in the sense that it can evoke not just similar sensations, or feelings, or emotions – but also even spur similar thinking.'

He offers as evidence that 'maybe there are wines with the majesty and dark power that drinking them could be like taking in *Tristan und Isolde*. After all, he points out: 'There are wines capable of taking our breath away and then plunging us into a kind of reverie that goes way beyond the glass and perhaps beyond the vineyard, the winery, the estate, the winemaker – a contemplation that calls up our mortality, our place in time.'

Among the winemakers I canvassed, Carlo Mondavi, the son of Tim Mondavi, who is making Sonoma Pinot Noir under his Raen label, does think of wine as art. 'Drinking a bottle of wine is experiencing the weather, a particular piece of land, the people who worked in the vineyard and cellar, all in a single beverage. That's unique. There's nothing else like this.'

THE MARKETING OF WINE AS ART

More and more frequently, producers of expensive wines are keen to promote a fuzzy overlap between art and wine, creating an aura of culture around their bottles and signalling how much their wines have in common with masterpieces of painting, drawing, sculpture, print-making and so on. A cynic would say it's all designed to manipulate you and make you think a $100 bottle of wine is a piece of art with a comparatively modest price tag.

As an industry insider once told me: 'In the luxury area, there's fierce competition for consumers. Logo fatigue has set in, and name alone is no longer enough. Buyers today are looking for something more: emotion and culture.'

Llewellyn Negrin, a senior researcher in the School of Creative Arts at the University of Tasmania, explored more reasons behind the increasing association between art and fine wine in her 2015 article 'Art and Fine Wine: A Case Study in the Aestheticization of Consumption'. Her take is that it's 'part of a wider phenomenon where art has increasingly been employed to market "lifestyle" commodities such as fashion and *haute cuisine*.' As more importance is placed on aesthetics in the process of consumption, in her view, art helps promote consuming as a way of life that transcends 'crass materialism'. But of course art, too, is a commodity.

Some examples? LVMH, the luxury goods conglomerate, once debuted a rare Hennessy cognac packaged in a special melted aluminum 'chest of secrets' created by French artist Jean-Michel Othoniel at the Musée des Arts Décoratifs at the Louvre in Paris. The cognac was a blend of the 100 greatest *eaux de vie* of the past century, and the 160lb (72kg) Art Nouveau-inspired chest looked rather like a mirrored casket designed to hold the relics of a sybaritic emperor.

The luxury company has long sought to associate its global champagne brands with art: Ruinart has been the official fizz at the New York City Ballet; Krug has stressed its connection with music; Dom Pérignon has relied on artist packaging from big names like Jeff Koons.

And then there are the images on labels designed to telegraph the quality of what's in the bottle. Following the lead of Château Mouton Rothschild (which also has one of the greatest collections of art related to wine), more and more prestigious wine estates commission celebrated artists to create paintings for the label. Julien de Beaumarchais de Rothschild – who now runs Mouton Rothschild with his brother and sister – once told me that the only requirement is that the artist has a global reputation

In good taste? Othoniel's 'chest of secrets'.

comparable to that of Mouton Rothschild. The long list of famous artists they've picked includes Pablo Picasso, Salvador Dalí, Marc Chagall and Andy Warhol.

Ornellaia chooses a different artist each year to create a site-specific artwork and labels that capture the essence and personality of the vintage, using art as an interpretation of the wine. The wines, sold only at auction, thus become two-pronged collectibles, the proceeds often going to museums.

Taittinger's unique angle is asking artists to transform the entire bottle into an artwork. The latest, released in 2016, is a 2008 Brut etched with an image of a leopard, courtesy of Brazilian photographer Sebastiaō Salgado.

Wineries themselves have been transformed into public art museums, with outdoor sculpture in the vineyards as at Château Smith Haut Lafitte, Château La Coste in Provence, Castello di Ama in Tuscany and Hall Winery in Napa. Also in Napa, the Hess Collection not only has a museum of serious art at the winery, but even its name has a double meaning – for their 'collection' of wines and the 'collection' of art.

Added to this is the push towards making the winery itself a contemporary art statement, another recent phenomenon that has changed the landscape even in traditional regions such as Bordeaux. Philippe Starck's metal boat-shaped cellar at Les Carmes Haut-Brion, for example, is more a sculpture than simply a place to make wine, and visually it echoes the idea that the wine made there is an artwork, too.

So, we're back to the big question with which I started: Is wine art? I'm still not sure. But does it really matter? The fact that there are so many connections and similarities to the way we regard both means that, for many wine lovers, the question is answered. Wine may not be art, but it's close enough. 🐾

*First published as 'Is Wine Art?' by Elin McCoy in **The World of Fine Wine**, Issue 64, 2019. Reprinted here with the kind permission of the author and of Neil Beckett, editor (www. worldoffinewine.com).*

Best Dressed and Bottled at Home

JOAN LITTLEWOOD (1984)

The early 1920s were down-beat times in the vineyards of Bordeaux, that is until Philippe de Rothschild arrived with an idea that would revolutionize the trade from the châteaux to the shop floor. Joan Littlewood – controversial theatre director, friend and writer of his memoirs – tells his story.

In the early 1920s the fortunes of My Lady Vine were in eclipse. Wine drinking was not the smart business it has become. A new invention, the cocktail, was the thing. For 'le six o'clock', the new girl with her Eton crop, long cigarette holder and tiny, straight skirt would demand gin or whisky. People even drank whisky with their meals. New concoctions were *à la mode* and wine was given away, *en carafe*, in the restaurants. It was a drink for the groundlings. Only a few connoisseurs seemed to care about the great old wines and there was nothing to attract the others. Labels were plain, old fashioned and dull, and often wine was badly treated – it could be 'off' when you uncorked it. With gin or whisky you knew where you were.

One fine day I was watching the barrels of new wine being loaded on to the drays. It was my second harvest at Mouton and I was disheartened. I had just driven from Paris, and every hoarding en route had been plastered with adverts for the zazzy new drinks: '*La Suze, l'amie d l'estomac*'; '*Picotin, Apéritif Américain, Honi soit qui mal y pense*'; '*St Raphael, Quinquina, c'est la Santé*'.

The drays went lumbering down the road to Bordeaux. They looked like an 1890s painting. Harvest home. Sunset on the road to Pauillac. The picture needed touching up or maybe scrapping altogether; it was dreary and old hat, what's more it was all wrong. It came to me suddenly, the simple, obvious, extraordinary idea that was to revolutionize the wine trade. They could keep their hoardings and their slogans. I would put wine right back at the top of the poll. I knew exactly how it should be done.

They would call it revolution, but it would be a revolution that had its roots in tradition. Always the peasant on his holding and the rich man on his estate had each cared for his own wine in his own way, and every plot had yielded its own distinctive flavour. The old locals swore they could tell which side of the railway line the wine came from.

Our *cuves*, the great wooden, iron-ringed vats in which the grapes ferment, were works of art, built in situ by a master craftsman. Wine for our own consumption was watched over like an only child during its three-year sleep in the oak casks, occasionally clarified with beaten white of egg, which Fleming, the penicillin man, told me adds lysozyme which protects the sight. Every year our store of oak casks was renewed, the wine gently moved from barrel to barrel, and when its time came the wine was bottled for us by our own *maitre de chai*. At our table, *en carafe*, it was labelled in his handwriting and its year of birth given.

Why then, in the name of goodness, were we shipping the wines we were selling to Bordeaux at the most critical period of their lives? Anything might become of them in the

Baron Philippe de Rothschild pictured in 1929 at the wheel of his racing car just before the start of the Spanish Grand Prix.

wine merchants' sheds. Three years' maturation in a strange environment, at the very time when we should be responsible for nursing the precious juice. Had we ever known exactly what was going into those bottles which carried our labels? It wasn't good enough. That was my wine rolling down to Bordeaux in those heavy barrels, and I wanted to be sure it was still mine when it was labelled. Why not put my name on the bottle? That would be an innovation – until now nobody had ever signed a bottle – but I, Philippe, intended to let the world and his wife know that my wine was the best. No criticism of the wine merchants intended: many of them were men of taste and integrity. (Not all of them, mind you, there's always somebody doing a bit of trafficking in the wine business, though they don't always get away with it; witness the Cruse scandal a few years ago resulting in a suicide and the disgrace of a house which had reigned in Bordeaux for over 100 years.) I believed that my idea would give the wine trade the boost it needed, put it back among the aristocrats so that the good man in Manchester or Maryland would know where his wine was born and nurtured and who its parents were.

I couldn't wait to tell the world, but first I had to put it right with the neighbours: Haut Brion, Margaux, Latour and Lafite. I hoped to convert all four of them without too much trouble but I'd begin with Pierre Moreau, part-owner of Margaux. He had taken a liking to me from the start; I knew I would be able to win him over easily. He was an old dear with a mop of white hair and splendid moustaches. I caught him in a good mood. Before I'd finished my sales talk he was bubbling over with enthusiasm. 'A superb idea. It will give a whole new boost to the wine trade!' Monsieur Moreau was a merchant as well as a grower.

'We'll call it chateau-bottling,' I said.

Together we went to see André Gibert, who owned Haut Brion, his beautiful French phrases slightly spoiled by the clicking of his new false teeth. Then there was the Comte René de Beaumont at Latour. What a character – huge beaked nose, meerschaum pipe, a shabby shapeless jacket and spats, every inch the run-down aristocrat. They were both delighted with the idea, so there was only Lafite left, but Lafite, being so to speak in the family, might prove difficult. Our two houses have a long and chequered history. I'm afraid I have to fill you in on part of it – I'll keep it short.

My English great-grandfather, Nathaniel, bought Mouton in 1853. In 1868 he was boasting of his 'extraordinarily good wine that I have sold at the fantastic price of 5,000 francs the barrel'.

Baron James, his uncle and father-in-law, youngest of the original Frankfurt brothers, was jealous, having already tried to buy the neighbouring estate, Lafite, and failed. He tried again, offering 4,140,000 gold francs, nearly four times as much as Nathaniel had paid for

Mouton. It was accepted. A few weeks later he died, just as he was trying to get a better price than Nathaniel for the wine.

That was the beginning of the family rivalry, which has existed ever since, sometimes blowing hot, sometimes cold; and since the two estates border on each other, and here and there overlap, it can be inflamed from time to time by squabbling among the estate workers over a fallen tree or a shattered wall.

Since 1905 the Rothschild bank in Paris had been run, discreetly and unadventurously, by two cousins, Edouard the elegant and handsome Robert. They also owned Lafite, but they were never there. If you had a problem, you talked to Monsieur Mortier, their manager. Should he consider it of sufficient importance he would go to Paris to consult his bosses, and await their instructions. On this occasion, having heard me out, he went to Paris.

I followed soon after, summoned to the Rothschild bank. Baron Edouard received me. He had a strange face, thin with a long, crooked nose. He was of my father's generation; they were distant cousins, but of very different stock. On my father's side, medicine, invention, art; on theirs, banking, politics, hunting. All the same, Baron Edouard had always been very kind to me; he seemed to have a soft spot for Henri's son, though not for Henri. I had been invited to Ferrières, his family home, several times – a monstrously ugly place, I must say.

'How now, my young friend,' said he. 'And what do you think you're playing at? How long have you been in the Médoc? You do realize, I suppose, that nobody has ever found fault with the way our wines are bottled. Very much to the contrary. In my opinion these merchant fellows do a first-rate job. Where would we be without them?'

'The wine passes through too many hands, Cousin Edouard – first it's offered to the brokers, then to the Bordeaux merchants, then to some wholesaler, who may be in the Antipodes, then to a retailer – the . . . We should be growers *and* merchants.'

'Very commendable, all these bright ideas, young man, but the traditions which govern the wine trade have developed over centuries. You may have heard of "Le Bureau de la Répression des Fraudes". It exists to put a stop to any mischief. There are laws to protect the consumer, my boy, the strictest control over quality. The large areas known as "Appellations" are carefully defined, so is the type of wine to be grown there, and even the number of vines which may be planted therein.'

'I do know about the wine laws, cousin. I also know that as things are it is the wine-grower who carries the loss and the merchant who makes the profit, living off the backs of the growers, as he does.'

'Now that is mere foolishness. Where would the poor producers be without the merchants' money? Most growers have no capital, they have to wait for the merchant to pay them before they can buy weed killer.'

'Because he pays them in dribs and drabs, he hasn't much capital to fall back on either. The whole industry wants tuning up.'

'I see. And I suppose you think your scheme is going to do the trick? Has it struck you that with your system the poor grower will be worse off? He'll have to wait three years before he sees any cash.'

'No, the brokers will still buy the wine at harvest time. Only we will look after it for the next three years, instead of sending it to Bordeaux.'

'But they're used to paying cash on delivery. Without the stock it's not going to be easy for them to raise the cash.'

'They could pay by instalments – three, let's say, spread over nine months.'

'And have you asked yourself how many growers will be able to afford the necessary outlay? Have you worked out how much this wonderful idea of yours would cost?'

He seized his slim gold everlasting pencil and made calculations on the blotter. He was right. It wouldn't be easy. Maybe it would drive some of the little men out of business. But they were going broke anyway. The main thing was to put some verve back into the wine trade, market the château wines for the aristocrats they were, and produce more wines of quality.

Cousin Edouard was getting his figures right. '...taking an average figure, say three harvests each of 400 casks, allowing three by four metres per cask, that's going to mean a large area...'

My thoughts flew out of the window to our little old *chai* at Mouton. It was scarcely big enough to manoeuvre the dray horses when we were shifting the casks.

'...plus space for storing, for approximately 100,000 bottles, add the cost of installing bottling equipment at each chateau...'

'It would be a guarantee of quality, it will give the wine distinction. Each owner would be responsible for his own wine. You know, cousin, many of the so-called châteaux are now nothing but a front, a name...'

I was repeating myself. Anyway, he wasn't listening, he was completing his calculations. He gave a flourish. 'Reckon on a million francs, at least. And what for? Simply to make a break with tradition and upset our old friends, the wine merchants. I'm going to give you a little advice, young friend, you go back home and hold your horses.'

I was dismayed, but not discouraged, at least not till the storm broke. Christian Cruse, of the most famous merchant house in Bordeaux, led the attack with an article in *La Petite Gironde*. He laughed the idea to scorn. 'In any case nothing will come of it, it would mean the ruination of the wine trade.'

Letters even appeared in *The Times* of London. Berry Bros, the English importers, declared that their reputation was under attack. They are still cross with me, even today.

You cannot imagine how much the idea of château-bottling upset people, especially the old dodos. 'Who is this young man? Is he questioning our capability or our honesty?'

Someone advised my father to take me away. 'Why?' he said. 'Let him cut his teeth.'

I might have given up but my dear old gentlemen at Haut Brion, Latour and Margaux, backed me all along the line, especially Pierre Moreau. He was great. Through him, the best of the brokers, the Lawtons, were won over. Then I heard that Lafite was having second thoughts.

The time had come for a get-together. Nobody ever got together in the Médoc. Nobody ever ate well in the Médoc either. They still don't. I invited my converts to dinner at the famous Chapon Fin in Bordeaux. Would Lafite come? That was the question. I received a letter from the bank, informing me that Monsieur Mortier, the manager, would be instructed to attend; so I booked a table in the name of 'The Five'.

Monsieur Mortier turned out to be a rather severe man and a Freemason, but we all sat down in friendly style. Luckily the food was excellent and the wine impeccable. I talked about publicity; they winced. I changed the word, tried 'glamour'. Accepted. We came to the topic of the day, château-bottling. To my amazement they were all for it, even Lafite. I proposed that we sign a document committing ourselves to château-bottling and engaging to help each other in all matters, technical and commercial, and that we call ourselves the Association of Five.

Monsieur Mortier enlarged on Lafite's knowledge and experience, then with a superior air informed us that the Barons Edouard and Robert never signed anything; it was not their custom. 'Our word is enough,' said he. The other four signed, Lafite never.

The storm began to die down as word of our agreement got about. We had already decided that our get-together should become a regular institution, as the first had been so pleasant and useful to us all. So we met once a month, exchanged ideas – and gossip, of course – mulled over problems and enjoyed a fabled cuisine under the Chapon Fin's spreading indoor tree.

Our club, if you could call it that, was the first of its kind in the Médoc. Everyone talked about the Association of Five – the name stuck.

I was worried about the storage problem at Mouton. I would have to patch up the old *chai* and extend it. I asked everybody if they knew of a good local architect. My progress report at the second dinner was a long moan about the chap who'd been recommended to me. I'd just received his plans for the extension of the *chai*, which were very 1910 art school, all shading and trees and suburban Tudor. I should have known this would happen: a rash of Swiss chalets and bizarre villas with bell towers and medieval windows had been appearing all over the Médoc.

I thought of Charles Siclis, busy on his pleasure space in the Rue Pigalle, and wondered what he would have done with a *chai*. Imagine his ideas in poor old broken-down Mouton. Would any artist work in these backwoods? It was worth a try. I called to see him.

'It's the sticks,' I told him. 'There isn't one decent building in the place, but there's room to make something happen, and no restrictions.'

He took a weekend off and we went to Mouton. One look at the old *chai* and, 'It's no use tinkering about with that,' he said. 'Erase it, build a new one.'

'Will you design it?' 'Yes.'

And when you come to Mouton you will see, as two white doors roll back, a glorious piece of décor, the great *chai* that Siclis built. It is 100 metres long and, as far as you can see, totally unsupported, the cool white length of its walls broken only by columns of light. At the far end, I have Mouton's coat of arms, two giant rams, rampant.

It took three years to build, from 1924 to 1927. The soil underneath was so hard it had to be dynamited. I had no intention of waiting for the new *chai* before I started the whole process of château-bottling. I stored my wine anywhere I could find, the barrels stacked one on top of the other. Villages were scouted for disused *chais* 'Mouton 1924, *mise en bouteille au château*' was going to make its début in 1927, no matter what it cost.

'More money than sense,' they said.

During the works, part of the old *chai* collapsed and went crashing down into the cellars. Nine-tenths of the 1925 vintage was destroyed.

'It's a judgment on him.'

It was a nasty big hole. There was only one thing to do, speed up the tempo. Not only would my bottles be ready for 1927, but I would give them a new look. I was sick and tired of seeing Mouton go out into the world badly dressed, sporting that dreary 19th-century label with no design about it at all, and no colour.

What would be right? It would have to be something special, my first label. Why not the latest thing, a Cubist design? Jean Carlu was famous for introducing Cubism into advertising, you could see his work on all the hoardings of Paris. Just the man. When he sent me his design I was thrilled with it.

'I'll keep it for ever,' I said.

In 1927 I stood and waited for the first château bottles to appear. The old hand-lift came groaning to a halt. There they were. The Carlu label, red, gold, green, grey and black, made a dazzling, dancing border. They would catch the eye anywhere. They did.

Whether it was the label or not, château-bottling did the trick. Within a year, '*Mise en bouteille au château*' was a sign of quality, Médocain. Now it's universal. 🌿

*Extract from **Milady Vine, the Autobiography of Philippe de Rothschild** by Joan Littlewood, Jonathan Cape (London) 1984.*

Fine wine meets fine art: the first of Château Mouton Rothschild's 'art' labels, by Jean Carlu.

FOR A PIECE OF THE GLAMOUR

TONY ASPLER (1997)

Toronto-based wine writer and author Tony Aspler revels in the grandeur of Bordeaux' biennial wine fair, Vinexpo, and finds himself in possession of a particularly special wine label.

In the entrance to Toronto's Eaton Centre on downtown Yonge Street is a bronze statue of Timothy Eaton, the founder of the department store chain. The toe of his left shoe is worn to a golden sheen by the myriads of people who have rubbed it over the generations for good luck. (Not that it has worked for the company's current directorate.)

This atavistic gesture of touching or rubbing an image for luck must be a universal need since I have seen statues in Italy with the same shining parts as Timothy Eaton's toe. One is in Florence at the entrance to a covered market square in the centre of the city. It is a large, beautifully executed, life-size bronze replica of a wild boar whose gleaming snout has been polished by the attentions of countless tourists.

The other memorable example is the statue of Shakespeare's Juliet in a courtyard under that celebrated balcony in Verona. The doors, the archway and the walls leading into this courtyard are covered with the names of lovers who no doubt hope for a more felicitous fate than the Bard's Gen-X'ers, Romeo and Juliet.

Juliet stands at the far end of the courtyard, a demure young thing who looks more like a statue of the Madonna, except that her right breast flashes like a beacon in the dimly lit forecourt. Tourists take turns being photographed fondling her breast. Herein lies the difference between Canadians and Italians. Our basic instincts impel us to touch the toe of an unrepentant capitalist while Italians go for the gusto. I'm sure the French would understand and sympathize: after all, they consider wine to be the liquid embodiment of the female sex.

While the French and the Italians may agree on some things, their attitudes to wine and wine shows are quite different. Just visit Vinexpo in Bordeaux and Vinitaly in Verona and you can see the differing national attitudes.

Vinexpo happens every other year, in odd years, in June at around the time of flowering if the vintage is good. Vinitaly occurs every year in April.

Vinexpo, while showing off the best that France can provide, also welcomes the world. It is the most international of wine shows; even Ontario and British Columbia wineries feel compelled to have a presence there. Vinitaly invites other wine regions to exhibit but basically it's an Italian event and in Vinexpo years tends to be overshadowed.

Vinexpo is located just outside Bordeaux, the undisputed wine capital of the world (after all, when you think of vintages, your first thought is red Bordeaux). The exhibition hall is a kilometre long, set by the side of an artificial lake. There are ancillary tents along the lake side for regional and national restaurants (which are uniformly very good and difficult to get into) and other tents and hospitality areas on the other side rented by the large companies.

Invariably it is hot in Bordeaux in June. Blazing hot. And those who were there in 1989 will never forget just how hot. The hall had no air conditioning and the build-up of heat made the place feel like a furnace. Corks rose like magic from the bottles as the alcohol expanded but no one wanted to taste the tepid wines anyway. All we wanted was water. The temperature was said to be 47°C and even hotter in those stands that had an upper deck. There were stories of oysters boiling on the half shell and winemakers collapsing with heart attacks – apocryphal, no doubt, but certainly it was terribly uncomfortable for those who attended. The stands that had their own air-conditioning were very much in demand.

My abiding memory of the 1989 Vinexpo will always be the sight of Roberto Anselmi, the fine Soave producer, in shirt sleeves with his trouser legs rolled up to the knees, sitting on the edge of a fountain with his feet dangling in the water. Bags of ice and bottles of his Capitel Foscarino and I Capetelli Soave were also chilling in the makeshift ice bucket.

Many of the châteaux have guests for lunch or dinner during Vinexpo, but an invitation to Mouton Rothschild is one of the most coveted. It is a black tie event, quite formal. The guests are transported by special train from Bordeaux to the station in Pauillac where they are greeted by the local band and then driven by bus to the château.

That year was my 50th birthday and I had been invited to dinner, along with some 200 other guests, to Château Mouton Rothschild. We lined up on the gravel driveway to be received by Philippine de Rothschild prior to a champagne reception outside and then into the cellars for a candlelit dinner.

I was staying at the Terminus Hotel in Bordeaux which is above the main railway station. It was not air-conditioned and I was forced to sleep with the windows open – which was the lesser of two evils since Vinexpo coincides with La Fête de la Musique when itinerant musicians can perform at all hours of the day and night. Mainly night.

I changed into my tuxedo and took a cab to the smaller local station from which the private train to Mouton was to leave. But the cab driver did not understand my French and took me to a station that was boarded up and abandoned. It did not take me long to realize that I was not going to join the party from there. The train was due to leave in 15 minutes from a station I had ascertained from a passerby was 'pas loin d'ici'.

It was blisteringly hot still and I looked around for a passing taxi but the streets in this part of Bordeaux were deserted.

I began to run.

Sweat was pouring off me in buckets. I felt like Niagara Falls. I had five minutes to make the train and I was a good half mile away from the station. I ran faster. My dinner shirt was drenched.

I arrived just as the train was about to pull away from the platform and jumped on board. I might as well have been in a Turkish Bath.

Every pore of my body gave up its fluids. The leather of my shoes felt sodden. The lapels of my suit jacket were steaming like the flanks of a horse that has been ridden hard and put away wet.

The party's over: autumn descends over Château Mouton Rothschild, Pauillac.

Two glasses of champagne helped to cool me down, and by the time the train arrived in Pauillac I was merely as hot as the rest of the gathering. In the reception line-up I ran into a fellow Canadian who worked for the Alberta Liquor Board. He had been a wrestler in his youth and when he had taken more wine than a liquor board executive should, he was prone to putting head locks on people in bars. We had drinks on Mouton's terrace and then moved into the cellar for dinner. The menu read as follows:

Mosaïque légumes au foie gras
Cuisse de canard en civet à l'ancienne
Pâtes au basilic
Fromages
Gourmandise à la vanille au coulis de framboise

The accompanying wines were:
Opus One 1982
Mouton Baron Philippe 1970
Mouton Rothschild 1939
Baron Philippe de Rothschild Mise de la Baronnie Sauternes 1987

The centrepiece wine, served with the cheese course, was the Château Mouton Rothschild 1939 in magnums. Since this was my birth year I was over the moon – even though the vintage received no stars at all from Michael Broadbent, who described it in print, having tasted it in 1978, as 'lightish in colour; sound and nice bouquet; with an acceptable twist of acidity'.

It hadn't improved in 11 years but it was fun to try. I asked Philippine de Rothschild if she would autograph the label for me, which she graciously did.

The dinner ended about one o'clock; by then the weather had cooled somewhat. We drank cognac on the terrace and my colleague from Alberta approached me, suggesting that I would be better off coming back to his air-conditioned hotel and sleeping there rather than embarking on the long journey back to Bordeaux and the Terminus Hotel. Recalling my sauna-like room and the street music, I decided to take him up on his offer.

He was staying at the Relais de Margaux, a luxury hotel, in a room with twin beds.

It was around two o'clock by the time we arrived back at the hotel. I have no recollection of how we got there. Someone must have driven; I hope it wasn't the Albertan.

I decided at that point that I had to soak the label off the magnum of Mouton 1939. Now the French have invented the ideal contraption for soaking labels off wine bottles: a bidet. I filled the bidet in the hotel bathroom with hot water and then filled the bottle with hot water so that it would lie immersed. The combined heat on both sides of the glass would melt the glue and the label would come away. (This method works for most wine bottles, except those with gold on the label. For some reason gold seems to stick limpet-like to glass.)

Mouton's magnum label came away very easily. It measured 6 inches by 4¾ inches, slightly larger than the label for a 750ml bottle; and as a 1939 bottling it bore the Rothschild crest surmounted by a crown and held by two rampant rams. It was not yet an art label (for every vintage since 1945 the late Baron Philippe de Rothschild, and latterly his daughter Philippine, have commissioned renowned artists to design the top band of the label.* Over the years the works of such luminaries of the art world as Pablo Picasso, Marc Chagall, Salvador Dalí, Joan Miró, Henry Moore, Andy Warhol and Jean-Paul Riopelle have graced that top band.

---

* The first Mouton Rothschild 'art label' was Jean Carlu's design for the 1924 vintage, but Philippe de Rothschild waited until 1945 before making the art labels an annual tradition.

The design for the 1993 vintage, by Hartung, caused something of a scandal in the States: a pencil drawing of a nude pubescent girl. The Bureau of Alcohol, Tobacco and Firearms, the federal department that polices wine labels (!) was outraged; so Mouton had a special label printed for the US: one with a blank white space in place of the buff-coloured image. This bottling has already become something of a collector's item.)

I placed the 1939 Mouton label lovingly on the flat surface next to the sink and patted it dry with a towel before wrapping it in a wad of toilet paper. It would make a fine memento of Vinexpo 1989. The wine of my birth year. By the time I had finished, my room-mate was already in bed, sitting bolt upright.

'Hurry up,' he said. 'I'm turning out the light.'

I undressed quickly and slid into the single bed next to his. The light snapped out and he said: 'Good night.'

Almost immediately there was the sound of a match being struck and a flame illuminated the room.

'What are you doing?' I demanded.

'Having a smoke,' he said. 'I always have a smoke before I go to sleep.'

'In the dark?'

'Yes.'

'I'd rather you didn't.'

'Okay,' he said, obligingly.

Scandalous: Hartung's 1993 Mouton Rothschild label.

There was the sound of a cigarette being stubbed out in an ashtray and the rustle of sheets as his head hit the pillow. Within seconds he began to snore. Great window-rattling inhalations that pierced through the pillow I used to cover my ears.

After 20 minutes I decided there was no way that I was going to fall asleep with the rolling thunder from the neighbouring bed.

I picked up the pillow and a blanket and walked to the bathroom. The bath itself was too short to sleep in so I made up a bed on the marble floor. Then it occurred to me that the sleeping volcano in the bedroom might want to get up in the night to use the bathroom. I would be in his direct path to the toilet. So I moved sideways until I was positioned under the wash basin and vanity unit. My ear was next to the pipes and when anybody else in the hotel that night flushed a toilet or turned on a tap I was jolted into consciousness by a noise even more devastating than my neighbour's snoring.

'How did you sleep?' he asked me the next morning over breakfast.

'As well as might be expected,' I replied. 'And you?'

'Great,' he said, 'but this morning when I went to the can I couldn't find any toilet paper so I had to use a god-damned wine label.' 🍂

*First published in Tony Aspler's **Travels With My Corkscrew,** McGraw-Hill Ryerson (Whitby, Canada) 1997.*

CHAPTER 10

Wine and the Poets

Wine and the Outcast Poet – Giles MacDonogh (2009)

Colette and Wine – Alice Wooledge Salmon (1983)

In Vino Veritas – Harry Eyres (2014)

WINE AND THE OUTCAST POET

GILES MacDONOGH (2009)

Wine was a constant source of inspiration for Charles Baudelaire, providing the subject for many of his most famous works. Giles MacDonogh traces the vinous influence on the life and work of one of France's greatest poets.

Charles Baudelaire is best remembered today as the author of the dark and decadent collection of poems of 1861 titled *Les Fleurs du Mal*, which contains a series of five poems dedicated to various manifestations of wine. Baudelaire was born in 1821 and died aged 46 in 1867: at the same age and from much the same causes as his early hero, the Prussian writer ETA Hoffmann – syphilis, gonorrhea and general debilitation brought on by a misspent life.

Baudelaire was born in Paris, but his father, an unfrocked priest who had cast off his clerical collar during the Revolution, hailed from Sainte Menehoud on the border of Champagne. His people had been vignerons and coopers for many generations, and his best friend at school was a Monsieur Pérignon. Baudelaire *père* was already an old man when he married Caroline Archimbaut-Dufaÿs, and he died while Charles was still a small child. The poet's mother remarried a career army officer with Irish origins called Jacques Aupick. Aupick's career took him to Lyon, where Baudelaire spent the years that bridged childhood and adolescence. Most of the rest of Baudelaire's life was spent in the French capital.

Baudelaire's existence was a bohemian one, but by common consent he was never actually either a drunk or an alcoholic. Despite his translation of de Quincey and his well-

Dark and decadent: an early 'Woodburytype' by Étienne Carjat of the poet Charles Baudelaire (1821–67).

documented brush with hashish, it was only at the end of his life that he took excessive quantities of opiates and drank deep of the wine of consolation.

Contemporaries were at pains to report after his death that his consumption of wine was generally limited to around half a bottle. 'He drank nothing but unadulterated wine,' said one, while another stated: 'He was sober by nature. We used to drink together; I never saw him drunk.' He was fastidious, drinking 'wine like an epicure, not like a plowman'.[1]

Little is known about his taste in wine. Once or twice burgundy is mentioned in his writings, but that is all. His friend Paul Emmanuel Auguste Poulet-Malassis used to entertain Baudelaire and others with lavish meals and lovely wines (though we don't know which) at the restaurant La Laiterie du Paradoxe in the Rue Saint André des Arts. One of his fellow *convives* was the gastronomic writer and poet Charles Monselet, but there is no evidence that Baudelaire was given to gourmandize. He was also known to drink porter and beer.

He frequented cafés, taverns and restaurants, where he composed over a glass of white wine: the Brasserie des Martyrs in the street of that name; Hill's Tavern in the Boulevard des Capucines; the Café Lemblin in the Palais Royal, where someone is supposed to have suggested the idea of *Les Fleurs du Mal*; and the Café Momus in the Rue des Prêtres St German l'Auxerrois – immortalized by Murger (and subsequently Puccini) in *Les Scènes de la Vie de Bohème*.[2]

CONSOLATION OF THE POOR

Baudelaire's best-known bacchanal is *L'Ame du Vin*. The poet presents wine in its symbiotic relationship with its creator, man – but not just a man; also the poet. It rekindles the charms of his wife and bolsters the puny strength of his son. Wine is sympathetic to the human condition. It is aware how much blood, sweat and tears have gone into its creation, and its moment of supreme joy arrives when its wax is removed and its cork pulled, and it falls 'into the gullet of a man worn out by toil'.

> *Et je serai pour ce frêle athlète de la vie*
> *L'huile qui raffirmit les muscles des lutteurs.*

> *[And I will be for this frail athlete they call life*
> *The balsam that oils the muscles of a wrestler.]*

---

[1] Joanna Richardson, *Baudelaire* (John Murray, 1994).
[2] Claude Pichois and Jean Ziegler, *Charles Baudelaire* (Fayard, 1996).

Wine also pays its dues to the 'eternal sower, / So that poetry be born out of our passion / that will spurt up to God like the rarest flower'.

In his 1851 essay *Du Vin et du Hachisch*, Baudelaire restates his case: 'Who has not experienced the profound joys of wine? Whoever has felt the need to calm a sense of remorse, to evoke a memory, to drown some sadness, to wallow in fantasy; all these have invoked you: mysterious God who lurks in the fibres of the vine.'[3]

In *Le Vin des Chiffoniers*, wine is the consolation of the poor, in an underworld of unfulfilled dreams. It was probably the first of the wine poems to be written, having been published in 1854 in the magazine *Jean Raisin, Revue Joyeuse et Vinicole*, which had a cover the colour of wine lees emblazoned with a picture by Charles Doré representing a harvest in Burgundy. It is the old story: A man who is drunk is as great as a king. God created sleep for the old and damned who die in oblivion, 'And man added wine, the sacred son of the sun'.

> *There exists an immeasurable number of people on*
> *the earth's surface, anonymous beings, for whom*
> *sleep suffices not to alleviate their sufferings. For*
> *them, wine composes their songs and poems.*[4]

'Sad drinkers, happy drinkers.'[5] Wine's lovers sport different faces: In *Le Vin de l'Assassin*, wine gives the murderer the courage to kill his wife and the oblivion he needs to evade conscience and responsibility. He will make wine into a shroud for his murdered wife:

> *She's dead. I'm as free as a sparrow!*
> *I can drink as much as any bloke.*
> *When I came back stony broke,*
> *Her cries pierced me to the marrow.*

Wine is a consolation in despair, to the poet slighted by a haughty beauty. In *Le Vin du Solitaire*, no woman can compare to 'the all-pervading redolence of [wine's] fertile belly'. Hope, youth, and life are in the poet's wine

> *– and self-esteem, riches for every rag –*
> *That renders us triumphant and divine.*

---

[3], [4], [5] *Du Vin et du Hashisch*.

In his poem *Le Tonneau de la Haine*, Baudelaire compares hatred to the harmless excesses of reasonable drinkers:

> *Mais les buveurs heureux connaissent leur vainqueur,*
> *Et la haine est vouée à ce sort lamentable*
> *De ne pouvoir jamais s'endormir sous la table.*

> *[But happy revellers know when they are licked,*
> *And hatred is destined for that pitiful fate*
> *Never to nod off when the night gets late.]*

In *Le Vin des Amants*, the last of his wine lyrics in *Les Fleurs du Mal*, wine is a portal through which the drinker passes into the imagination and comes face to face with the divine.

> *Today skies are huge and splendid!*
> *Cast aside saddle, spurs, and bit,*
> *And let us ride away on wine*
> *To a heaven magical and divine.*

THE INFLUENCE OF HOFFMANN

Baudelaire had derived an important message from one of the most significant literary wine lovers of the older generation: ETA Hoffmann. He had learned the need to escape – by whatever means – from the banality of the humdrum. Before he discovered Edgar Allen Poe, Hoffmann had been one of Baudelaire's heroes, and the Prussian writer's portrait had hung on his wall in his flat in the Rue Pimodan in Paris. He knew of Hoffmann's works through the translations made by Hamburg-born Jew François-Adolphe Loève-Veimars.[6]

Baudelaire's wine is Dionysian not Apollonian. It is the effect rather than the taste that counts. 'In the worker's stomach I shake up the household, and from there I climb invisible stairways to his brain where I perform my great dance'. He is thinking of the Dithyramb and the terrible destructive passion of the Maenads – the female followers of Dionysus – rather than something like the Saintsbury Club, where gentlemen in dinner jackets sit around a table comparing the relative merits of 10 vintages of Château Lafite.

---

[6] Pichois and Ziegler, *Charles Baudelaire.*

Dionysus is also the god of poetry, and Baudelaire pays him his dues: 'Our intimate bond will create poetry. Together we will make a god and we will fly up towards the infinite like birds, like butterflies, children of the Virgin, perfume and all winged things.'

Baudelaire's thinking was coloured by the German romanticism he found in Hoffmann. It is tempting to believe that he had read Goethe, too, but there is no evidence to confirm this was the case. His position comes close to Goethe's in his prose poem *Enivrez-vous*: 'You must be constantly drunk... To anesthetize yourself against the horrible burden of time that breaks your back and makes you stoop towards the earth, you have to be drunk non-stop'. But once again this drunkenness is a metaphor for passion. You can get drunk on wine, poetry or virtue.

Just as Goethe labels childhood 'drunkenness without wine', Baudelaire refers to the effects of wine as 'second youth', 'illuminated by an inner sun'.

Unlike Hoffmann, however, Baudelaire sheds no light on the wine of his day: it is a pure symbol. The boorish Belgian prefers his beer to burgundy in *Sur les Débuts d'Amina Boschetti*. For Baudelaire, the Belgian attitude to wine is one more nail in their coffins. As is often the case today, the Belgians possessed marvelous cellars, but 'Belgians show off their wines. They do not drink because of taste, but for reasons of vanity and conformism: They want to look French'. Belgium is a 'paradise for commercial travelers selling wine'. In reality, the people drink philistine tipples like gin and beer.[7]

Once more there is an allusion to Hoffmann, who thought beer the drink of the philistine.

> *I am what is looked forward to on Sundays. Work makes for prosperous days, wine makes joyful Sundays. Elbows on the family table and rolled-up sleeves, you will proudly sing my praises, and you will be properly happy. Let him suffer – the man whose selfish heart, impervious to his brothers' suffering, has never heard this song!*

AN APOLOGY FOR DRUNKENNESS

Baudelaire's most reasoned statements on wine are to be found in *Du Vin et du Hachisch*. Baudelaire is particularly scathing in his condemnation of Brillat-Savarin's book *La Physiologie du Goût* of 1825, an examination of all aspects of taste that is admittedly skimpy in its treatment of wine even if the author – a winemaker and a hedonist – knew a lot more about it than he let on.

---

[7] Pauvre Belgique! in Claude Roy and Michel Jamet (eds), *Baudelaire Oeuvres Complètes* (Laffont, 1980).

Baudelaire falls into the same trap as most subsequent readers of *La Physiologie du Goût* in that he believes the book is about eating, when in reality it is a pseudo-scientific treatise dealing with all aspects of taste, gastronomy included. Brillat-Savarin had been heavily influenced by the *philosophes* who penned the prefaces to cookery books in the 18th century, as well as by his own readings in the natural sciences. The resulting treatise is, at times, an uncomfortable mixture between kitchen philosophy and self-indulgent anecdote.[8]

Baudelaire opposes Brillat-Savarin with the sodden Hoffmann, who had gone through a rough patch in Bamberg, where he sought oblivion after Napoleon's invasion of Prussia had put him out of work and his passion for an underage pupil had been thwarted by the girl's mother. 'The divine Hoffmann' had tabulated a strange system of wine and inspiration in his *Kreisleriana* of 1814, deciding just what was necessary to get the composer Johannes Kreisler in the mood. To write a comic opera, for example, Hoffmann proposes champagne: 'There he will find the bubbly gaiety and frivolity the genre requires.' Religious music calls for hock or Jurançon.[9] 'Just as there is at the bottom of [all] profound ideas, there is an intoxicating bitterness.' Heroic music, on the other hand, requires just one sort of wine – Burgundy: 'It has a serious ardour and leads to patriotism'.[10] Baudelaire salutes an impartiality that does credit to a German.

Baudelaire also recounts the story that at the end of his life Hoffmann had demanded that a part of his royalties be paid in French wine. There was some truth in it, but the wine was not French – it was a Rüdesheimer Hinterhaus (now the eastern half of the Schlossberg) from the Comet Year of 1811.

In fact, Kreisler's views were – as ever – a reflection of Hoffmann's own.[11] Already to his friend Hitzig, in 1812, Hoffmann had recommended Chambertin for its 'poetic' nature; and, like Baudelaire, Hoffmann developed early on the habit of writing in a wine-steeped tavern. It may have been this that inspired Baudelaire, for Hitzig recounts in his life of Hoffmann that he drank 'to give himself strength. He was never idle in the tavern, and studied everyone with his falcon eyes...'[12] Hoffmann's characters also derive strength from wine, while others become more evil under the influence.

---

[8] *See* Giles Macdonogh, *Brillat-Savarin: The Judge and His Stomach* (John Murray, 1992).
[9] 'French wine' in the text: see *ETA Hoffmanns Werke in Zwei Bänden* (Vienna; nd).
[10] Hoffmann suggests 'very good burgundy' for serious opera and Italian wine for cantatas. For highly romantic works like Don Giovanni he prescribes a 'good glassful of a drink produced by the salamander and the god of the earth'.
[11] See, for example, GilesMacdonogh, 'ETA Hoffmann, Dionysos, Vin, Ivresse,' in Gilbert Garrier (ed), *Les Rencontres de Dionysos*, Actes de Colloque (1993).
[12] Idem.

Baudelaire is aware that he lays himself open to a charge of immorality; that he is writing an apology for drunkenness and alcoholism. Wine, however, is cast in the mirror image of man, and like man it possesses its virtues and vices. Under the effects of wine, 'a bad man becomes execrable, just as a good man becomes excellent'. Its benefits greatly outweigh its defects. The abstainer is dismissed as a hypocrite: 'A man who drinks only water has a secret to conceal from his fellows.'

At the end of his writings on wine in *Du Vin et du Hachisch*, Baudelaire returns to the shortcomings of Brillat-Savarin and the symbiotic relationship between man and wine that is the theme of *L'Ame du Vin*: 'Once we have a real medical philosopher, a rare bird indeed, he could write an important study of wine; a sort of dual analysis in which man and wine are two linked themes. He would explain how and why certain beverages possess the capacity to increase beyond measure the personality of the thinking being; or in other words to create a third person: a mystical operation where natural man and wine – an animal and a vegetal god – perform the roles of father and son in a trinity thereby engendering a holy spirit who is a superior man proceeding in equal parts from both.'

Besides the pseudo-Christian terminology, there is also here an element of Hegelian synthesis. While the view that man can be transformed by a measure of wine would be accepted (but hardly approved) today, the next point that Baudelaire makes – that wine can actually increase physical efficiency – would almost certainly be rejected by the new puritans of our own time. Indeed, Baudelaire's Dionysian message seems sadly out of fashion now. But he must have struck an enormous chord with youth in the more carefree days of the 1960s and 1970s, before that morning call from Mount Olympus told us to put down our glasses and get back on our bikes. 🍂

*First published as 'Vin et le poète maudit' by Giles MacDonogh in **The World of Fine Wine**, Issue 26, 2009. Reprinted here with the kind permission of the author and of Neil Beckett, editor (www.worldoffinewine.com).*

COLETTE AND WINE

ALICE WOOLEDGE SALMON (1983)

Nobel Prize-nominated French author, actress, controversial social commentator and adored citizen, Colette (1873–1954) was born in Burgundy and always gloried in the wine and food of her region. Alice Wooledge Salmon reveals the mastery with which she described them.

was very well brought up. As first proof of such a statement, I'll tell you I was no more than three when my father offered me a glassful of the sun-burnt wine from his native Midi: le Muscat de Frontignan.

Illumination, capsizing of the senses, revelation for the tastebuds! This baptism made me wine's worthy convert. A little later, I learned to drain my tumbler of mulled wine, perfumed with lemon and cinnamon, while dining off boiled chestnuts. Hardly able to read, I spelled out each drop of aging and graceful Bordeaux rouges and dazzling Yquem. Then came the murmuring froth of champagne, springing in pearls of air across birthday and first communion banquets to celebrate the grey truffles of la Puisaye… A good education, from which I progressed to judicious familiarity with wine, never gulped and swilled, but measured into slim glasses and absorbed by sips at reflective intervals.

Colette presents her credentials, the same Colette who died a French monument, had a state funeral, and is famous in many languages for extreme love of animals and flawless writing about wayward, ambiguous men and women.

The most casual reading of three or four of her 50-odd books and sheaves of essays proclaims that Colette was *gourmande*, emotionally attached to large loaves of crusty bread and hand-pressed butter, lacquer-red cherries, honeyed figs, and the slow-cooking dishes of rural Burgundy, their secrets whispered among housewives at vinous country weddings and rarely recorded. She loved cheese, water chestnuts and a bewitching old *daube* from Provence which simmered beef, bacon and garlic with 'oil that lurks in the sauce and wine which gives it splendour, a special fragrance'.

Many pages and a fair amount of nonsense have been written about Colette and her marriages, numerous liaisons, and career in the music-hall, the notoriety that with age turned to fame and adulation. Her life was extraordinary, her personality lacking in banality to a degree which most people would find hard to tolerate – 'You can't imagine what it's like to live with a woman who is always barefoot', said her second husband – and just as one's pleasure in rare wine can be blunted by undue dissection, so various critics have taken Colette to absurdities in their haste after 'psychoanalysis' of both woman and achievement.

Not so the Burgundian oenologist and wine writer Pierre Poupon, who by way of endorsing her vinous credentials simply judges Colette 'our most perceptive wine writer' and suggests that the Collège de France should have named her *Professeur de Dégustation*: 'Her works ought to be the bedside books of professional and amateur tasters, to their much greater benefit than all those pages which preach the mechanics of tasting and never divulge the spirit'.[1] In 1951, Pierre Poupon was secretary and member of the jury in charge of awarding the *prix littéraire* at the Paulée de Meursault, one of 'three glorious' November feasts which celebrate the Burgundy vintage; that year Colette was chosen for the excellence of her Burgundian writings and the particular essay *Ma Bourgogne pauvre*. She neglected to accept this distinction, and many startled inhabitants of la Maison de Vieux Artistes Retraités de Ris-Orangis were soon delighting in the contents of 100 bottles of Meursault that should have been her recompense.

Well, I said she was extraordinary. It was Sido, Colette's mother and inspiration, who taught her to 'divine the hidden treasure' in every aspect of the physical world through fullest employment of the five senses, of which the 'noblest, most lucid and uncompromising' became to Colette the sense of smell. Folded away in the 1870s and 1880s at Saint-Sauveur-en-Puisaye, a market town near Auxerre in the Basse-Bourgogne, 'bereft of vines' save for some lighthearted *vin de Treigny* whose stock did not resist phylloxera, the child shot up nimble and receptive, her intuition schooled to the significance of '*le monde matériel, sphérique, bondé de saveurs*'. Lessons well-learned; one fragment of a sentence from the autobiographical *Maison de Claudine* engages all alert senses: 'the echoing house, dry, warm and crackling as a newly-baked loaf'.

---

[1] Pierre Poupon, 'Colette, ou l'art de la dégustation', *Mes dégustations littéraires*, Nuits-Saint-Georges, 1979.

Colette as Le Petit Faune in 'Le désir, la chimère et l'amour' *at the Théâtre des Mathurins, Paris, 1906, where her provacative performance and revealing costumes caused a scandal.*

And Sido contributed some *grands crus*, vintage pre-phylloxera, to that 'good education'. As antidote to the possibility of adolescent pallors, Colette was given unusual tonics: from the dry sand of her granite *cave*, Sido unearthed bottles she had hidden from invading Germans at the time of the Franco-Prussian war: '...wine left by my first husband. Château Larose, Château Lafite, Chambertin, Château d'Yquem. Bottles already 10, 12, 15 years old (at the moment of burial). That good dry sand made them even better', and glass after glass escorted Colette's afternoon *casse-croûte* of cutlet or cold chicken as Sido watched her cheeks flame with the 'vinous glories of France'.

Colette grew up to write ripe, full-bodied prose, savoury with archaic words and racy dialogue, which 'improves with age like wines that grow rich in the bottle', as described by Pierre Poupon. The vineyard and *cru* appear so often in her work – a rapid mention, a chapter, the metaphor for complex emotions – that the present tasting must be selective.

Three essays form the heart of this writing. *Vins* is based on that vinous education, *En Bourgogne* evokes Burgundian cellars in winter, and *Ma Bourgogne pauvre*, the prize winner, moves from childhood wines to the Côte d'Or. The three overlap, as often occurs with Colette, and reveal qualities of vigneron and *caviste* that complement the taster.

She felt wine as a great mystery, but attentive, she learned secrets: its different translations of the soil's 'true flavour', the tastes of flint or chalk or that of a Sauvignon graft from Bordeaux which sugared and lightened Algerian wine of quite another character.

She sensed that sap quickened in the sleeping vine of a stripped winter vineyard despite all visual evidence, marvelled at snake-like Provençal stock apparently nourished by dew alone, and observed grapes, 'clear and cloudy agate or silver-dusted blue' as a fine summer brought them to splendid maturity. Tasting wines *sur place*, finding six bottles of Jurançon – 'fiery, imperious prince, treacherous as all great seducers' – at a village auction taught Colette more geography than any professor, just as 'glorious' wine once drunk in a dark old inn delighted her like the stolen kiss of an unseen stranger.

She was soothed by winter industry in the cellars of an *éleveur* where one man racked wine, another fined it by rocking a *dodine* to distribute egg white, and a third scoured casks by means of heavy chain. Here was quiet, rhythmic work, in no particular hurry, whose midwifery brought forth 'His Royal Highness the Wine of Burgundy' on which she'd been raised but whose Côte d'Or she never knew till much later. It was a case of love at first sight. 'My initial visit, at the height of a glowing September, the hills all laden with their vintage, landed me in a Dijon which local festivities, the hot Indian summer and its jollifications had set alight, ashamed neither of being rich nor of lavishing the treasures of a city given over to gastronomic pleasure and running with eternities of wine.'

Translation is hard on Colette's sumptuous, multi-layered vocabulary and pell-mell of images, the words chosen for their exact and often double or triple meanings. The following sentence from *Ma Bourgogne pauvre* shows why she gains when read in the original: '*La veine qui charrie les crus illustres passe assez loin de la Puisaye, bifurque puis tarit*'. The word *veine*, in French, indicates both 'vein' or 'seam' and 'underground stream'; *charrier* means to 'bear' or 'carry' and is often associated with transport on rivers; *bifurquer*, to 'fork' or 'divide', applies equally to seam or road and to stream; and *tarir* means to 'dry up', 'cease', or 'peter out'. Four words that give both a geological concept – the 'seam' of soil and subsoil that bears and nourishes the great wines of the Côte d'Or – and the idea of a hidden river, even a source or a spring, one of Colette's symbols of the life force with which, by inference, wine is allied. Translation to 'The seam that bears the illustrious growths passes nowhere near la Puisaye, divides and then peters out' must sacrifice the second meaning.

But often the message arrives. In *Vins*, Colette evokes a 'violet-perfumed Bordeaux', colour of the '*rubis balais*' or balas ruby, a rose-red variety from north-eastern Persia near

Samarkand. That's quite an image; not just 'ruby', but arrayed with connotations both specific and exotic, bringing all sorts of echoes, pipe dreams of adventure to the well-regulated slopes of the Gironde.

And now let's roam. Colette is first-rate on *vendanges*, grape-pickings in the Beaujolais, the Limousin, and Provence – where for 12 years or so she owned vines that yielded up to 2,000 litres a season. *Automne* brings the whole department of the Var out to 'save' the grapes of a vintage whose clusters trail on the burning August earth; the women sing, their voices carried by the wind from Mediterranean gulf to gulf, drunken and defenceless wasps fall about sticky vats, and folk in all sorts of kitchens boil the new wine to make into *vin marquis*. *Mon amie Valentine* sits down to a large harvest lunch: *la soupe, poule au pot*, pork 'pink and white as a breast, veal in its goodness'. In September 1941, gripped by wartime shortage, Colette encouraged readers of her newspaper column to reflect on the coming vintage, the autumn sun which stimulates late-ripening grapes, and the lure of good bottles, for the moment empty but as ready to put up 'the tomato and the *haricot vert*' as to welcome fresh wine (*De ma fenétre*). And much of *La Naissance du jour*, an essay-like novel about renunciation in middle age, is based on the *vendange* as a metaphor for the culmination and reflective aftermath of love, gathered up and put aside to slumber in the memory like the 'cloistered new wine'.

Colette's voice, with its rugged and rolling Burgundian 'r', spoke of wine as both intoxicant – like opium, perfume, silk and velvet, the music of speech, sexual love, all the '*enivrant superflu*' – and a symbol of restraint: 'And drink little, if you don't mind. We have a saying, where I come from, that during a good meal one isn't thirsty but "hungry to drink"'. Not just restraint, but positive order and sometimes elegance, even among marginal people, the 'bourgeois bohemia' who were Colette's recurring subjects. If she alluded to *lorettes* – the rank and file of Parisian kept women, circa 1840 – as drawn by Gavarni with 'shoulders in the shape of Rhine wine bottles', and to fusty, political, all-male luncheons washed down in dim restaurants with Richebourg and other oh-so-respectable growths, she used champagne as a kind of passe-partout. Weddings and birthdays – her 75th brought a jeroboam – New Year's *réveillon*, courtship (honourable and otherwise), a moment of ambiguity were refreshed with Piper-Heidsieck, a good *brut* of 1906, a Pommery, or – not so successfully – a night-club brew 'that tastes metallic'.

Pommery is the champagne of Colette's to me best-realized creation: Léa de Lonval, courtesan of the *belle époque* and light of *Chéri* and *La Fin de Chéri,* stories of the sentimental education and extinction of Chéri, ' *jeune home riche au petit coeur*'. Léa, handsomely 50, has 'kept' the boy, aged 25, for seven years; they part, he marries, and in losing each other both relinquish the finest possession either will ever have. It's a world of

Colette in later life, drawn by the Austrian artist Benedikt Fred Dolbin (1883–1971).

money, love and small curiosity, as respectable as milieux less irregular, and Léa, whose career has been sure-footed and profitable, is a woman of great if somewhat hot-house style.

'*Elle aimait l'ordre, le beau linge, les vins mûris, la cuisine réfléchie.*' (She liked order, good linen, wine that has mellowed and well-considered cooking.) She lunches alone, 'with a smile for the dry Vouvray and the June strawberries, served with their stalks on a Rubelles plate, green as a tree-frog after the rain', the dining room assimilates Louis XVI mirrors, English furniture of the same period, heavy silver and a butler whose 'restrained glance' announces '*Madame est belle*' and does not displease her. Léa's *eau-de-vie*, refined by seven decades, is poured from cut-glass into goblets of the thinnest crystal, served with iced water and shortbread biscuits on a cloth of old embroidery.

But it's Pommery which signifies the essence that Chéri, grieving and rudderless, can't bear to lose. 'And he breathed in, remembering, as he opened his nostrils, the rose-perfumed sparkle of an old champagne of 1889 that Léa kept for him alone.' Chéri, whom Léa had mocked as a *petit bourgeois* when he counted up her bottles, tells her at the end of volume one, 'In the very wine I drank I looked for you, and never found a Pommery like yours', before they part finally with bittersweet sorrow.

Appropriately, Colette spent her last 16 years in the rue de Beaujolais in Paris, dying there, aged 81, 'after a small sip of champagne'. Three of her windows, on the first floor of the graceful Palais-Royal, overlooked the semi-private world of its gardens, and her final handful of years, when she was crippled with arthritis and never out of pain, were cheered by the proximity of the Grand Véfour, restaurant returned to quality in the late 1940s by Raymond Oliver. Colette and husband made it their 'local', met friends, entertained there, and as she couldn't walk, Oliver used to have her collected by two liveried waiters and a sedan chair. Her favourite Véfour lunch was salmon *coulibiac* – with champagne, *bien sûr*.

A final word from Colette? 'A difficult page, the conclusion of a novel, are advantageously served by an exceptionally well-filled glass.' ❧

*Alice Wooledge Salmon, a New Yorker long at home in London, is a short story writer and essayist. She has written about food and wine for **House & Garden** (UK), **Gourmet** (New York), and publications beyond. Her essay Colette and Wine was first published in **Christie's Wine Companion 2**, Christie's (London) 1983.*

IN VINO VERITAS

HARRY EYRES (2014)

Horace's Odes *are a collection of lyrical poetry capturing the essence of Roman life. Tennyson called them 'jewels five-words long, that on the stretched forefinger of all time, sparkle for ever'. Harry Eyres addressed the Horatian Society with the following exploration of the poet's fascination with wine.*

thought of many possible themes for this research, because Horace is in his subtle way one of the most wide-ranging of all poets. One phrase kept popping up in my mind: '*irasci celerem*', quick to anger, from that brief self-portrait in the envoy poem, *Epistles* 1 20. This would be a fascinating topic. The supposedly even-tempered Horace, the man of the golden mean, was in fact irascible (though also easily appeased). It happens, unfortunately, to be a trait I share with Horace and I have speculated about its causes. But I will leave that for another day.

In the end I chose something else as my subject: Horace's love of wine – evinced in so many poems, especially in the *Odes*. Wine is something we find easy to enjoy on the whole – in fact, it might seem easier to appreciate and enjoy than Horace, at least when one is young.

Wine was, in fact, the first means of connecting with Horace that I discovered, when I found him hard to understand, and pretty hard to construe, as a schoolboy. I struggled with Horace, as quite a few have done before and since. Byron was one; toiling at Harrow School he wrote: 'Farewell Horace whom I hated so,/ Not for thy faults but mine; it is a curse/ To understand, not feel thy lyric flow,/ To comprehend, but never love thy verse.' Byron perhaps didn't live long enough – though he already felt old, or so he said, by the time he died at Missolonghi at 36 – to come back round to him; that's another theme.

Beatus ille qui procul negotiis.

Horaz.

Horace, who eschews romantic love (with rare exceptions) and extremes, appeals more to middle-aged people than to adolescents and young adults. Ezra Pound, never known for his opposition to extremes, was especially rude about Horace; Pound was not even young when he attacked Horace for being 'neither simple nor passionate…bald-headed, pot-bellied, underbred, sycophantic, less poetic than any other great master of literature'.

Horace didn't need Pound to tell him that he was underbred: '*ut me libertino patre natum*.' Touchingly he made his humble origins a badge of pride. He would not have swapped his humbly-born but excellent father for a grand senator. The bald-headed and pot-bellied bits also come from Horace's own self-portrait. Pound's friend Yeats had a thing about bald heads as well: 'Bald heads, forgetful of their sins/ Old, learned, respectable bald heads/ Edit and annotate the lines/ That young men tossing on their beds/ Rhymed out in love's despair/ To flatter beauty's ignorant ear', as that splendid tirade *The Scholars* begins. But a full head of hair does not a poet make. Most amazing, I think, on this sub-theme of how one comes back to Horace in middle age is the testimony of Rudyard Kipling, who in his autobiography *Something of Myself* relates how his classics teacher, Mr C (the model for the teacher in that marvellous story 'Regulus' from *Stalky & Co*), taught him to 'loathe Horace for two years, to forget him for 20, and to love him for the rest of my days and through many sleepless nights'.

But back to wine. I was wary about Horace when we studied *Odes, Book One* at school. Like Pound I found his closeness to the Augustan regime a bit creepy. Weren't poets supposed to be outsiders? I preferred Catullus (doesn't everybody?) – the frankness and power of the emotion, the rude bits (there are some in Horace too), the magnificent disdain for politics and political leaders (I don't care if Caesar is fair or swarthy). Some of Horace's poems even seemed close to being propaganda – the Cleopatra ode, for instance – as if some contemporary poet were to write an ode about George Bush's great victory in Iraq.

You might well say that I was missing the point. The Cleopatra ode, which begins in what you might think of as unseemly triumphalism, ends very differently, with an extraordinary, intense, magnificent picture of Cleopatra's courage in the face of death. More precisely, of course, the Cleopatra ode begins with those famous words '*Nunc est bibendum*', which have given the name to at least one excellent wine company. And it is not just any old wine that Horace is suggesting the time has come to broach: it is Caecuban, one of the top Roman *crus*. Caecuban, like most the wines the Romans valued highly, came from the south, near Naples. Horace himself was a southerner.

Here was the thing. In my last term at school, finally free of exams, I found myself writing an essay for the rather pompous Essay Society, which met once a month in the Head Master's drawing room, on the subject of Wine and Western Civilization.

I was the son of a wine merchant, who had introduced me to the heady stuff rather young, and had instilled in me a love and fascination for it which went beyond the desire to get blotto. My father, brought up partly by a British Israelite teetotal grandmother, thought wine was a civilized and civilizing thing, and I had gone round various European wine regions with him, tasting and drinking. The wine business was run from home, from my parents' rather lovely and poetic early Victorian villa on the edge of a village in the Chilterns, which possessed an excellent cool cellar. The house was benignly cluttered with the paraphernalia of wine, with sweet-smelling wooden cases, labels soaked off and stuck on walls, corkscrews and decanters.

Wine was in my blood and in my soul, and I quickly realized that was the case with Horace too. Maybe scholars and teachers who were not the sons of wine merchants were less sensitive to this (though remember that Eduard Fraenkel, perhaps the greatest of all Horatian scholars, though apparently not entirely safe in a room with a female undergraduate, was also the son of a wine merchant). But to me it was blindingly obvious. Horace, who was born in Venusia, modern Venosa, centre of production of the excellent fiery, mineral red wine Aglianico del Vulture (ancient Voltur, the extinct volcano Horace wandered on as a child, where he was kept safe from bears and snakes by a blanket of leaves woven by doves), was one of the greatest wine-lovers of all time. Wine is many things for Horace: a topic of conversation, a status-symbol perhaps, but above all especially in the Odes wine is something like the master-symbol of the poetry, the thing which gathers the maximum of meaning to itself, through which so many truths are told.

Take that deceptive ode from Book One addressed to Maecenas, the one that begins '*Vile potabis modicis Sabinum/ Cantharis*'. *Vile sabinum*, my Sabine plonk, refers to the wine made by Horace himself at his Sabine farm, the country estate gifted to him by Maecenas in the early 30s BC, the place that became his spiritual home.

How many things the wine means here. It is first of all connected to friendship, the deep and probably rather complicated friendship Horace has with his grand and important patron Maecenas. This intimate get-together between poet and statesman is a celebration both of Maecenas's triumph and his return to health. The wine Horace is offering is not grand and important – quite the opposite: Sabine wine was considered by Galen the thinnest of all Italian wines. It is probably not that much better today. But Horace is stressing the value of the home-grown and authentic. And beyond that this humble wine stands for the humble poet, the freedman's son, and beyond that for the poetry this man wrote, which was a kind of transformation of humility into eternity.

So was Horace 'a typical nouveau riche wine snob' as our fellow-Horatian the Mayor of London rather unkindly put it?

Surely he was much more than that. Wine was certainly a topos of snobbery in ancient Rome, as it is in other consumer societies including our own. At the same time that he defends the local and home-grown, the *'vile Sabinum'* (vile, here, meaning cheap), Horace also displays his familiarity with much grander *crus*. But Horace's view of wine goes much deeper than that.

Let me show you one of my pesky modern versions, this time of the great Ode 3.21, which I find to be strangely neglected by scholars. It was even neglected, in his great tome on Horace, by Eduard Fraenkel, the wine-merchant's son, though not apparently in tutorials, when he frequently spoke movingly about it. Mysterious, that. Maybe it was just too close to the bone.

Horace Ode 3.21

Your time is up, my faithful aged
Margaux, contemporary, my twin –
just think of it, you were vintaged
the year of Supermac's shameless spin,
that 'you've never had it so good' guff –
Oh come, descend: old friend
Jim has called for smoother stuff.

Heaven knows what havoc or ferment –
what vehement argument
or crazy love obsession
or merciful slumping
into snores you have in store.

Though philosophically inclined
and aptest to peruse
abstruser tomes by Plato
I know my friend will not refuse
a little tipple of the warming kind
not scorned by stern old Cato.

In vino veritas, they say; you,
venerable vintage, have the subtle knack
of mellowing tough nuts; such a dusty
bottle can unlock from the most crusty
the best-kept secret and release the craic.

And that's not all; you can restore
to a desperate mind the balm of hope;
give strength and sustenance to the poor
man faced with all the aftermath of war;
one wee dram and he'll feel potent as a pope.

Your presence brings diviner traces –
goaty Bacchus and the gorgeous Venus,
if she's willing, and the gang of Graces,
so slow to untie their virgins' girdles,
all dance around us while we drink till dawn.

This ode sums up everything Horace thought was important about wine, which means most of what he thought was important about life. First, friendship: the ode is addressed to his old comrade-at-arms from the field of Philippi, Marcus Valerius Messalla Corvinus. Surely Philippi – the battle where Horace and his friend fought against his future protector, Octavian/Augustus – was something you wouldn't mention in a poem at least partially directed at Maecenas and Augustus. But Horace, perhaps recklessly, keeps going back there and this poem is, I feel, full of memories of Philippi. Friendship is about differences as well as similarities and closenesses. One senses from reading the ode that

The Romans in Their Decadence *by Thomas Couture, oil on canvas, 472 x 772 cm (186 x 304 in), Musée d'Orsay.*

Messalla Corvinus was a very different character from Horace – he was crusty and difficult where Horace was warm and voluble.

This leads on to the second thing, philosophy. Corvinus is 'steeped in Socratic lore', to give C E Bennett's Loeb translation. As was Horace himself. Wine is a philosophical thing, as well as a sensuous, even riotous one. That is to say it helps us to live well, however strange that notion may seem. This was also something my father taught me.

Third, divinity – that wine is a commerce with the divine. This may seem even more far-fetched. But this is what Horace is saying in the final stanza. Wine, the right wine, and as we will see this is no ordinary wine, takes us beyond ourselves, to magical places. Wine, as the Spanish philosopher Ortega y Gasset recognized, is not just vino, something you glug in a bar, but *vino divino*, something which transports you to another realm.

Which brings us to the fourth thing, mortality. Horace, as I'm sure you will notice, is always banging on about mortality. *Eheu fugaces*. He will not let us get away with thinking we are immortal, though he does allow himself a flight of fancy, imagining how if that falling tree on his estate which narrowly missed him had in fact dispatched him, he might have met Alcaeus and Sappho holding the throngs in Hades spellbound as they sang to the lyre.

Perhaps the most important and moving words in this wonderful poem are the first three, '*O nata mecum*'. This special jar of Massic was vintaged the year Horace was born, the year of consul Manlius, 65BC. Wine is born with us and dies with us. It is not *aere perennius*, more lasting than bronze, as the poetry will prove to be. 🍃

ACKNOWLEDGEMENTS

The publishers would like to thank the following people/organizations for their invaluable help in preparing this book:

For kindly letting us use articles first printed in their publications, our grateful thanks go to Neil Beckett of *The World of Fine Wine*, Dan Keeling of *Noble Rot* magazine and Merlin Holland of The Saintsbury Club. For sourcing copyright details of some of the better known and lesser known texts, we are grateful to Rachel Thorne of RN Permissions who has been patient and persevering from start to finish.

To Tony Aspler, Bartholomew Broadbent, Michael Broadbent, Andrew Caillard MW, Harry Eyres, Randall Grahm, Justin Howard-Sneyd MW, Ben Howkins, Dan Keeling, Simon Loftus, Jane MacQuitty, Jonathan Miles, Fiona Morrison MW, Dirk Niepoort, Jason Tesauro and Peter Vinding-Diers, thank you for being ready with ideas for a 2020 readership (and for bouncing around a few others). To Gerald Asher, Kathleen Burk, Giles MacDonogh, Elin McCoy and Alice Wooledge Salmon, thank you for your wonderful contributions from across the art and wine scene.

Most of all, thank you to Hugh Johnson, Steven Spurrier and Simon McMurtrie for creating the Académie du Vin Library in the first place. Their original intent was to provide a forum for exploring wine writing from across the ages – from bringing back the brilliant authors of the mid-1900s whose carefully crafted words crave rediscovery, to introducing intrepid new wordsmiths, well worthy of our attention. *In Vino Veritas* attempts to begin this in one volume, inspired by Cyril Ray and his *Compleat Imbiber* series of the 1960s–90s. With luck and a following readership, perhaps our book with see a run of annual editions too?

Thank you to Hugh for generously sharing the original copies of Henry Vizetelly, André Jullien, Thomas Jefferson, Maurice Healy and more from his wonderful library at home – inspiration aplenty! And to Steven for knowing how to strike just the right balance between old and new; quirky and irreverent; art, wine and poetry.

PICTURE CREDITS